# NORTHERN IRELAND:

# THE THATCHER YEARS

# NORTHERN IRELAND: THE THATCHER YEARS

## Frank Gaffikin and Mike Morrissey

**Zed Books Ltd.**
London and New Jersey

*Northern Ireland: The Thatcher Years* was first published by
Zed Books Ltd, 57 Caledonian Road, London N1 9BU, UK, and
171 First Avenue, Atlantic Highlands, New Jersey 07716, USA,
in 1990.

Cover designed by Andrew Corbett.
Cover photograph by Joanne O'Brien/Format.
Printed and bound in the United Kingdom
by Biddles Ltd, Guildford and King's Lynn.

**Library of Congress Cataloging-in-Publication Data**

Gaffikin, Frank.
    Northern Ireland: the Thatcher years/Frank Gaffikin and
Michael Morrissey.
      p.    cm.
    Includes bibliographical references (p.
    ISBN 0-86232-906-X. – ISBN 0-86232-907-8 (pbk.)
    1. Northern Ireland—Politics and government—1969- 2. Thatcher,
Margaret. I. Morrissey, Mike. II. Title.
DA990.U46M72    1990
941.60824—dc20                      89-25027
                                       CIP

**British CIP data is available from the British Library.**

# Table of Contents

Introduction . . . . . . . . . . . . . . . . . . . . . . . 1

**Thatcherism and Northern Ireland** . . . . . . . . . . . . 7
 Thatcherism: An Elusive Concept.................................... 7
 Paving the Way......................................................... 8
 The Challenge of the New Right ................................... 9
 Selling Thatcherism ................................................. 11
 The Four Phases...................................................... 12
 Understanding Thatcherism....................................... 14
 Leadership Style ..................................................... 21
 The Falklands Factor ............................................... 23
 Good Fortune......................................................... 24
 A Broader Perspective ............................................. 26
 Northern Ireland: A Distinctive Politics?....................... 27
 Thatcherism and Northern Ireland............................... 34

**Economic and Social Change since 1979: An Overview** . 40
 Basic Comparisons ................................................. 43
 Public Expenditure and GDP...................................... 45
 Household Income and Expenditure ............................. 49
 Employment, Unemployment and Earnings .................... 53
 Social Services....................................................... 60

**The Economy: Accounting for Change** . . . . . . . . . . 63
 Economic Performance: Key Indicators........................ 64
 What Has Happened to Manufacturing? ........................ 70
 The Thatcher Economic Record: A Summary ................. 72
 What Has Happened in Northern Ireland? ...................... 74
 Employment and Unemployment................................. 75
 Output and Growth ................................................. 78
 The Public Sector.................................................... 79
 Recent Developments .............................................. 81
 Northern Ireland: The Economic Problem ..................... 82
 Industrial Policy: A Greater Pragmatism?...................... 87
 A Different Agenda ................................................. 94

**The Tories and Poverty: Privatising the Poor** . . . . . . 96
 The Nature of Poverty .............................................. 97
 The Conservative Assault on Poverty ........................... 100

Poverty in Northern Ireland................................................. 107
The Reform of Social Security ............................................ 108
The New Poverty: The Underclass...................................... 110

## The Tory City: Urban Blues . . . . . . . . . . .112
Urban Development Corporations in Britain ....................... 112
Planning in Belfast: A Brief History ................................... 115
The Belfast Urban Plan 1989 .............................................. 117
Prospects for the Retail Sector ........................................... 119
On the Waterfront................................................................ 120
Planning for Post-Industrialism? ........................................ 121
The Urban Plan and Job Creation....................................... 123
Thatcherism and the Belfast Urban Plan ............................. 125
Belfast: A Different Politics ............................................... 126
Thatcherism and Urban Change: An Overview ................... 127

## Inner City Strategies: Reclaiming the Core . . . . . . .130
The Experience of Inner City Programmes: Britain and
Northern Ireland.................................................................. 130
Thatcherism and the Inner City .......................................... 132
The Role of Local Government ........................................... 134
Enterprise Zones................................................................. 136
The Inner City: A Law and Order Problem? ....................... 139
An Image Problem?............................................................. 139
Bringing Employment to the Inner City: Making Belfast Work ........ 140

## Housing Policy: Accommodating Thatcher . . . . . . .150
Hitting Home ...................................................................... 150
Some Political Implications................................................. 154
Housing in Northern Ireland................................................ 155
Public Spending on Housing ............................................... 157
Housing in Northern Ireland 1979-87: Sheltered from the Market?... 161
Policy Changes in the Late 1980s ....................................... 162

## Education: A Testing Time . . . . . . . . . . . . .166
Education Resources............................................................ 166
Education Policy.................................................................. 167
The Content of Education.................................................... 169
The Management of Schools ............................................... 170
Higher Education................................................................. 174
Education in Northern Ireland............................................. 175
Education Reform: The Northern Ireland Version................ 176
More Parent Power? ........................................................... 178
The Role of Local Education Boards ................................... 179
Segregated Schooling.......................................................... 180

The Business of Education? ....................................................... 182
Higher Education in Northern Ireland............................................... 183
The Current Agenda ...................................................................... 184

# Health Care: Operating Under Thatcherism    . . . . . . .187
The Northern Ireland NHS. ............................................................ 187
Health Care: Britain and Northern Ireland Compared ....................... 188
The Economics of Health Care....................................................... 189
Thatcherism and the NHS.............................................................. 190
The NHS Review .......................................................................... 192
Rationalising Health Expenditure in Northern Ireland ...................... 195
Privatising Ancillary Services ....................................................... 197
The NHS Review and Northern Ireland............................................ 197

# Conclusion    . . . . . . . . . . . . . . . . . . . . . . . . . .199
Thatcherism and Northern Ireland: An Agenda of Change or a Change
of Agenda?................................................................................. 199

# References    . . . . . . . . . . . . . . . . . . . . . . . . . .209
Chapter 1....................................................................................209
Chapter 2....................................................................................211
Chapter 3....................................................................................212
Chapter 4....................................................................................214
Chapter 5 ...................................................................................216
Chapter 6....................................................................................219
Chapter 7....................................................................................220
Chapter 8....................................................................................222
Chapter 9....................................................................................223
Chapter 10..................................................................................224

# Bibliography    . . . . . . . . . . . . . . . . . . . . . . . .226

# Index    . . . . . . . . . . . . . . . . . . . . . . . . . . . .236

# List of Tables

Table 1     Incident Statistics, 1972-1987 ........................... 41
Table 2     Basic Profiles: English Regions, Wales
            and Northern Ireland ...................................... 44
Table 3     Real % Changes in Selected
            Public Expenditure Programmes, 1979-80 to 1989-90 ... 46
Table 4     Average Weekly Household Incomes
            by Region (£) ............................................. 49
Table 5     The Proportion of Households on
            Low Incomes by Region .................................... 50
Table 6     Average Weekly Household Expenditure
            by Region (£) ............................................. 51
Table 7     Personal Incomes Before Tax by Region .................. 52
Table 8     Civilian Working Population, 1974-1988 ................. 53
Table 9     Employment By Industrial Sector, 1971-1989 ............ 55
Table 10    Rates of Unemployment by Region (%) .................... 56
Table 11    Unemployment: Department of Employment
             (DE) Count and Unemployment Unit (UU)
            Index June 1989 (Seasonally Adjusted) ................. 57
Table 12    Average Weekly Earnings, Full Time
            Adult Men, 1979 and 1988 by Region .................... 58
Table 13    Average Weekly Earnings, Full Time Adult
            Females, 1979 and 1988 by Region ..................... 59
Table 14    Mis-estimates in Recent Government
            Income and Expenditure (£billion) ..................... 69
Table 15    UK Manufacturing Performance 1979-1987 ................ 71
Table 16    Macro Economic Indicators by Party
            in Power 1951-1988 (annual average) .................. 74
Table 17    Changes in Employment: Northern Ireland
            and the UK, 1979-1988 (%) ............................. 75
Table 18    Civil Employment, by Sector 1974-1988 ................. 76
Table 19    Industrial Output: The UK and
            Northern Ireland, 1983-89 (1985=100) ................. 78
Table 20    Public Spending Per Capita in
            Northern Ireland as a % of Britain, 1980-1986 ........ 80
Table 21    Indicators of Recent Economic
            Performance, Northern Ireland ........................ 81
Table 22    IDB and LEDU Job Promotions, 1987-1989 ............... 85
Table 23    Employment in the Retail Sector in
            Northern Ireland, 1979-89. ........................... 120

Table 24    The Costs of Enterprise Zones
            (from designation to 1987) (£Million) ........................... 136
Table 25    Job Analysis by Industrial Sector:
            Belfast Inner City ............................................................ 137
Table 26    Job Analysis by Industrial Sector:
            Belfast North Foreshore .................................................. 138
Table 27    Deprivation Index for Belfast, 1985 ............................... 141
Table 28    Expenditure on Making Belfast Work ........................... 145
Table 29    Housing Tenure: Northern Ireland (NI)
            and Britain (GB), 1966-1986 (%) .................................. 156
Table 30    Completed Permanent Dwellings in
            Northern Ireland, 1977-1987 ......................................... 159
Table 31    The Operation of Housing Benefit, 1984-87 ................. 161
Table 32    Changes in Housing Conditions in
            Northern Ireland, 1974-1987 ......................................... 161
Table 33    Total Real Expenditure By Northern Ireland
            Education and Library Boards, 1978-79 to 1988-89 ..... 167
Table 34    Infant Mortality Ratios as a % of the UK
            Average by Region ......................................................... 188
Table 35    Hospital Beds per 1,000 Population
            by Region, 1986 ............................................................. 188

# Acknowledgements

Our thanks go to: John Freeman, Pat McGinn, Laurence Moffat, John Pinkerton and Robin Wilson who read drafts and made constructive criticism; Robert Molteno for his exhaustive editing of first drafts: Les Allemby and Hazel Morrissey who provided data; and Colette Gaffikin and Liam Lynch for help in layout and Desk Top Publishing.

# Foreword

For a number of years the Amalgamated Transport and General Workers' Union has been concerned to widen the political debate on Northern Ireland beyond the conventional terrain of constitutional dispute. We have been keen to address the rapid changes taking place in the economy and social provision in a region particularly vulnerable to unemployment and poverty. This is not to ignore the importance of the distinctive local politics, but simply to acknowledge that other issues are frequently driven from the agenda by the intensity, and sometimes the horror, of the conflict. These also merit detailed, objective research and equal public attention.

To that end we have sponsored a series of pamphlets and articles dealing with the problems of restructuring the regional economy, developing economic relationships with the Irish Republic and anticipating the impact of the European Single Market.

In the same spirit we are pleased to cooperate with Zed Press in bringing out this book. An assessment of the impact of the Thatcher government on Northern Ireland's economy and welfare state is timely and valuable. Its two authors combine a rigorous academic background with extensive experience in voluntary and trade union activity. As such, they are well placed to evaluate this critical period. Without necessarily endorsing all of their views, I find the wealth of material contained in the book informative and stimulating. Somewhat uniquely, the scope of the analysis embraces both the economic and the social, identifying the two as complementary rather than in competition for resources. In this respect, it offers a perspective in contrast to that of the present government.

My primary consideration is to encourage debate within the Trade Union Movement, but a venture in conjunction with a major publisher thankfully offers the opportunity to reach a wider audience.

*John Freeman*
Regional Secretary
Amalgamated Transport and General Workers' Union.

# Introduction

In the British media, Northern Ireland draws attention mainly because of its political violence. After two decades of conflict, even though the daily minutiae of events have ceased to be newsworthy, there is a sufficient number of incidents whose peculiar horror is such as to attract periodic surges of media interest. The epitome of this process occurred in 1989 when the SAS killed three unarmed members of the IRA in Gibraltar and so fuelled the prolonged debate about the existence of a 'shoot-to-kill' policy. At the funeral for the victims in West Belfast, a Loyalist gunman infiltrated the crowd and began to hurl grenades, killing three mourners and injuring many more. At the subsequent funeral of one of these new victims, two men, at least one of whom was armed, crossed the cortege in a car, were dragged out, horribly beaten and shot. They were later identified as two British Army corporals. This chain of events, which reflects in a gruesome manner the intense contradictions of the Northern Ireland conflict, constitutes the predominant media picture of the region.

From this perspective the conflict is inter-communal, almost tribal. The British government and the security forces stoically stand between warring factions and get no thanks for it. The terrorists are an evil minority attempting to enforce an undemocratic solution on the mass of ordinary citizens.

From the Republican perspective, the situation is equally uncomplicated. In its view the central cause of the conflict is British imperialist interference in Ireland, which has been pernicious and long term. The desire of the Irish people for self-determination, evidenced in the results of the 1918 General Election, has been systematically frustrated. The interests of imperialism are primarily economic (profits are still extracted from Ireland) and geopolitical (Ireland remains strategically important because of its location on the extreme West of Europe). The IRA, with small membership and fewer resources, has fought imperialism to a standstill and, despite imprisonment and shootings, demonstrates a sustained capacity to carry the war to Britain. Loyalists are the witting or unwitting allies of imperialism, their loyalty secured by better access to jobs and their almost exclusive membership of the local security forces. Only in the era of the Anglo-Irish Agreement have they been put aside in the

1

search for more reliable allies for the domination of Ireland. The solution to the conflict is equally simple: Britain must withdraw from Ireland; Loyalists will at last recognise that they have no alternative but to co-operate with fellow Irish citizens to build a better Ireland; the deformed political system in Ireland will be reconstructed on Left/Right lines.

Opinion in Britain tends to polarise around these two positions, with sections of the Left, in particular, supporting the Republican analysis. Policy prescriptions are not so easily dichotomised. Some, who hold that the conflict is essentially inter-tribal and that the terrorists are 'the scum of the earth', want the British Army to adopt a more positive counter-insurgency strategy. Others, who hold essentially the same analysis, suggest, however, that the Army be brought home to 'let them get on with killing each other'. Those who see British intervention in Ireland as the cause of the problem also propose the withdrawal of troops.

The proponents of the two positions would argue that the above descriptions are caricatures, which significantly underestimate the sophistication of their analysis. Perhaps that is so, but, no matter how further elaborated, they remain deficient in two respects: their account of the conflict is essentially one dimensional, reducible to a single cause whether that be British intervention in Ireland or the irrationality of the Irish. It is unlikely that a set of problems of such intractability could be so easily understood. Secondly, they both take the view that the political conflict completely determines all else. Social and economic developments are either merely disguised forms of the conflict or insignificant. Yet, Northern Ireland in recent years has undergone profound changes which are not simply the result of its political conflict. And their importance remains under-appreciated by such blinkered perspectives.

If, for example, the IRA is a small band of evil terrorists, where do they derive the support to sustain such a high level of campaigning? Other groups, like ETA, are more sporadic and less widespread in their operations. How does Sinn Fein, the political wing of the IRA, regularly obtain between 8% and 10% of the popular vote in Northern Ireland elections and elect one MP to Westminster? Similarly, if the situation can only be understood via the concept of imperialism, what other population suffering imperialist exploitation actually receives greater social spending per head than in the mother country? Some theories of colonialism suggest that the repatriated profits of imperialist investment were used, in part, to buy off working class militancy within the imperial power. Northern Ireland, whose total public spending is subsidised by around 40% from the British Exchequer, would seem to be the reverse of that thesis.

The overwhelming attention generated by the political conflict ignores the fact that the North East of Ireland was one of the first regions in the world to industrialise with the consequent production of a class system. Its form of industrialisation was similar to that in British regions. It intensively developed a limited number of industrial sectors like linen, shipbuilding and engineering.

While this development was affected by political relations within Ireland and between Ireland and Britain, it also influenced the course of key political struggles. The developed economic base of the North East of the island, integrated with the British economy, was an important factor in generating the Unionists' intense desire to remain British. Connolly's belief that the connection with Britain served the interests of no class in Ireland was fundamentally naive. However, for most of its existence, Northern Ireland has seen the erosion of that economic base, with profound social consequences. It has had an endemic problem of unemployment, which, even in years of substantial growth, was alleviated rather than resolved. It has been the location of considerable concentrations of poverty. Efforts to revitalise its ailing economy have had little long-term success.

This other dimension, the social and the economic, is the subject-matter of this book. A substantial literature already exists on the nature of the conflict within Northern Ireland and on issues like discrimination in the labour market. There is little point in merely replicating that material. Our starting point is the contention that there are two crises in Northern Ireland — the political and the economic. The latter tends to be neglected because of the intensity of the former. Yet, the economic problems in Northern Ireland are sufficiently severe that they demand urgent attention and cannot await the resolution of the political conflict. However, we do not argue that economic and social issues can exclusively account for the conflict. There is a perspective on Northern Ireland which holds that the primary concern should be with 'bread and butter' politics, partly because the political conflict appears so irresolvable and partly in the belief that deprivation and discrimination alone account for a propensity to support political violence. Thus, to address these issues seriously would undermine the support for terrorism.

In our view, Republican ideology is not reducible to such factors, but is also rooted in a long history of grievance and struggle. Those who are deeply committed to the ideal of Irish unity will not be pacified by social and economic improvement. Accepting that the political conflict has this measure of autonomy does not imply that deprivation and discrimination are subsidiary issues. Rather, we argue that tackling these should not be viewed simply as instrumental to the achievement of other political goals, such as the containment of the current Republican challenge. Thus, we subscribe neither to the view that the resolution of social and economic problems in Northern Ireland must wait for an answer to the political conflict, nor to the idea that the struggle over nationalisms is a diversion from the urgent project of social and economic reconstruction. The nationalist contest cannot be wished away by a concentration on social reform. Equally, the problems of a small and weak region, vulnerable to current global economic shifts, require immediate attention.

Both the Nationalist and Unionist perspectives on Northern Ireland benefit from an uncomplicated analysis from which it is relatively easy to prescribe appropriate solutions. Political intervention thus becomes clear-cut and directed towards readily identifiable objectives. Such clarity becomes more difficult if it is seen that there is not just one crisis, but two, which inter-penetrate, yet retain an autonomy. While this does not permit the same incisive set of prescriptions offered by the main protagonists, it does recognise the more ambiguous and contradictory nature of the conflict. This also involves understanding the degree to which general processes of change — such as industrial restructuring — impact on Northern Ireland and in turn are mediated by the specifics of its local politics.

Our intention is to examine economic and social change in a political context, but a broader one than the politics of the region itself. The focus is on the last ten years, the decade of Thatcherism. Since the election of the Conservatives in 1979, a great deal of material has been written on the significance of this period. The term 'Thatcherism', coined to describe a distinctive style of government and a Radical Right approach to public policy, has become commonplace. Its objectives have been about reversing the downward trend of the British economy, partly through reducing what it sees as a swollen public sector. It has also consistently adopted a strong posture on 'law and order', emphasising the need to protect the ordinary citizen from the 'criminal element'. In one sense, Northern Ireland would appear to have been a prime candidate for the Thatcher treatment. Its economy had been suffering long-term decline, while the relative size of the public sector was much greater than in Britain. Moreover, its 'security' problem posed a major challenge to the authority of a strong government. In these ways, it might have been the ideal test case for the new approach. An article in *Labour Research*, February 1990 — **Northern Ireland: A Double Dose of Thatcherism** — suggests that the region has been on the hard receiving end of the Thatcher treatment. We wish to qualify this typical assessment.

Essentially, this book analyses the degree to which recent Conservative policies have been applied to Northern Ireland. It does so:

☆ first, by a critical examination of the concept of Thatcherism, exploring its relevance to Northern Ireland politics;

☆ second, by examining certain key areas of social and economic change in the region,

☆ and finally, by looking at a range of case studies, documenting the British experience and evaluating the extent to which a parallel course has been taken in the region.

The subjects chosen have been the economy, poverty, urban policy, inner urban renewal, housing, developments in education, and reform in the Northern Ireland NHS. Where the Thatcherite policy approach has been more pragmatic, or less severe than in Britain, possible explanations for the differences are examined. The intention is to throw more light both on the complexity of Northern Ireland and of Thatcherism. Moreover, it recognises that the process has not simply been one of applying British policy to the region. In some respects, developments within Northern Ireland have been exemplars for

British policy-making. This refers not merely to issues like riot containment, but others such as reduction of local government powers. This is an opportune time for such an assessment, coinciding as it does, not merely with a decade of Margaret Thatcher as Prime Minister, but also with two decades of British troops on the streets of Northern Ireland.

# 1. Thatcherism and Northern Ireland

## Thatcherism: An Elusive Concept

In February 1975 Margaret Thatcher assumed the leadership of one of the most traditional and patrician of parties in the Western liberal democracies. Just nine months previously she had herself scoffed at any such prospect:

"It will be years before a woman either leads the Party or becomes
Prime Minister. I don't see it happening in my time."[1]

In the mid 1970s the Conservatives were in a state of despondency, having experienced four defeats in the previous five general elections. Since then, Margaret Thatcher as Conservative leader has faced three different Opposition leaders, achieved a triple success in the 1979, 1983 and 1987 general elections — a feat unequalled by any Prime Minister since Gladstone — and blithely boasted of her intention to "go on and on and on". The Tory Party of the paternalistic grandee has been radically recast in her own image of the aspiring and self-made suburbanite.

The political agenda has also been refashioned so that previously eccentric advocacies about money and markets have been converted into new orthodoxies. Whole institutions and professions, for long immune from scrutiny and challenge, have been subject to significant review, and in some estimates, major change:

"The old guard at the BBC has been turfed out. The universities have been so alienated that Oxford will not grant Mrs Thatcher an honorary degree. The glittering prizes in the civil service go to can-do meritocrats, not to elegant wordsmiths. The legions of local government have been chopped down; the ermin'd gowns of the law are next on the list to be reduced to rags."[2]

Her electoral pre-eminence has survived the kind of traumatic events which scuppered her predecessors — over three million unemployed, major urban riots and a bitter year long confrontation with the miners. She has pursued a doctrinal course with a stridency and relentlessness which has disturbed even sections of the British Establishment. While other attempts within the Conservative Party, such as Powellism, to rally and harness a New Right movement failed, and Edward Heath's earlier flirtation with Selsdon Man proved equally abortive, Mrs Thatcher has in fact managed to secure a restoration of reactionary politics. It is a formidable performance.

Yet the very concept of Thatcherism is itself contestable. For some, it mistakenly accords current Conservatism an undeserved distinction and mystique, at once elevating a particular leader and hypnotising opposition to her into political paralysis. This amounts, they argue, to personalising politics to a point of frivolity. To such critics, the Thatcher administrations have simply adopted policies demanded by the 'logic' of a crisis-ridden capitalism, geared to radical restructuring. While they concede that they have pursued this class interest with a single-minded resolution, they infer that any Conservative government — and probably even a right-wing dominated Labour government — would have performed similarly, confronted with similar imperatives.

Those for whom the concept of Thatcherism does have currency represent it as a qualitative departure from the social democratic consensus which emerged after the Post-War Settlement. It is not just that Mrs Thatcher is perceived as someone contemptuous of the indifference of consensus compared to the commitment of conviction politics. It is also that the policy agenda of the last decade has witnessed a significant break with the universalist and redistributive principles of welfarism and the interventionism of Keynesian economics.

## Paving the Way

The intellectual ground for Thatcherism had been constructed for some time before Mrs Thatcher's ascendancy. Hayek and Friedman[3] had delivered numerous tracts decrying the economic inefficiencies and political tyrannies contingent on the distortion of free markets. The primary cause was judged to be escalating government intervention. Back in the 1950s, the Bow Group had been established inside the Conservative Party to challenge the pre-eminence of Fabian nostrums. Its magazine, *Crossbow*, operated under editorial principles such as the need for a classless Conservatism and for social and economic policies derived from the free market. In the 1960s Enoch Powell stood out as a champion of de-regulation and traditional Toryism, and attained a brief, though potent, notoriety by tying these elements into the issue of race. The early years of Heath's administration were characterised by its adherence to Selsdon principles of reduced state support for industry. However, after two years, Heath largely retreated to conventional economic management and reflation in the face of soaring unemployment and mounting industrial unrest.

From the mid 1970s, a series of publications from bodies such as the Centre for Policy Studies and the Institute of Economic Affairs established an embryonic strategy for a new and more confident Radical Right. Their critique of the old consensus amounted to an effective and caustic demolition. These ideas were elaborated by journalists such as Samuel Brittan and Peter Jay in the quality media and subsequently propagated in a more accessible form in the popular press. Meanwhile, on the political stage itself, Keith Joseph was evangelising the efficiency of a market-led restoration for an economy stagnant in the quagmire of corporatist ineptitude.

The momentum for change had a peculiar 'back to the future' strain — a rediscovery of past virtues as a pre-requisite for future prosperity. It was both radical and reactionary, a form of politics some commentators later dubbed 'regressive modernisation'. An example of this is Mrs Thatcher's fondness for acclaiming a mythic Victorian age when a resilient people with resourceful spirit were supposed to have prospered on the virtues of enterprise, thrift, discipline, morality and patriotism. The years of socialism had been corrosive of that spirit to a point where today people faced with adversity were passive and supplicant for state handouts. "Dependency corrupts, absolute dependency corrupts absolutely", she has warned.[4] Only a rediscovery of Victorian values can redeem the nation from disarray and inexorable decline.

## The Challenge of the New Right

Challenging the Beveridge-Keynesian precepts on which post-war social democracy was constructed, the New Right platform comprised certain central propositions. In its view, government management of the economy was a case of the undesirable in pursuit of the unachievable. The concentration on demand rather than supply side economics was detrimental to sustainable growth, while the key policy objective to maintain full employment eschewed other economic goals such as the control of inflation. An ever expanding role for nationalisation — despite its transparent inefficiency — had become accepted since the concept of the mixed economy had itself been mistakenly accorded legitimacy. Moreover, the credibility given to trade unions under the drift to corporatism had enhanced their militant capacity to organise workers into 'labour monopolies'. In turn, this had distorted the labour market and restricted the scope for employers to deploy their workforces flexibly and profitably. Under welfarism, wealth redistribution had been allocated greater priority than wealth creation. This had led to a profligate public sector, borrowing beyond its means in a vain attempt to catch up with ever more generous definitions of social need and poverty. The ratchet effect of a universalist welfare system had increasingly crowded out the private sector, feather-bedded the work-shy, demeaned the work ethic, and imposed a penal tax burden on the risk-taking entrepreneur. The more impoverished the economy became due to the subsequent profit and investment squeeze, the greater the levels of unemployment and welfare dependence. In turn, this increased burden demanded escalating welfare expenditure, which only further eroded the capacity for wealth generation. It was a pattern which could only portend a grave fiscal crisis for the state. In other words, the relentless drive to egalitarianism not only dissipated enterprise, it also created a demoralising dependency on a state whose decreasing tax base could not support an increasingly claimant society.

Competition between the two 'monopoly' parties for votes in the political market had contributed significantly to this process. The spiral of increasing promises had become politically inflationary. It had produced a government overload, whereby the expanding scope of responsibility was unconducive to effective performance in any particular administrative sphere. Incompetence and equivocation had inevitably accompanied attempts to appease sectional interests, resulting in widespread public disenchantment with a politics which failed to deliver the high expectations it raised. In such circumstances, the legitimacy of the system itself was vulnerable. Yet, given what in right-wing apologetics[5] was perceived as the 'institutional sclerosis' in Britain, the capacity for a welfare-based state to respond flexibly to these pressures was retarded.

To the New Right advocates, the underlying strategy behind welfarism had ventured well beyond its original claims of modest incremental change. It had become, in fact, a social engineering project, tantamount to 'creeping' socialism. Their reappraisal suggested that the liberation of an enfeebled and fettered capitalism demanded an unambiguous disengagement from these spurious policies. It demanded a rolling back of the state to a more minimalist role in economic policy, and the conversion of an untenable welfare state into a more manageable residual service.

In general terms, the rhetoric was one of less government, less welfare, lower taxation, and curbed trade union power. Business would be less regulated but also less subsidised. Government would get off people's backs and out of their pockets. But, in return, individuals would have to rediscover the virtue of self-reliance.

More specifically, an incoming Thatcher government would apply the combined tenets of monetarism and supply side economics. This included the imposition of tight monetary control through fiscal restraint, and also, if need be, through high interest rates. Such discipline would pressure both labour and capital into a more innovative and exacting pursuit of efficiency and competitiveness. It would help achieve a better link between increased money supply and consumption on the one hand and increased output on the other, and between increased output and increased productivity. Thereby, obstacles such as inflation and balance of payments deficits, which had previously bedeviled the attainment of sustained growth, would be removed.

In the pursuit of this objective, many firms in the 'sunset' industries might falter and founder. But, they would either slim down to a fitter and more viable form, or else their demise would in time make way for a new vanguard of lean and mean 'sunrise' alternatives. To facilitate this transformation, the supply side of the economy would have to be freed from excessive regulation.

Incentives would have to be restored and the functional benefits of social inequality rediscovered. Also crucial was the reinstatement of the market mechanism as the most effective determinant of prices, wages, profitable investment and so on. This opening up of the economy would reinvigorate the private sector, and indeed promote opportunities for the privatisation of industries, services and assets currently trapped in the public sector.

It was apparent that the pressurised pace and scale of industrial restructuring inherent in this strategy would have a dislocating impact on individuals and communities, not to say whole regions. However, it was felt that the shockwaves of redundancies which might accompany the diminution or removal of state assistance to industry, might well alert people to economic realities from which they were customarily cushioned. Implicit in such an approach was an assumption that government should abandon responsibility for, if not indeed the goal of, full employment.

## Selling Thatcherism

Since in Thatcherism the medium has often been as significant as the message, it is interesting to note how this free market gospel has been sold to the public. After all, a philosophy which seemed to promote acquisitive individualism and to assess everything in terms of value for money was vulnerable to the charge of greed and philistinism. No political party could blithely risk its electoral fortunes by appearing immune to compassion and indifferent to the democratic deficits alleged by opponents. Mrs Thatcher has attempted to resolve this in several ways.

In the early years of her premiership she was keen to present herself as some kind of hybrid housewife cum warrior queen. The housewife could package the monetarist medicine in terms of domestic homilies about living within one's means. The warrior queen could herald the crusade against the male-dominated world of trade union barons and civil service empire builders. The policy of selling off council houses to sitting tenants was elevated into a grand design to create a property-owning democracy. Later, when the initially hesitant programme of privatisation designed in part to raise government revenue, was judged successful, it was projected in terms of extending a share-owning democracy of popular capitalism. In a similar way, very modest strategies to encourage self-employment and the growth of small business were boosted by being associated with the rhetoric about the enterprise culture.

This packaging of sometimes relatively minor programmes in large boxes has been adroit. Whereas understatement has traditionally been more palatable to fastidious Conservative taste, this Tory leader has been ebullient in the praise and significance she has awarded to her own policies. When her opponents have raised objections to the efficacy of this or that policy, she has been able to raid the repertoire of New Right dictums to respond with a novel political vocabulary. Her answers have invariably implied that the question is the trite product of a stale political imagination, which remains resistant to the new agenda.

For example, the case has been repeatedly made that the trend towards greater market determination in such areas as urban development and social services has increased centralisation, dismantled local democracy and impaired standards of provision. Mrs Thatcher's riposte does not address the issue in those terms. Rather, she conceptualises it in terms of consumer sovereignty. The individual directly affected, more than the distant politician or interfering bureaucrat, is best placed, she argues, to exercise choices about his/her own life. Markets can sensitively register that demand and the private sector can interpret the signals and respond appropriately. The extent to which the private firm can offer efficient and competitive service delivery will determine whether the consumers vote with their money to elect it again as a suitable candidate for their custom.

Of course, the argument is seriously flawed. It refers to demand rather than need. The choice is for those with money who can jump queues of more deserving applicants. It assumes that individuals separately pursuing their-self interest add up to a common social good. It attributes a responsiveness to markets and a level of competition among firms which are inoperable in an age of greater monopoly as well as market manipulation by means of advertising.

However, regardless of its threadbare logic, the relevant point is that the way Margaret Thatcher chooses to engage astutely shifts the terms of the debate. The Opposition finds itself in terrain where it is vulnerable because of its ambiguous attitude to the virtues of markets or the redefined notion of democracy.

Another notable aspect of selling Thatcherism has been the role played initially by Saatchi and Saatchi, and subsequently by a plethora of public relations consultants, who advised the Prime Minister to temper her strident voice, restock her wardrobe, reset her teeth and restyle her hair. The same advertising agencies were responsible for the Americanisation of Tory Party presentation. They bestowed a new razzmatazz and orchestration to showpiece rallies, which highlighted the authoritative image of Mrs Thatcher before her flag-waving devotees.

## The Four Phases

One problem with the loose application of the term Thatcherism is that it suggests an ideologically driven force, which has remained undaunted and consistent, whatever the prevailing political turbulence. A more accurate reading of the period under Mrs Thatcher illustrates the extent to which a reluctant pragmatism occasionally intrudes and prompts her government to retrench and consolidate rather than press forward precipitously. One example relates to her dealings with trade unions. Despite her impatience for their early emasculation, she acceded to Jim Prior's inclination to pursue change incrementally. Within five years the government had achieved a legislative framework which substantially left unions bereft of effective industrial sanctions. A more cautious and gradual approach had delivered the desired objective. Similarly, a contrived showdown with the miners was delayed until the strategic contingencies for its successful outcome could be secured. So the trait of impulsiveness often attributed to Mrs Thatcher is overstated.

On the other hand, the implementation of a deflationary 1981 budget at a time when the economy was already reeling from recessionary pressure provoked widespread incredulity and opposition. It appeared to many as a provocatively blind adherence to monetarist dogma despite the looming prospect of a crash landing for the economy. This period proved critical for Thatcherism. Under intense pressure after 1980 to ditch her strategy, she defiantly declared: "You turn if you want to. The lady is not for turning."

For all the manipulative expertise of the public relations consultants, the remodelling of the Tory leader and party could not avert the slump in their popularity registered in successive opinion polls in the early 1980s. Yet, in the course of the last decade, Thatcherism has succeeded in recovering from such periods of deep unpopularity. The Westland affair in 1985-86 was, by Mrs Thatcher's own admission, a crisis which brought her near to resignation. Successful management of these periods does, for some, indicate that Mrs Thatcher possesses a statecraft, to which she is capable of subordinating her more instinctive inclinations.

So the ups and downs of her political fortunes over the decade have been reflected in what we may call the phasing of her policy agenda. At least four distinct periods are discernible. The first stage, 1979-82, witnessed the beginnings of the dismantling of corporatism, the implementation of monetarism and supply side economics, and the creation of the strong state headed by the resolute leader. It was also a period when Mrs Thatcher was personally keen to associate herself with the anguish felt by those of a moral majority mentality about declining virtue. The radical credentials of the Thatcher regime were firmly established:

> "It was less concerned simply to shift the balance between capital and labour with the crumbling framework of the Post-War Settlement than to abandon the whole project in favour of a new edifice more favourable to capital."[6]

The second stage, 1982-87, saw the retreat from monetarism, a reflationary budget in 1982, a greater emphasis on supply-side economics, with references to the liberating and energising features of an enterprise culture and, of course, the jingoistic triumph of the Falklands. In other words, this chapter marked something of a strategic withdrawal from radicalism to consolidate the political ground captured in the early 1980s. For example, despite Festivals of Light

13

and other similar events, the moral majority never secured the prominence and influence in Britain which it did at this stage in Reagan's America. So, although there continued to be sporadic government tirades against the boorishness generated by a Labour-inspired permissiveness in the Sixties, Mrs Thatcher's association with the crusade faded.

The third stage, 1987 to October 1989, saw the re-application of the radical agenda with a packed legislative programme, which included privatisation, a community charge representing a major step in regressive taxation, and totally reshaped health and education services subject to the rigours of markets and competition. The package has been controversial in both content and the pace of change involved, and has prompted nervous Tory backbenchers to reassert some dissent in the face of improving electoral performance by Labour.

The most recent phase has seen a considerable degree of conflict within the government and a related decline in popularity. The dramatic departure of Nigel Lawson from the Chancellorship typified the mounting problems. As the resignation of a senior Minister, it echoed the Westland crisis. Losing one Minister in acrimonious circumstances might be considered unfortunate; losing two, careless! Moreover, the dispute was over the handling of the economy, a matter central to electoral success. And this at a time when the flagging fortunes of the economy were evident in a massive trading imbalance, a volatile exchange rate, high interest levels and renewed problems of inflation. It also exemplified the fissures in the Tory Party over Europe, which has become an increasingly tricky issue for the party managers. Coming as it did just weeks after a Cabinet reshuffle which turned into a debacle, her reputation for both competence and efficiency suffered. Nor did it benefit her posture as a principled politician, given the ambiguities which emerged concerning the reasons for the Chancellor's resignation. As in the immediate aftermath of the Westland affair, Mrs Thatcher, under public and party pressure, did show some contrition and resolved to operate more of a team government. But previous experience suggests that this reluctant repentance is likely to prove very transient.

Despite the distinctive periods in her decade-long administration that can be identified, it has been imperative for Mrs Thatcher to insist that no policy reversals or retreats have been sanctioned in the long haul of her grand mission. The bitter memory of Ted Heath's notorious 'U-turn' is writ too large in her political consciousness to permit her any such admission. Moreover, it is important for her that she is perceived as an unusual politician, one who is committed to unfaltering principle rather than electoral expediency.

# Understanding Thatcherism

In the expansive literature on Thatcherism, it is notable that a preponderance emanates from the political Left. Its analysis has developed considerably over the last decade. This is not only because the nature of Thatcherism has itself changed. It is also related to the way that the political opposition has been compelled to address the phenomenon more seriously, the longer it has persisted.

In the initial stage, to many in the labour movement the electoral appeal of neo-conservatism was somewhat bewildering. How could the public be deceived by such platitudes and certitudes, when they were in fact brimming with contradictions? Why could they not penetrate the insincerity of the pieties, particularly since they were delivered in Mrs Thatcher's husky tones of confected sentiment? Moreover, the critics could plausibly point to several key incongruities. Here was one of the most political of governments determined to depoliticise many areas of social life; one which espoused non-interventionism, at times almost anti-statism, yet which enhanced state power through increased centralisation and harsher measures relating to law and order and official secrecy; one which elevated the role of the family as a counter to supposed trends in permissiveness and child neglect, yet whose family policy was fatally deformed by social spending cuts; one which demanded greater civic responsibility and patriotism, yet proclaimed that there was no such thing as society; one which appeared libertarian in its promotion of individualism, yet was censorious in its moral prohibitions; a government which promised tax cuts, yet raised the total tax burden for most people through increases in VAT and national insurance payments; talked of reducing public expenditure in real terms, yet raised it to pay for its real increases in military spending and for unemployment benefits to the million and a half additional unemployed its policies helped to create; espoused competition, yet privatised monopolies; extolled self-reliance, yet persisted with subsidies for the pampered middle class such as mortgage interest tax relief; embraced monetarism and then presided over the rapid expansion of the money supply; adopted Europe yet remained fervently Atlanticist; and all of this from a Conservative government committed to a frenetic pace of change and challenge to Establishment institutions.

The implication was that Thatcherism would be short-lived, its demise merely requiring the labour movement lucidly to proclaim a confident radical alternative. However, the Alternative Economic Strategy developed in the early 1980s failed to articulate a programme with popular appeal. It never found a persuasive means of integrating its three main strands — reflation, restructuring and redistribution. While some Labour sympathisers continued to rationalise their second election defeat in 1983 in terms of the post-Falklands triumphalism and the dispirited presentation of Labour policy, wider recognition of the credibility and durability of Thatcherism caused it to be accredited with more considered assessment.

Several writers on the Left had been long advising their fellow adherents to examine Thatcherism and the rise of the New Right in a more self-critical gaze. Hobsbawm,[7] for example, addressed the long-term decline of labourism, which he controversially characterised as 'the forward march of labour halted'. At one level, this involved a process whereby the social and class recomposition of Britain in recent decades had eroded the natural electoral base of Labour's support. Put at its simplest, the manual working class, which for generations had constituted the bedrock constituency of the labour movement, was in an irreversible decline. The conventional appeal of Labour was primarily pitched at the white male manufacturing worker, whose electoral significance was being overtaken by other social groups more responsive to Tory concepts of individualism, opportunity and mobility. Moreover, the early idealism of the labour movement was being more critically evaluated in the light of its flawed performance in government. This type of analysis attempted to explain the apparent incongruity of why a Labour Party, which in the recent past could boast of itself as 'the natural party of government', now appeared to be demoted again to a party of protest and opposition. Others have since located this reversal in a more international trend:

> "The historic exhaustion of the Left is rooted in the exhaustion of its idea of progress. This exhaustion is evident in the lack of vision of socialist governments in France, Spain, Greece and Australia, and the rethinking underway in Eastern Europe."[8]

In this view, Thatcherism emerged in the context of a declining public confidence in the inevitability of a linear model of progress. The hope was fading that the physical world could be reshaped unproblematically and predictably by the white heat of new technology. Likewise, there was greater scepticism that the social world could be improved incrementally by a benign state, applying the sophisticated tools of social science. The welfare state, designed to help manage crises in capitalism, was itself deemed to be in crisis,[9] thus posing a fundamental threat to the legitimacy of the old social order — a "crisis in crisis management".[10]

According to this perspective, Thatcherism is not exclusively culpable for the current vagaries of welfarism. Its inadequacies preceded Thatcherism and indeed helped to create a political space for a New Conservatism, which could articulate the widespread disenchantment with the public sector. In this respect, Stuart Hall was perceptive in asserting that the Radical Right was not only a problem **for**, but also a problem **of**, the Left.

Stuart Hall has been credited with coining the term Thatcherism. His influential article **'The Great Moving Right Show'**[11] preceded Mrs Thatcher's first election victory, when her grip on her colleagues, never mind her ascendancy over the Opposition, was still less than assured. Nevertheless, Hall was one of the first to appreciate that Thatcher-led Conservatism was earnestly intent on a radical transformation of Britain, that its programme was comprehensive and ambitious in scope, coherent in content, and would be confrontational and persistent in application. Accordingly, assessment of its impact should be similarly extensive:

> "....it should be judged in terms of its success or failure in disorganising the labour movement and progressive forces, in shifting the terms of political debate, in reorganising the political terrain and in changing the balance of political forces in favour of capital and the right".[12]

In this view, Thatcherism could be electorally defeated while remaining politically successful. It could achieve a sufficient hegemony that would, at the very least, determine the terms on which any Opposition secured victory. For some, the extent of this hegemony is already evident. They point to the way in which Labour has been compelled to abandon previous strategies on defence and the economy. They highlight the new reverence accorded to markets and competition in its remoulded programmes derived from its policy reviews, and the generally more defensive tone in Labour's advocacy of the public sector and trade unionism. It is a metamorphosis well symbolised by the Red Flag furling into the Red Rose. This in itself is indicative of Labour's enthusiastic embrace of public relations and personality cults. And so Mr Kinnock has forsaken his instinctive and appealing humour and amiability in his imitative quest to acquire Mrs Thatcher's gravitas and authority.

But there remains an enigma about any extravagant claims about a Thatcher hegemony. On the one hand, successive opinion polls register a widespread public opposition to many of her values, record an ongoing concern for high unemployment and an under-funded health service, and continue to hold it to be a government responsibility to redress these short-comings. Yet, as Hugo Young[13] has noted, this same public has continued to re-elect the very representation of all that they appear to reject. So, to what extent has a new hegemony been securely established?

Jessop et al[14] contend that Stuart Hall concedes too much success in this respect to Thatcherism. They argue that by presenting it as a homogeneous force, he tends to universalise its impact to an exaggerated degree. He has spotlighted what he sees as the success of the New Right in substituting its 'common sense' for the conventional social wisdoms in place since 1945. This achievement springs not just from its intellectual assaults on these verities, but also from its ability to offer an alternative social vision. In Hall's view, Thatcherism arrived at a critical conjuncture when the already grave debilita-tion of the UK economy was accentuated by global recession, the reserves of social democratic solutions seemed exhausted and discredited, and the Cold War was once again reaching freezing point.

With the perception of an unruly world in which both security and living standards were increasingly vulnerable, Thatcherism offered a more robust national defence and public order, together with economic renewal. The package was popularised by its capacity to appropriate themes such as 'nation' and 'family', while exploiting public resentment at bureaucratic inertia in face of cumulative decline.

The sensitive political antennae which helped Mrs Thatcher resonate with this public disquiet, the avowedly austere medicine she prescribed, and her steely determination to ensure steadfast adherence by the patient have been characterised by Hall as 'authoritarian populism'. It is a politics which attempts to combine acquisitive individualism with a centralised state strongly led, without confessing to any contradiction. It does this mainly by suggesting that the major impediment to the legitimate pursuit of individual advancement lies in organised blocs of sectional interests. Only the state can arbitrate in this circumstance and act for the individual by compelling the sectional interest to succumb to the national interest.

This dual nature of Thatcherism has since been addressed by other commentators such as David Marquand:

"A society of atomistic individuals, relating to each other only through the mechanisms of free exchange, in which intermediate associations are seen as conspiracies to distort those mechanisms and treated accordingly, is easy meat for state power."[15]

Thus, Thatcherism appears to abandon social democratic/liberal conservative statism by championing the people against the state and its bureaucracies, and against the experts and other patronising members of the cultural elite. Yet it is in fact reinforcing of state authority to free individuals from intermediary forms of power.

However, for those like Hall, who have emphasised the ideological aspects of Thatcherism, it is insufficient to dismiss her convictions as contradictory or to perceive her populism as provincial and moralistic. The appeal she makes extends beyond suburbia. It has a cross-class character built upon what Raymond Williams[16] has described as 'mobile privatisation'. This refers to the way in which modern production and consumption patterns tend to at once pressure, seduce and facilitate people into a more home-centred privatised life style. It is one conducive to the appeals of Neo-Conservatism. Mrs Thatcher may be rebuked for an imagination insensitive to social compassion. But for her the call for social compassion is misplaced. There is no such thing as society — only individuals and their families. In this new world, state welfare is largely redundant. The privatisation of public housing, education and health accords better with an age of consumer-oriented individuals, largely apolitical, adapting flexibly to changing patterns of work and leisure and motivated by personal opportunity and mobility.

This perspective emphasises the economic basis for the ideological and social changes addressed by people like Hall. It suggests that Thatcherism can appear to make a classless appeal because it offers something for everyone — cut-price shares for workers, cut-price houses for public sector tenants, greater incentives and restoration of management authority for business, and so on.

Some, like Krieger,[17] suggest that though this appeal was pitched in a form that seemed to transcend sectional interests, it was in fact a fairly calculated and targeted series of programmes designed to secure electoral support from specific groups. In this process of 'arithmetical particularism', electoral success depends on placating merely a sufficient section of the public. It can afford to marginalise some groups, for example, blacks, because their membership of the mainstream is not numerically necessary for securing an electoral majority. Thus, an 'underclass' of the excluded and impoverished is politically expendable.

Jessop et al[18] accept that Hall's interpretation helps explain how the Thatcher government's policies are popularly endorsed and politically legitimated. However, they claim that it is less illuminating when it comes to the analysis of the roots of those policies. The concept they advance instead is that of the "dual crisis of the British State", the crises in parliamentarism and corporatism which created the political space for Thatcherism.

In the case of the parliamentary crisis, they show how an increasingly volatile electorate was becoming less tied to the traditional two-party system. This de-alignment was occurring alongside growing sectionalism. Both processes eroded the capacity of the major parties to speak with authoritative mandates or adequately meet the requirements of representative democracy. These changes in turn were reflected in varied ways, from demands for new voting procedures to mounting intra-party factionalism. The ultimate effect was government confusion, loss of direction, indecision and unseemly bartering with specific interests to secure an uneasy consent. Jessop et al regard Thatcherite populism as a means of transcending this discord and uncertainty by achieving a government which was effective and which commanded legitimacy:

> "....Thatcherite populism is indeed predominantly plebiscitary and
> ventriloquist in character: Thatcher speaks in the name of the people
> against all sectional interests, including those in her own party."[19]

The other element of the crisis was the unpredictable and ineffective corporatism which tended to immobilise rather than facilitate flexible responses to rapid economic change. The tripartite agreements needed in the system, involving government, business and unions, were cumbersome to attain and fragile in their execution. This was exemplified in the deterioration of industrial relations into the 'winter of discontent' in 1978-79, following the optimism of the Social Contract. Thatcherism again seemed to represent a way of dispensing largely with corporatist machinery and operating the economy in a way which gave clear signals to, and predictable and sympathetic policy execution for, international capital.

Overall, while acknowledging the relative coherence, force and relevance of Thatcherism as a strategy for contemporary capitalism, Jessop and his colleagues are wary of the claims made for its success and durability. In particular, they argue against a pessimistic retreat by the Left into a New

Realism, which would effectively concede considerable political terrain to the New Right.

Further light is thrown on Thatcherism by Andrew Gamble who sees it as a composite of the social market economy and the strong state. It represents a strategy to escape from the cycle of economic decline by restoring favourable conditions for profitable capital accumulation. This implies industrial restructuring which facilitates an adjustment of the UK economy to the highly volatile and increasingly competitive global economy. Government's role in this transformation amounts to the fostering of the entrepreneurial spirit, restoration of incentives, taming trade unions' excessive power, and opening up the economy to unrestricted flows of international capital. Gamble comments:

"As an accumulation strategy this is fraught with risk, since it depends on ceding ground in most areas of industry to foreign competitors, and trusting to the ability of British companies and new entrepreneurs to seize opportunities in whatever new regime of accumulation emerges that will maintain Britain's status as an advanced industrial society."[20]

In the context of the internationalisation of production and the supposed shift away from the old Fordist mass assembly line production methods, economic modernisation depends on substantial investment and strategic planning. Considering the directorial role adopted by the governments of many of Britain's industrial competitors, Gamble is sceptical about the capacity of unregulated markets to protect, never mind advance, the UK's relative position. Interestingly, he concludes that:

"This is not a strategy for reversing decline so much as seeking to come to terms with it, and to reorganise British economy and society to fit a permanently reduced status".[21]

This is certainly not the impression created by the inflated influence Mrs Thatcher frequently accords Britain's new geopolitical role. The almost obsessive adherence to the concept of a British nuclear deterrent is a telling indicator of the failure of Britain — or more specifically, governments like those of Mrs Thatcher — to reconcile itself to a more realistic and humble global status.

The other component Gamble concentrates upon is 'the strong state'. His contention — not dissimilar to Stuart Hall's — is that the social convulsions consequent upon the reorganisation demanded by economic modernisation will inevitably displace and alienate many people. Those exiled from the new production systems as surplus to its needs have to be policed and contained in a manner supportive of public order and the security of those who are the beneficiaries of the new free economy. This element had particular appeal within the ranks of the Tory Party, where 'the hang them and flog them and short sharp shock' brigade has long been aggrieved at how the erosion of discipline and compliance has denigrated state authority.

Gamble also sees Thatcherism as a hegemonic project, though he takes hegemony to mean more than ideological supremacy. Rather, he understands it as an integrated form of ideological and political/economic domination. On this basis he concludes that Thatcherism should be seen not as a new hegemony as much as a prelude to a new hegemony.[22] Appreciating this distinction, he feels, helps resolve some of the central contradictory tendencies within Thatcherism. For example, while Toryism is accustomed to endorsing traditions and institutions, Mrs Thatcher never sees a British institution without wanting, in the words of Julian Critchley, to hit it with her handbag. Gamble explains this unusual historical position of Thatcherism as follows:

"The crusading style and the ideological certainties evident among Thatcherites seem alien to traditional conservatism. But understood as statecraft, aimed at determining the Conservative party interest and restoring the freedom of action and the authority of the party in government, Thatcherism is placed firmly in the most central Conservative tradition of all."[23]

Gamble argues that, to do justice to the complexity of the New Conservatism, a distinct examination is needed of its policy programme; its intellectual doctrines; the interest bloc it represents; the popular movement it mobilises; and the style of its leadership.

## Leadership Style

The issue of leadership style raises an interesting question — does Thatcherism depend upon Thatcher? Undoubtedly, there is much in her personal style which has become inseparable in the public mind from the substance of what her party now professes. Her abrasiveness and petulance signal an impatience with the old Toryism, which seemed resigned to managing Britain's decline. When she disparages her critics in depressed regions as 'moaning minnies' or those who 'drool' their compassionate concerns, she does so in the uncompromising tones of stern rectitude. When she affirms that "there is no alternative" to her policies, it is in the form of a haughty dismissal intended to browbeat any challenge. In other words, the hectoring voice and overbearing attitude convey an image which crystallises Mrs Thatcher's personal preferences: decisiveness rather than prevarication; efficiency rather than equality; self-assertion and self-reliance rather than dependency. The tenor of her remarks and demeanour of her delivery blend in with her message.

She has been called the most disloyal member of her Cabinet. This refers to how she frequently allocates herself a political position which transcends the government itself, almost as if she sees herself messianically destined to confront and subdue two oppositions — Labour and her own Cabinet. Indeed, there has been much comment about the extent to which she exemplifies Lord Hailsham's dictum about the premiership as elective dictatorship. It is plaus-

21

ible to argue that while the party system in this century has displaced Parliamentary with Cabinet government, she has often replaced the latter not so much with prime ministerial as with presidential government. By the early 1980s, she had largely filled the Cabinet and other public posts in her patronage with people who demonstrably qualified in her terms as being 'one of us'.

This inclination to be not simply primus inter pares but rather in a convenient contortion to be both of, and above, the government, allows Mrs Thatcher to appeal to the public over the heads of her colleagues and party. In this way, she can signal her sympathy with the popular mood without being hamstrung with the responsibility of delivering the popular demand. For example, she has declared herself in favour of capital punishment and, on the issue of immigration, she has empathised with those who feel 'swamped', a term laden with obvious racial connotations. The presidential tendency has occasionally caused her to speak of herself in the royal plural, so that with no evidence of self-parody she recently declared to the world that "we are a grandmother". Such pretensions, which can be interpreted as usurping a monarchical privilege, have apparently incurred considerable disfavour in the Palace. It is one thing to relish the image of the Iron Lady and the comparisons with Boadicea, it is less acceptable to indulge such vanities and actually impersonate the image.

In originally making her bold and stunningly successful leadership bid, she had tapped the bitter frustrations harboured by many backbench Tory MPs, particularly those on the Right. They had witnessed what they took to be a cowardly and calamitous loss of nerve under Heath. Their faith in the radical Conservative prescriptions of the early 1970s had never wavered.

Success simply demanded a more obdurate advocacy, and Mrs Thatcher could convincingly claim the necessary credentials. From this moment, she could rely on their fervent loyalty and zealotry to brace her for battle not only with a heathen Opposition but also with the agnostics and heretics within her own ranks. Those whose sentiments reflected more the traditions of One Nation Toryism, and who remained unchastened by the new creed, were cynically christened as Wets. The Thatcherites have always been mindful of how a failure or retreat on their part would permit these sceptics to deflect them from their course and reclaim the party for their brand of Butskellite conservatism.

The extent to which Mrs Thatcher has confronted rather than placated this internal party opposition is a significant measure of her intent to discharge a more distinctive stewardship than that of her post-war predecessors. The extent to which she has mostly managed to subdue or disperse this dissident faction is a testament to her political daring and dexterity. Unquestionably, it has been a high risk strategy played for high stakes. Traditionally, in the Tory Party, the leader, particularly when Prime Minister, can command an almost abject obedience from the rank and file. However, in return, the party faithful tacitly expect the leadership, in the exercise of its authority, to be respectful of its views. Mrs Thatcher, consumed by the imperatives and pace of her personal crusade, has exploited the former obligation, without indulging the latter responsibility.

All told, there have been some very grand theories concerning Thatcherism. The most recent and eccentric in this genre[24] consists of a psycho-analytical probe into how Mrs Thatcher's politics relate to her private anxieties, generated by an emotionally unexpressive mother and an idolised father. For example, in this perspective, her notorious 'milk snatching' when Education Minister was settling scores for the milk privation she experienced at the maternal breast.

But interestingly, amid all the academic debate devoted to understanding Thatcherism, she herself is keen to disavow the influence of any grand abstract philosophy:

"My policies are not based on some economic theory, but on things
I, and millions like me, were brought up with: an honest day's work
for an honest day's pay; live within your means; put a nest egg by for
a rainy day; pay your bills on time; support the police."[25]

Indeed, there are some analysts of Thatcherism who also disown any grand theory. Journalists like Riddell[26] and Young[27] and wet ex-government Ministers like Gilmore[28], Pym[29] and Prior[30] tend to record events in the Thatcher era and to deduce more modest and specific explanations for its emergence and endurance.

In this vein, the success of Thatcherism over the last decade can be attributed to prevailing circumstances at particular crucial periods. For example, it may be argued that its victory in 1979 was due less to the public's attraction to its programme than to the sense of drift and despondency in the Labour camp generated by its experience in government. By that stage, the Social Contract negotiated with the trade unions had collapsed into a bitter winter of discontent. Previously, in the aftermath of the IMF intervention, the Labour government had resorted to public spending restraint and had adopted the rhetoric of tighter monetary control, if not its efficient practice. In this respect, since it prefigured Thatcherite remedies, albeit in a diluted and more apologetic form, its subsequent criticism of the new Tory agenda sounded less than convincing. This analysis is also proclaimed by those on the Left who believe that the 'treachery' of the Labour leadership in the mid 1970s paved the way for the Thatcher years. In this view, most lucidly articulated by Tony Benn, Labour failed because it tried to manage the crisis in capitalism rather than use the crisis as an opportunity to transform the system towards socialism. The second election victory in 1983, which all but eliminated Labour representation in much of the South, tends to be explained largely in terms of the Falklands factor, despite the signs of economic improvement.

## The Falklands Factor

Following the Suez debacle in 1956 it was widely acknowledged that the days of Britain's gun-boat diplomacy in far distant waters were finally at an end. Mrs Thatcher's adventure in the South Atlantic seemed to dislodge that political touchstone.

The Falklands war represented a critical watershed in realising Mrs Thatcher's vision of a reinvigorated Britain, in which the people, for too long mesmerised by socialist delusions, could be reawakened to a nobler destiny beckoning from their glorious past. But the war not only helped to revive the old fundamentalisms about Britain's spirit and greatness. It also provided Mrs Thatcher with a victory to brandish before the sceptics and fainthearts she denigrated within her own ranks. And more menacingly, it allowed her to evoke the threat of the 'enemy within' when confronted by militant industrial resistance, in particular the miners' strike. The triumphalism behind her exultant command that people 'rejoice, rejoice' contrasted with the more sombre and circumspect tones of institutions like the Church. Its call that consideration also be accorded to the vanquished appeared to her as all too typical of a modern Britain, used to celebrating achievement with the apologetic contrition of a penitent rather than the justifiable jubilation of a victor. As such, it mirrored the wider welfare system which she derided for rewarding both the feckless and the successful with indiscriminate magnanimity.

For those analysts who prefer more pragmatic explanations, the hat trick success represented by the 1987 election victory poses greater difficulty. In general, they find the reason in the widespread popular perception of an economic upturn. There was good economic growth. Interest rates were down, while profitability, productivity and employment were all on the increase. Inflation seemed to be under control. With overseas assets increasing, even the spectre of declining North Sea oil revenues seemed manageable. In these apparently favourable circumstances, the government could present itself as both generous and responsible when it cut taxes, and increased public expenditure, while still maintaining a budget surplus.

## Good Fortune

Apart from the specific positive circumstances which pertained for the Tories over the three general elections, many of the pragmatic analysts emphasise the sheer good fortune enjoyed by Mrs Thatcher. Not only did she enjoy the uncritical acclaim of a largely sycophantic press; the assent, however begrudged at times, of a submissive party and Cabinet; and an easy political passage courtesy of a divided Opposition, so that on a mere 42.5% of the popular vote she has been able to command parliamentary majorities of over 100. She also benefited from economic good fortunes, for example, the lucrative revenues generated by North Sea oil and the global conditions for lower inflation resulting from price reductions in commodity markets. Those who emphasise these extenuating circumstances — whether Tory Wets or Hard Left — infer that there is no sound reason to be bewitched by Thatcherism. In disputing the claim that it has installed a New Right national consensus, they point to successive polls which demonstrate that the values held by a majority of the public regarding the importance of collective welfare, the need for generous social spending, and government responsibility for economic management, are at variance with Thatcherism. On this basis, those on the Hard Left specifically refute the suggestion of the New Realists within the labour movement that adaption to the seismic shifts of 1980s politics is imperative for survival. Instead, they contend that Thatcherism, far from representing a new era of confident assertion for capital, signals a risky last-ditch manoeuvre to address the deep seated tendencies to crisis in the system.

The advocates of this position— Miliband[31] for example — place less emphasis on the ideological under pinnings of Neo-Conservatism. In their view, the crucial context for understanding Thatcherism is not only the relative decline of Britain's political and economic status in global terms, but also the wider issue of the weakness of 'old' Western capitalism relative to the vibrancy of Japan:

"....Western management was unable to import wholesale the highly successful Japanese organisation of labour. Worker resistance remained too powerful for individual firms to impose their will. The project of smashing trade unions and atomising the labour movement devolved increasingly on to governments. The most determined of these were the Thatcher and Reagan administrations."[32]

This view tends to regard Thatcherism as a class politics intent on seducing or subjugating the working class into bearing a disproportionate burden of capitalist modernisation. As such, it represents nothing new, neither in the liberalism of its economics nor conservatism of its public policy. It has recourse to the usual instruments of class discipline and retribution such as unemployment to weaken labour organisation and to penalise resistance. To some, like Tony Benn, it is simply a further step along the road from corporatism in the harsher measures it is prepared to deploy to win or enforce working class acquiescence.

One of the debates within this class reductionist perspective concerns the moot question over which specific class Thatcherism represents. There is a recognition that it hasn't been universally and consistently endorsed by all factions of capital. In the early stages, it could be seen as most evidently reflecting the frustration and disaffection of the petty bourgeoisie. Squeezed between big business and big government, without the established organisations representing a large section of the working class, the discontent of small enterprise and the lower middle classes cried out for attention. Thatcherism seemed sympathetic, at least rhetorically. Policies to reduce taxes and regulations, raise incentives, and elevate the status of those who were risk-taking and enterprising seemed assured.

Yet, as commentators like Gamble have made clear, the central direction of Thatcherite economic policy has been mostly oriented to the interests of high finance and international corporations. Much of the modest changes in taxation and regulation for the benefit of small business has been offset by high interest rates, increased VAT and, most recently, by the new industrial rates policy under the Poll Tax. Besides, the deflationary policies pursued for a good while under Mrs Thatcher depressed home demand upon which small business largely depends. Of course, there is no simple dichotomy between international versus domestic capital. Global capital has clearly appreciated decisions such as the abolition of exchange controls and the relaxed attitude by government to mergers and take overs. But there is often a difference of interest between big and small capital and also between the productive industrial sector and the finance and services sector. The former has, under corporatism, benefited from subsidies and other forms of state intervention. Its representations through organisations like the CBI have indicated that it is not exactly ecstatic to forego these supports while at the same time being burdened with costly borrowing and high exchange rates. On the other hand, financial services, typified by the City of London, have enjoyed a deregulation and expansion which have made them understandably appreciative of Thatcherism.

## A Broader Perspective

The majority of the commentaries examined here have tended to view Thatcherism as a product of the specific features of British politics. However, it also needs to be understood in the more general context of international economic developments and changes in the processes and location of production. For example, it has been argued that in the core economies there has been a move away from Fordist volume manufacture of standardised products in highly unionised mass assembly plants. The scale of this process is open to debate, but it is claimed that its direction is towards Neo-Fordism, which is geared to more flexible specialisation and batch production responsive to rapidly changing demands in affluent consumer markets.

In this respect, Lipietz[33] suggests that the recomposition of production and the relocation of capital are linked, in that the latter is a consequence of the failure of Fordism to sustain a growth in productivity and profitability. At an early stage, the phenomenon involved investment by major firms in depressed areas within the advanced economies, where, supported by regional policy incentives, subsidiary firms, using relatively unskilled and low waged labour, engaged in component assembly operations. This so called branch plant tendency was to prove inherently unstable for peripheral regions, due to the opening up of alternative sites for production in the newly developing economies and to the transfer into Neo-Fordist systems by many firms remaining in the Centre. Under the impact of these changes regional specialisation of industrial sectors has given way to new and starker regional differences. As Doreen Massey has argued: "....the old regional specialisms [cotton, coal, cars] are gone. The main regional contrast.... is between control and conception on the one hand and execution on the other, between the sunbelt and the rest."[34] This polarisation is sometimes represented spatially as the North-South divide.

According to this perspective, production has been progressively relocated and its processes reorganised. The spatial consequences have been to the benefit of some regions and to the detriment of others. This has not been an exclusively British phenomenon, but it has had its reflections within British politics. Economic changes have generated severe social costs, made new demands on the flexibility of the labour force and reinforced capital's tendency to become more international. Mrs Thatcher's government can be viewed as accommodating and facilitating these developments. It has been prepared to tolerate the growing inequalities in British society, assault the power of trade unions, accept unemployment at over three million and free up the economy for the easier operation of transnational capital.

Moreover, in the 1970s the Left analysis of welfarism suggested that collective social consumption was functional to the needs of capitalism by providing a reasonably healthy, well educated, workforce. For this reason, it was assumed that the welfare state would persist, even under Right Wing governments. But, as the needs of capital changed, so the value of social consumption declined. The Conservative government had therefore greater scope to restructure the welfare system. However, while Thatcherism has to be understood in the context of these fundamental economic changes, it clearly has an independent existence and is not merely their political expression.

The above review indicates the diversity of analyses of the Thatcher phenomenon itself. Accordingly, when the complexity of Northern Ireland politics is introduced, any assessment becomes even more difficult. Not only is there a large number of contesting theories about the nature and significance of Thatcherism, but there is an equal variety of conflicting interpretations of Northern Ireland politics.

## Northern Ireland: A Distinctive Politics?

The conflict in Northern Ireland stems from a fundamental contest of two nationalisms — Irish and British. The nature of the state in the region is therefore central to the dispute. From one perspective, it is an anti-imperialist struggle, in which Republican forces represent a progressive challenge against a reactionary and repressive British state in Northern Ireland. To the adherents of this position, the political division of the country in the 1920s was an illegitimate violation of Irish national integrity, which ever since has thwarted the right of Irish people to self-determination. Particularly from a left-wing Republican position, Partition was a deliberate instrument employed by a British ruling class, intent on stifling revolutionary politics in post-colonial Ireland.[35]

Contemporary Irish Republicans regard many of Northern Ireland's current ills — including the high unemployment and poverty endured disproportionately by Catholics — as legacies of the uneven development which typically accompanies imperialism. The Sinn Fein President Gerry Adams, has described Northern Ireland and the Irish Republic as "two artificial statelets" which were formed on a sectarian head count and, in the case of the North, sustained by sectarian repression.[36] Moreover, Partition, the instrument of British imperialism in this century, is held responsible for the debilitation of both politics and economics in the whole country. In the words of Sean McBride:

"Partition has distorted the economic and social life of this country. It has been responsible for destroying both the rule of law and the legal system, North and South. Political life has been completely distorted-Ireland does not have a normal alignment between the Right and the Left, divisions are based on the politics of the Civil War. Partition is completely responsible for today's tragedies in the North."[37]

The differences in wealth and status, derived from this sectarian distribution, provides no material basis on which a valid working class politics can be constructed. In this respect, the Northern Ireland state is beyond reform. The attainment of socialism is contingent on the achievement of an independent nationalism for the whole of the island. This involves not just a disengagement from the British State, but also from the European Community and largely from international capital, which are also judged to erode Irish sovereignty.[38]

From an opposite vantage point, Unionism is not so easily consigned to being the blinkered stooge of clever imperialist strategy in Ireland. In this view, Partition was arguably not Britain's preference as the most secure guarantee of its strategic and capitalist interests. Those who contend otherwise are seen to underestimate the relative autonomy of Unionism, and the pressures it exerted on a hesitant Britain. Moreover, the opposition marshalled against Home Rule amounted to more than just a ploy by a Unionist ruling elite to entrench its ascendancy. The Protestant working-class, though usually characterised in Republican analysis as the manipulated victims of false class consciousness, also perceived their economic interests being best protected by the British connection. Republican failure to appreciate the rational basis of the Unionist position, in this view, has doomed their appeals for a common Irish identity. In Unionist interpretation, it is a coercive demand for them to forsake their heritage and subordinate themselves in a Catholic-dominated and economically vulnerable state.[39]

Judged from this position, the persistent Republican challenge to the existence of Northern Ireland cornered the Unionist working class into a beleaguered reactionary response. As evident in times when this pressure ebbed, Unionist workers were amenable to bouts of progressive policies, which offered material improvements beyond the more typical sectarian distribution.[40] One example was the pressure they exerted for the full implementation of the British welfare state, which despite some reluctance, the Unionist leadership had ultimately to concede if only to maintain the cohesion of the Loyalist bloc.

Much depends on which of these two broad perspectives one believes to accord most closely with the reality of the conflict. For those who accept the imperialist model, "Northern Ireland is a British problem".[41] The best contribution that Britain can make is to declare a clear and irreversible intent to withdraw. In other words, Britain is the problem. If she takes her leave, the problem will largely leave with her.

From the other viewpoint, this conveniently conflates many problems into one. It addresses the divisions between Britain and Ireland with little sensitivity towards the real divisions which exist within Ireland itself:

"They (the Republicans) struggle for the right of the Irish people to self-determination but ignore the fact that the Irish people are divided as to how that right should be exercised."[42]

To the Northern Ireland Protestants, talk of "getting rid of the British" is a semantic expression for getting rid of them. Yet, Irish Republicanism has confidently assumed that Protestants will 'come round' once the British guarantee underwriting their position has been removed:

"We are talking about the Irish who are Protestants. Some of them are misguided enough to adopt a Unionist position. We will have to persuade them to do otherwise."[43]

This sounds very like making people an offer that they cannot refuse. It hardly squares with the promise to acknowledge existing cultural and political diversities in the construction of a New Ireland, though of course, some who aspire to Irish unity do distinguish between cultural and political pluralisms. As expressed by a member of the Irish Sovereignty Movement, Northern Protestants "have a right to be Unionists in that they have a right to their culture and to their religious beliefs, but they do not have a right to keep the sovereignty of a foreign power on this island."[44] In our judgement, this is an oversimplified account of a very difficult set of political/economic/cultural problems. It is concerns like these which figure most prominently in our reservations about the Republican case. A highly complex situation is reduced to the transgressions of a single villain. The loose application of the concept of imperialism facilitates this summary evaluation. A more elaborate understanding of the concept is necessary if its current relevance for the Irish-British relationship is to be upheld.

We take the process of imperialism to include the export of surplus capital from advanced industrial nations to less developed ones, and the super-exploitation of those subjugated regions, including their political and military subordination. In addition, their hopes of independent industrialisation are systematically frustrated, particularly in those sectors perceived by the imperial power to represent a competitive threat to its domestic industry. From this perspective, many of the relationships within Ireland and between Ireland and Britain, pertinent to the conflict, predate the age of imperialism.[45]

The modern historical development of the North East of Ireland involved a highly autonomous form of industrialisation. Its dependence on City of London finance and Britain's imperial markets was no greater than that of industrial regions in Britain such as the North East and North West.[46] Indeed, as we have argued elsewhere, it shared many characteristics with these British regions:

"It built up an independent manufacturing base with specialisation in certain sectors such as shipbuilding and textiles. The decline of that base in this century reflected similar trends to those in weak British regions like the North East of England or South Wales. The integration of the Northern Ireland economy with the British has been much greater than with the rest of Ireland. Like certain regions in Britain, the need for Northern Ireland is to reindustrialise rather than complete industrialisation, as is the case in the Irish Republic. Attempts to change and spread the mix of industries in Northern Ireland in the 1950s and 1960s were modelled on British regional policy. Amongst other things, this led to a high level of dependence on outside capital.

Northern Ireland, like other depressed regions in Britain, became more and more vulnerable to changing investment patterns at British and global levels. Finally, while there has been a move to some similarity between the two economies in Ireland, the Northern one remains more like British regions in terms of employment, unemployment and industrial structure."[47]

This distinctive development formed a material basis for the loyalty of the North East of Ireland to Britain, and ultimately for Partition. In more recent decades, the pre-eminence of transnational capital and the related demotion of local capital in both parts of Ireland have thrown up new kinds of dependency not satisfactorily subsumed in the traditional concept of imperialism.[48]

The long-standing relationship of Britain to Ireland has not been the same immutable one over the centuries, as can be suggested from Republican platforms. For example, in the 18th Century it still largely had a strategic purpose. Ireland was perceived as a convenient and willing stepping stone for an invasion of Britain by her European enemies such as France and Spain. In the contemporary geopolitics of Europe, the relevance of this military concern is well past. Similarly, in the current global economy the role of international capital has eroded the integrity of nation states and diluted the purity of sovereignty. As mentioned earlier, even Mrs Thatcher is having to reconcile herself to that reality in Britain, a country which some of its politicians like Tony Benn now see as a colony of the United States!

The assumption that Britain presently enjoys a material benefit from the maintenance of Partition, either in terms of profit repatriation or geomilitary advantage, has yet to be substantiated. Indeed, it has to be squared with the high levels of subsidy — around £1.6 billion annually — the Westminster Exchequer contributes to the upkeep of the Northern Ireland economy. Yet, some suggest that Britain should disengage not only militarily and politically, but also economically, without satisfactorily addressing the implications of this shortfall for the welfare of people in Northern Ireland.

Moreover, generalised claims about what is 'the British interest in Ireland' tend to underplay the differentiation and potential dissensions within Britain as between the British government, the British State, the British ruling class, and British multinationals. There is a substantial literature[49] which refutes the kind of deterministic analysis which is heedless of the fractions that exist in capital, class and state.

For these kind of reasons, we contend that any monocausal analysis of the problem, with its attendant one-dimensional solution, though seductive in its clarity and simplicity, is basically flawed. It fails to do justice to both the complexities of the situation as well as the diversity of the arguments.

Many ironies can be identified amid the complexities of this ancient quarrel. For instance, there is the dutiful indulgence in 'verbal' Republicanism by successive governments in the Irish Republic in their claim of constitutional authority over Northern Ireland. Yet, they have attempted neither the risk of military force to subdue Unionist opposition, nor the reform of their theocratic political culture which might make the prospect of Irish unity more appealing to them. The Irish Republic has largely contented itself with posturing and protesting, as in the inclusion of territorial claims to the North embodied by De Valera in the 1937 Constitution. This only served to demonstrate: "The weakness of their position, for these articles were no more than a legal fiction, designed to reconcile the contradictory abstractions of an ideology rigidly bound to a utopian world which bore no resemblance to that in which they found themselves. The Constitution represented a further retreat from reality into the refuge of hollow rhetoric and pragmatic partitionism".[50] Moreover, despite the attention devoted to the conflict in the Southern Parliament and media, there is a great deal of evidence from elections and opinion polls to suggest that most Southern Irish voters are either indifferent, circumspect or downright hostile to the political and economic costs of accommodating one million recalcitrant citizens in any new unified state. This ambivalence is shared by a section of Northern Catholics who also appreciate the unpredictable social dislocation consequent upon such a scenario. Meanwhile, Britain administers its responsibility for Northern Ireland, often only with the enthusiasm of a reluctant paternity. Again, successive polls demonstrate a desire by a majority of the British public to be rid of the burden. In other words, both governments feel compelled ritually to proclaim parentage of what they would each probably prefer to see in the foster care of the other.

Other contradictions in the situation abound. The main Churches in Ireland disclaim the significance of any religious dimension to the conflict. Yet their power in many influential institutions such as education is considerable. The Protestant churches declare their fidelity to a tradition of civil and religious liberty, yet they were notably silent about the abuses of civil liberties which occurred under the fifty years of unbroken Unionist rule. The Catholic church has allowed itself to be identified with the cause of Irish unification. Yet as an institution, it is in a certain way a beneficiary of Partition. It has, on the one hand, attained a dominant influence in a confessional Southern state, while in the North it has for long enjoyed the intense adherence typical of a congregation alienated from other social institutions.

The postures and practices of the paramilitaries are also demonstrative of a certain double-think. Loyalist paramilitaries have on occasion been prepared actually to fight British soldiers to illustrate their allegiance to Britain. Though they keenly recognise the authority of the British Parliament, virtually every major initiative that Parliament has sanctioned in relation to the conflict they have perceived as threatening to their interest. Meanwhile, they make sporadic and tentative overtures to their Catholic counterparts in Northern Ireland to establish a new and maybe independent Ulster, jointly governed by the two communities. Yet their record hardly makes the offer very credible. They have in the past been vehement opponents of power sharing, and have waged a brutal and random sectarian murder campaign against Catholics. They have yet formally to disassociate themselves from that strand in Unionism which depends almost exclusively on a virulent anti-Catholic politics.

On the other side, the Republican force similarly portrays itself in a confused dual personality. In one incarnation it comprises non-sectarian freedom fighters, legitimate inheritors of the Wolfe Tone tradition of achieving a new Ireland in the unity of Protestant, Catholic and dissenter. Yet, at the same time, it presents itself as the specific defender of the Northern Catholic community. Its success in realising either has not been notable. As John Hume recently commented:

"....the Provisional IRA and other Republican groups have killed six times more people than have the British Army. They have killed 2.5 times more Catholics than the British Army, the RUC and the UDR put together, and in the last 10 years have even killed more Catholics than the Loyalist paramilitaries. Somewhere along the road defending the Catholic community seems to have been lost sight of."[51]

With no electoral mandate for violence from either the North or South of Ireland, the Provisionals have executed a campaign noted for its elastic range of 'legitimate targets':

> "The IRA strategy is very clear. At some point in the future due to the pressure of the continuing and sustained armed struggle, the will of the British government to remain in this country will be broken....We will never fall into the trap of easing their military nightmare by restricting ourselves to specific sets of targets whatever their nature."[52]

At the same time, while still professing the irredeemable character of the Northern Ireland state, Sinn Fein has been adept at pressuring for claimant benefits awarded by this same state. Specifically, its call for more jobs, while its military wing blows up places of work, rings hollow to its political opponents.

Part of the reason for the protracted — and indeed maybe even intractable — nature of the 'troubles' is that these kinds of inconsistency are perceived by all the key actors in the situation. For instance, the paramilitaries are not likely to heed sermons from Mrs Thatcher about the cruelties of terrorism when they can point to her responsibility for the civilian deaths and injuries caused by the US bombing mission against Libya which took off, with her blessing, from British bases. By the same token, the valid complaints from the paramilitaries about British State's abuses of civil liberty and appalling miscarriages of justice, illustrated by the recent disclosures relating to the Guildford Four, can be countered by government references to the paramilitaries' use of torture in 'romper rooms' and the summary executions that follow their kangaroo courts, not to mention the deaths and mutilations resulting from bombing campaigns. In the course of this kind of verbal tit-for-tat, the moral high ground in the conflict tends to be rendered invisible in the mists of cant and recrimination.

In our view all of the actors in the present conflict need to reflect seriously on the assumptions with which they operate:

☆ The British public needs to be disabused of the notion that Britain's role in Northern Ireland is one of playing the thankless task of a benign referee, patiently arbitrating between two unreasonable tribes locked in some obscure 17th Century religious struggle. Britain is part of the problem and resolving the crisis in Northern Ireland demands that the fundamental relationship between the two must be firmly on the British political agenda. There has been some movement in this respect in recent years. A Tory government has declared that it will not obstruct the process of Irish unity, should it obtain the consent of a majority within Northern Ireland. Moreover, the Northern Ireland Secretary of State, Peter Brooke, made a significant statement in October 1989 to the effect that Sinn Fein's voice in a political settlement would be legitimate should the IRA first desist from its campaign. Labour has gone further, committing itself to work actively for constitutional change. This is a welcome break in the bipartisanship which has stifled debate in Britain for much of the last two decades. However, many of the key issues in the debate remain undeveloped.

☆ The Irish Republic is now in a more active role of responsibility towards Northern Ireland under the terms of the Anglo-Irish Agreement. That experience may help it to appreciate more the complexity of the situation and develop a more sophisticated political response.

☆ Within Northern Ireland, those who wish to convert others to an Irish identity have to recognise that narrow definitions of Irishness operate to exclude rather than welcome their potential audience. For Irish unity to be attained that is worth achieving, Republicanism needs to shift its strategy away from military coercion towards political persuasion. While Sinn Fein has become much more sophisticated and flexible in its tactics, it has retained a fundamentalist approach to strategic questions. In the 1970s Sinn Fein produced an **Eire Nua** programme which hinted at the idea of regional self-government. Now, this concession to the complexities of the Northern situation has been abandoned in current policy statements. Sinn Fein would prove itself more responsive to the demands of contemporary politics if it demonstrated greater flexibility at the strategic level.

☆ We have already indicated our differences with the general Republican analysis of the problem. It is committed to an armed struggle which offers little prospect of being winnable within a reasonable time span, and for the majority the level of violence is not proportionate to the level of repression being addressed. Further, the human and political costs in terms of life and limb, the brutalisation of the paramilitary participants and the greater polarisation of the community have to be assessed in terms of potential benefits, and these cannot be specified with any certainty. As Wickham comments:
"...a strategy of socialist transformation based on elitist forms of popular acclamation, such as those of old style European Stalinism or new 'Third World' nationalist liberation movements, is now as impossible in Ireland as elsewhere in Europe."[53]

☆ Conversely, those who believe in the long-term benefits of continued union with Britain have to demonstrate that it is no longer conditional on the preservation of their sectarian advantage. Those who condemn 'Republican outrages' but who remain silent when leaked security material is employed to set up Catholics for assassination can hardly expect political endorsement on any broad basis.

In other words, change in Northern Ireland, even from a hostile government, might best be achieved by a population prepared to recognise and accommodate both political and cultural diversity.

# Thatcherism and Northern Ireland

Northern Ireland is customarily presented in the British media as a place apart. This is not just a function of the ambiguity in Britain generally about its relationship to Northern Ireland. It is also an ill-disguised contempt for its perceived political obscurantism. So, it is hardly surprising that when comment is made about the impact of Thatcherism in Northern Ireland, there is a ready assumption that the region's peculiar circumstances have prevented the full application of Neo-Conservatism:

"Somehow it was fitting that the leader's final act in this completion of her ascendancy, after a thirty month passage of arms with the Conservatism she was determined to uproot, should be to call Prior's bluff (transferring the Secretary of State for Employment to the Northern Ireland Office).... Belfast was, in all circumstances, a natural terminus for this apostle of the old paternalism."[54]

The two interesting points in this observation are that Stormont Castle is a convenient exile for troublesome or mediocre colleagues, and that the writ of the old Toryism continues to run in that region. A similar comment has come recently from another seasoned political correspondent, Ian Aitken, in his reference to "the Independent Keynesian Republic of Northern Ireland, where monetarism remains unknown."[55]

If it be assumed for the moment that the conclusion of these commentators is accurate, and that Thatcherite public policy has indeed been given short shrift in Northern Ireland, this would amount to an outcome which would seem at odds with the very nature of Thatcherism itself.

For one thing, at a superficial level, Mrs Thatcher has frequently professed a respect for politicians inspired by conviction. Northern Ireland politics provides an arena where convictions and principles are found in abundance. It is a feature which has seduced fellow right-wingers like Enoch Powell, who perceive in its conflicts, central and engaging political questions. Moreover, the style of Northern Ireland politics offers many of the discordancies and drama in which Mrs Thatcher seems to revel. The patronising disdain with which she often repudiates the arguments of opponents departs from the etiquette of conventional political discourse in Britain. It is a tone conveying the kind of combative approach which prefers to decree rather than negotiate, and to impose by attrition rather than convince by persuasion. In its abrasiveness it echoes the tenor of political engagement in Northern Ireland, which British politicians are keen regularly to denounce.

Yet there is no evidence to suggest that Mrs Thatcher is attracted by either the content or the style of Northern Ireland's politics. The scarcely disguised relish she showed in facing down the challenges of Galtieri and Scargill has not been demonstrated in the cases of Ian Paisley or Gerry Adams. Sporadic events such as the hunger strikes and the Brighton bombing have certainly summoned her attention. But mostly she gives every indication of wishing, like her predecessors, that the problem would just go away.

Nevertheless, Unionists remain bewildered by her attitude. Many of their leaders have called on the Thatcher government to exercise the same fortitude and aggression in subduing the Republican challenge in Northern Ireland as it showed in the Falklands campaign. For them, the failure of the government to achieve this objective doesn't square with the image of an Iron Lady determined to restore the strong state, respect for authority and public order. The patriotic card she plays to perfection, enrapturing Union Jack waving audiences in Britain, resonates with the Ulster Loyalist, who similarly associates with 'Great' Britain and its imperial past.

There are, too, other examples of Thatcherite concerns which find a favourable response in the Ulster Protestant. That strain in her 'regressive modernisation' which extols the relevance for a prosperous future of a rediscovery of the values of discipline, hard work, enterprise and thrift, reflects a lot of the self-image in Northern Unionists. Likewise, her periodic moralising, particularly denunciations of permissiveness, meets with ready approval from a region prone to greater religious observance and abstemiousness. The following example of Mrs Thatcher's sermonising was well reported in the local Northern Ireland press:

"These people — like born-again prophets of the permissive society — are the ones who blurred the distinction between right and wrong; who showed more concern for the criminal than for his innocent victim.... It is not advice we require from these people. It is an apology. They not only left us an economic ruin, they left us a culture in decline."[56]

Those sentiments venerate the kind of moral world held dear by Ulster fundamentalists. So, in many respects, if Loyalists were to invest their trust in any modern British politician, she should have been an exemplary candidate. And for a brief period she seemed likely to occupy this heroine role. During all the awesome moral and emotional ambivalence evoked by the 1981 hunger strikes, in which ten Republicans died in agonising succession, she portrayed an imperious immutability. From her standpoint, they, as members of a movement which endorsed the brutal taking of innocent life, were taking a voluntary decision not afforded to the victims of Republican violence. Nevertheless, her apparent indifference to their plight touched a raw nerve in the Catholic Irish psyche, accustomed to equating the personal sacrifice of life with noble martyrdom. From this perspective, her stance was not merely devoid of compassion, it was also full of all the old colonial arrogance. This characterisation was confirmed for them when a few years later, in reaction to the policy options offered by the main constitutional Nationalist parties through the New Ireland Forum, she dismissed each in turn with a derisive "out, out, out".

Yet, in 1985, only a year after the Brighton bombing, which Loyalists might have expected to stiffen her resistance to any concessions to Irish Nationalism, she signed the Anglo-Irish Agreement. The governments of the UK and the Irish Republic signed an accord which appeared to permit the latter a formal say in the decision-making process for Northern Ireland. It represented a significant recognition by Britain that a substantial minority in Northern Ireland did not regard its authority as wholly legitimate and deserving of consent. In effect, Britain was recruiting another government, to which it was assumed most moderate Northern Nationalists felt a closer affinity, to assist it in securing stability. Though, in its present development, the Agreement falls far short of actual joint government, it does unquestionably amount to a qualification of British sovereignty.

As such, it was a remarkable decision by Margaret Thatcher. After all, isn't sovereignty this indubitably sacrosanct political substance, for which young soldiers were dispatched to Goose Green to devote life and limb to defend? Isn't sovereignty the kernel of Thatcherite resistance to aspects of the EC's internal market, perceived to be intrusive into the domain of British Parliamentary autonomy? And isn't sovereignty the key factor behind her unyielding denial of the validity of Scottish devolution, never mind Scottish Nationalism?

Indeed, it is difficult to identify any concept more revered in the lexicon of Thatcherism. Of course, the protection of the integrity of the United Kingdom has been long presumed to merit priority from a party which is called the Conservative and Unionist Party. It explains the particular betrayal felt by Ulster Unionists when Tory Party leader Ted Heath suspended Stormont and subsequently approved the Sunningdale Agreement, which also conceded a role for the Irish Republic in the Northern conflict — a so-called Irish dimension. Accordingly, for Mrs Thatcher to step even further in this direction, and without any consultation with the Unionists, has been for them incredibly disconcerting.

However, to appreciate better why Thatcherism is not such a predictable force in the way it operates in Northern Ireland, the distinctive features of the latter's administration and politics need to be clarified.

In 1972 the Stormont-based government of Northern Ireland was prorogued in the context of a deteriorating security situation. It was also in the aftermath of a counter-productive internment policy introduced in 1971, and sporadic military coercion, exemplified in the killing of 13 unarmed civilians in Derry on Bloody Sunday. The British government's role in Northern Ireland seemed both ineffective locally and tainted internationally. Unable to persuade the Unionist government to transfer responsibility for security to the exclusive preserve of the British government, the Stormont regime was suspended and Direct Rule from Westminster established. Apart from the brief period of a Power-Sharing Executive from January to May 1974, this status has continued.

The result would appear to place Northern Ireland in the same relationship to the British Parliament as Scotland or Wales. However, there are several significant differences. For one thing, neither Wales nor Scotland have ever experienced devolved government. Indeed, some opponents of the devolution proposals for them in the late 1970s pointed to Northern Ireland as a forbidding example of this form of government. Another difference is that Scotland and Wales typically have Secretaries of State who represent constituencies in the country concerned. That is not the case in Northern Ireland, a fact which accentuates the impression of a locally unaccountable overlord dispensing decrees in his appointed fiefdom. By contrast, it has been argued that because someone like Malcolm Rifkind hails from, and represents a seat in, Scotland, he has both the motivation and capacity to monitor the changing political mood there. Accordingly, his judgement about what is acceptable to the electorate has an authority which commands Cabinet attention. Whether or not this is actually the situation, it is at least very different from that pertaining in Northern Ireland for which legislation is enacted at Westminster in the form of unamendable Orders in Council. This has provoked criticism about the inability of local MPs to participate fully in the legislative process. A recent report from the Queen's University Ulster Unionist Association[57] argues that this procedure demotes the region to the status of 'an internal colony' within the UK. It recommends that a Select Committee on Northern Ireland should be set up, similar to that operating for Scotland.

Of course, another major difference compared to Scotland or Wales is that Northern Ireland developed its own political parties and discourse during the fifty years of its own self-government. The major political parties which contest elections in Britain were unrepresented in Northern Ireland. Critics of this state of affairs have pointed out that this makes the province the only part of the United Kingdom where people cannot exercise the basic democratic right to vote for a party which may form their government. In what may turn out to be a significant departure from traditional practice, on the 9th of November 1989, the National Union Executive Committee of the Tory Party granted official recognition to four constituency organisations in Northern Ireland. And in January 1990, representatives from these organisations met with senior Party officials in London, subsequently claiming that full support and subsidy would be forthcoming. It remains to be seen whether the Tories will actually allocate resources and personnel to construct an electoral machine. In a reflection of how different Northern Ireland politics can be, the deputy leader of the more extreme Unionist party, Peter Robinson, warned:

> "Conservative candidates will now have to face the electorate and explain health and housing cuts, the deplorable Tory policy of depriving senior citizens of a satisfactory level of pensions and the crippling mortgage rates".[58]

Under Direct Rule, the Northern Ireland Office, presided over by a Secretary of State, is responsible for the 'transferred' powers once exercised by Unionist governments. These include all the typical functions of government with the exception of so-called 'reserved' powers, such as general taxation, foreign relations and trade, and defence, which have always been the responsibility of the Westminster Parliament. In effect, one person with the assistance of several junior Ministers substitutes for the whole Cabinet of the old Northern Ireland government. Accordingly, many departments which used to be separate have been collapsed into new bigger departments. Moreover, a junior Minister is likely to be in charge of more than one of these enlarged departments. This centralisation has tended to make real political accountability difficult to achieve, and has accorded a lot of influence to the Northern Ireland Civil Service, which was, and remains, separate from the so-called 'Imperial Civil Service' in Britain.

So, considerable power is invested in the Secretary of State, who is represented in the Cabinet. Partly because the Northern Ireland post is widely seen in British politics as a taxing and thankless task, the occupant often appears to have some latitude in the implementation of government policy. This personal power, supported by the enhanced influence of the Northern Ireland Civil Service, has been further increased by the diminished role for local government in Northern Ireland.

Following the McCrory Report, the functions of local government were changed in 1973. Whereas in Britain, local authorities have responsibility for a wide range of services such as housing, education and social services, this is not the case in Northern Ireland. There the most obvious role retained by local government is the emptying of dustbins, the burying of the dead, and the administration of leisure and community centres. Impelled partly by the accusations of discriminatory practices on the part of certain local councils[59] and influenced also by the administrative urge to organise a more cost-effective form of service delivery, the decision was taken to remove many of the councils' functions. Accordingly, public sector housing throughout Northern Ireland is the responsibility of one central authority known as the Housing Executive. The provision of Health care, Social Services and Education is administered by Boards, whose membership is mostly appointed by the Northern Ireland Office. Thus, while one of the key imperatives behind Thatcherite public policy in Britain has been to curb the perceived excesses and obstructions of high-spending Labour-controlled local authorities, no such concern can be relevant in Northern Ireland.

In summary, any attempt to comprehend developments in Northern Ireland during the Thatcher years faces three sets of problems. First, there is considerable ambiguity and dispute generally about the impact of the ten years of Tory rule and the role of the Prime Minister herself. Second, there has been a long running and unresolved debate concerning the very existence of Northern Ireland and the source of its problems. Third, much of the analysis of the Thatcher project has emphasised its attempts to restructure the economy and welfare state; yet these two areas in Northern Ireland are different in both structure and significance.

# 2. Economic and Social Change since 1979: An Overview

## Politics Rules!

The special circumstances in Northern Ireland meant that the incoming Thatcher government retained the essential political priorities of the previous Labour administration: the continuing effort to contain, if not defeat, its Republican opponents; the quest to find some form of devolved government that would allow local politicians to accept a greater responsibility for affairs in the region; and the need to increase the level of co-operation with the government of the Irish Republic, particularly with respect to security issues. These priorities were primarily determined by the situation within Northern Ireland. Although the very high levels of violence of the early 1970s had abated by the end of the decade, the IRA and other Republican paramilitaries still demonstrated a capacity to sustain a bombing/assassination campaign, periodically exported to Britain as in the case of the car bomb that killed Airey Neave MP. Since the collapse of the Power-Sharing Executive under the impact of the Ulster Workers' Council strike, efforts to find an alternative system of devolution had been unsuccessful, as they continue to be even now. Moreover, it was believed within the British Army and the RUC that security co-operation along the Border was an essential prerequisite to defeating the IRA. It was argued, though without a great deal of evidence to support the contention, that the bulk of arms and explosives were moved from the Republic to be used in Northern Ireland. Equally, it was claimed that the Republic offered a safe haven for terrorists on the run. The question of extradition was therefore of some importance.

In all of these concerns, there was a virtual absence of a concerted strategy to resolve the political impasse. The IRA was regarded as a small group of terrorists, with a minimum of support and abhorred by all 'decent people'. Yet, its ability to maintain a military offensive showed it to be the most effective guerrilla organisation in Western Europe. The essence of the Irish problem continued to be viewed as an irrational conflict between warring communities. Only recently has there been any sensitivity to the deep structural inequalities between the two communities and the perception of the unequal application of the law, which help sustain the conflict.

At the same time, even a cursory glance at the 'terrorist crime' statistics (see Table 1) shows that the intensity of paramilitary activities has been less during the Thatcher years.

| Table 1 | Incident Statistics, 1972-1987 | | | | | | |
|---------|----------------------|------------|-----------------|------|------|-----|----------|
| Years | Shooting Incidents | Explosions | Armed Robberies | Deaths | | | |
| | | | | RUC | Army | UDR | Civilian |
| 1972-79 | 25,127 | 5,123 | 5,927 | 117 | 284 | 93 | 1,289 |
| 1980-87 | 4,392 | 1,912 | 4,869 | 120 | 62 | 68 | 372 |

*Source: Northern Ireland Annual Abstract of Statistics, 1989.*

These figures indicate a reduction in violent activity in the 1980s compared to the 1970s. The earlier period was distinguished by a Republican bombing blitz on Belfast, the resistance to internment and a sustained campaign of sectarian assassination, conducted mainly by Loyalist paramilitaries. The subsequent period was dominated by the IRA's attempts to consolidate itself within certain Catholic areas, an increase in punishment shootings, and the growth of protection rackets and armed robberies. The only group to suffer great casualties in the 1980s was the RUC. This reflects the IRA's efforts to destroy the policy of Ulsterisation of security responsibilities, whereby the RUC rather than the British Army was given the central role. From the statistics, however, it would appear that Northern Ireland for most of its residents was a safer place to live in the 1980s than in the previous decade.

In some respects, the adoption of certain new policies by the Conservatives only exacerbated their problems. The Northern Ireland Office's attempt to criminalise its Republican opponents by changes in the prison regime precipitated a hunger strike in which ten men starved themselves to death. The degree to which the Thatcher government remained unmoved by this suffering, and the mythic place held by hunger strikes in Irish Republican popular consciousness, combined to give a huge boost to the political support for Sinn Fein. When Sinn Fein then decided to contest elections, and, in the case of local authorities, actually take up seats they had won, it became a significant force, commanding about 10% of the vote. The presence of Sinn Fein councillors in local government has not merely been an embarrassment for government, but has provoked hysteria among Unionists.

Equally, the Anglo-Irish Agreement, signed by the British and Irish Republic governments in November 1985, was designed to usher in a new era of co-operation between the two. Nevertheless, the path to easy extradition has not been achieved, while Unionists have steadfastly opposed the Accord ever since. Although Unionist opposition does not have the force of the early 1970s, there remains little evidence that the Agreement commands any general support within Northern Ireland. A poll conducted by the magazine *Fortnight* indicated almost total opposition among Protestants and disappointment among Catholics that it had failed to deliver anticipated reforms. This is perhaps a reflection of the inherent tensions in the Accord. If the British government permits particular policies to be interpreted as concessions to Catholics obtained via the Agreement, it further alienates Loyalists. On the other hand, if it fails to attribute any significant change to the impact of the Agreement, it loses even more legitimacy among Catholics. Thus, even during the Thatcher years, the particular politics of Northern Ireland have remained the government's dominant concern in its efforts to develop policies for the region. Nonetheless, there have been significant economic and social changes which directly stem from the general strategies of the Thatcher government.

First, the recession of 1979-81 had a profound impact on the region with unemployment escalating and manufacturing falling into sharp decline. While the second oil price shock contributed to that recession, the tight monetary policies of the Thatcher government exacerbated its effects. The continuation of such policies until at least the 1982 budget, created a negative environment for manufacturing with predictable effects. Indeed, only the reversal of these monetary policies, permitting a growth in effective demand through the relaxation of credit controls, halted the remarkable fall in output experienced between 1979 and 1981. Northern Ireland could not be insulated from this recession. Its already fragile economic base proved particularly vulnerable. Redundancies tripled, unemployment doubled and many of the firms attracted in the 1960s and 1970s either contracted or closed. The artificial fibre industry, largely dependent on crude oil base as raw material, virtually disappeared. Northern Ireland's electricity generating capacity also depended on oil, so increased prices fed through into higher industrial costs. Only substantial subsidy maintained electricity prices equivalent to those in the most expensive region in Britain. The fall in regional output and the growth of regional unemployment were sharper than for the UK as a whole.

Second, the Conservative government set about reconstructing key elements of the welfare state and tax system. Social security provisions are applied universally in the UK and so Northern Ireland residents have also suffered as a result of these reforms. The shift in emphasis from direct to indirect taxation disproportionately affects those on low incomes who are well represented in Northern Ireland's population.

Nevertheless, certain policies in Northern Ireland have been operated less rigidly. It can be argued that it has actually been relatively protected compared to other parts of the UK. For example, in a report published in 1989 the Northern Ireland Economic Council contended that:

"Public expenditure in Northern Ireland (excluding social security), has grown by about 1.3% per annum in real terms over the past five years. This compares with an average annual decrease nationally of approximately 0.5%."[1]

The increased emphasis on Law and Order spending does not account for the whole of the difference. As a result, certain characteristics of Northern Ireland have improved, particularly relative to the poorer British regions. The apparent paradox that the citizens of Northern Ireland have, in a sense, benefited from a government generally castigated for its approach to the poor, reflects but one of the ambiguities of the concept of Thatcherism.

The purpose of this chapter is to document some of the economic and social changes that have taken place in Northern Ireland over the last decade. Comparison will be both with the previous period of the Labour administration and with other UK regions in the contemporary period. The intention is to provide an overview in which to situate the detailed case studies to follow.

## Basic Comparisons

Because of the very substantial difference in population, Northern Ireland does not easily compare with Britain. Instead, comparison will be made between Northern Ireland and selected British regions. At the same time, these regions also exhibit remarkable differences, as evidenced, for example, in the debate about the North-South divide. Accordingly, four varied regions have been chosen to reflect such differences: the North and Wales as examples of peripheral regions suffering serious decline; and the South East and South West as two currently prosperous regions. Table 2 provides basic information about the four regions and Northern Ireland.

The small size of Northern Ireland is immediately evident, with a population of only two-thirds that of Wales and less than an eighth of the South East. Also, like Wales, it has a low population density and is thus more rural than the other regions. Its population structure is distinguished by having a high proportion aged less than fifteen. Young dependents are thus an important segment of its population. To the degree that this is reflected in household size, there are implications for household income. Moreover, figures for Gross Domestic Product (GDP) per head will be artificially lowered, since those under 15 play almost no role in the production of GDP. Conversely, there is also a lower proportion of those aged 65 or more, a reflection of very high rates of emigration in previous periods. With its higher birth rate, Northern Ireland is likely to have a greater proportion of young people than other regions for some time to come.

| Table 2 | Basic Profiles: English Regions, Wales and Northern Ireland | | | | |
|---|---|---|---|---|---|
| | North | South East | South West | Wales | N.Ireland |
| Population (1986) (000s) | 3,080.0 | 17,254.0 | 4,543.0 | 2,821.0 | 1,566.0 |
| Persons Per Sq. Km. (1986) | 200.0 | 634.0 | 190.0 | 135.0 | 111.0 |
| % of Population under 15 | 19.2 | 18.5 | 18.0 | 19.3 | 25.6 |
| % of Population 65 and over (1985) | 14.8 | 15.2 | 17.8 | 16.0 | 12.0 |
| Birth Rate (1987) | 13.1 | 13.9 | 12.4 | 13.3 | 17.7 |
| Death Rate (1987) | 12.2 | 10.6 | 11.8 | 12.0 | 9.7 |
| Employment (1987) % in: | | | | | |
| Agriculture | 2.8 | 1.4 | 3.3 | 3.0 | 7.3 |
| Industry | 34.4 | 28.4 | 28.8 | 34.0 | 28.0 |
| Services | 62.8 | 70.2 | 67.9 | 63.0 | 64.8 |
| Unemployment Rate (%) (Eurostat 1987) | 14.7 | 8.2 | 8.7 | 12.9 | 18.9 |
| GDP (1986) | 92.0 | 121.0 | 97.0 | 87.0 | 81.0 |
| Note: The average for the whole of the European Community is taken as 100 | | | | | |
| Source: Regional Trends, 1989. | | | | | |

Curiously, for a region with a long industrial history, Northern Ireland has a low proportion of its employment concentrated in production. In that respect, it is more like the South East and South West than the other regions whose industrialisation was more similar. Whereas industry has been crowded out by a concentration on traded services in the Southern regions, in Northern Ireland it has simply declined. The employment slack has been to some extent taken up by the public sector which today accounts for over 40% of all jobs. But its unemployment rate remains substantially higher than in any other region, while GDP remains low.

Thus, quite apart from the particular form of its politics, Northern Ireland demonstrates distinctive differences from other UK regions. These include size, population, employment structure, levels of GDP and unemployment. Given also the tradition of a separate political administration, it is perhaps unsurprising that in certain policy areas, as we shall see, the application of Thatcherism has been less stringent.

## Public Expenditure and GDP

The first policy statement of the Thatcher government on public expenditure commented: "Public expenditure is at the heart of Britain's present economic difficulties."[2] It is clear that monetarist theory had a distinct influence on public policy. Since inflation had become the most important problem within the economy and the inflation rate seemed to vary with changes in the money supply, the key to tackling the problem lay with its control. Two steps were regarded as important: first, the imposition of a tight monetary policy through increases in interest rates; second, the reduction of government expenditure, which had been previously financed by excessive borrowing and the printing of money. However, cutting back on public expenditure was less easy than supposed. The impact of certain policies necessitated greater expenditure.

Allowing unemployment to rise, as the government did after 1979, resulted in greater demands on social security, even though the government also allowed the real value of social security benefits to fall. The much greater number of claimants still resulted in an increase in overall expenditure despite official intentions. Also, changes in demography compelled more expenditure. The health needs of an ageing population mean that more resources are required, even if the level of service delivery remains constant. Finally, pre-election promises to increase expenditure on defence and law and order had to be kept.[3] For all these reasons, Conservative claims that public expenditure would be brought under control in the short term, were unlikely to be realised. Thain and Wright, for example, claim:

"They did not achieve the Conservative government's initial aim of cutting public expenditure in real terms, nor even its second less ambitious objective of holding public expenditure steady. They were successful, however, in relieving the pressures for more spending which increased in the economic recession of the early 1980s...."[4]

Nevertheless, there were real attempts to control social expenditure where possible. The sale of council houses and a virtual embargo on local authority house building programmes created large reductions in that area of expenditure. Overseas aid also saw a real fall. In other areas, when inflation and demographic change are taken into account, the expenditure increase has been marginal since 1979 compared to the previous period. How did public expenditure in Northern Ireland fare over the period? Table 3 provides an indication of annual rates of increase in real terms since 1979-80. The figures for Northern Ireland are taken from the Coopers & Lybrand Deloitte review of the regional economy in January 1990. The comparative figures for Britain come from the government's expenditure White Paper, January 1989. To some degree the comparison is vitiated by the fact that expenditure categories are not identical in each case and the different sources may have employed different methods to identify change in 'real terms'.

| Table 3 | Real % Changes in Selected Public Expenditure Programmes, 1979-80 to 1989-90 | |
|---|---|---|
| | Northern Ireland | Britain |
| | 1979-80 | 1979-80 |
| Agriculture | -19 | 6 |
| Industry, Energy, Trade & Employment | -46 | -68 |
| Transport | -31 | -11 |
| Housing | -27 | -79 |
| Environment | 36 | -13 |
| Education, Arts etc | 19 | 10 |
| Health & Personal Social Services | 23 | 37 |
| Social Security | 37 | 36 |

*Sources: Coopers & Lybrand Deloitte 1989, the Guardian 31 Jan. 1989*

Comparison of Northern Ireland public expenditure over time is difficult because of definitional and accounting changes. Nevertheless, most programmes enjoyed less support under the Conservatives than Labour. Support for Industry was declining in real terms under both administrations, but since 1979 the fall was nearly half. The most general reason given has been the decline in new outside industries coming to Northern Ireland so that the funds available have not been taken up. Moreover, the Industrial Development Board's annual report for 1988-89 claims that the proportion of public subsidy required to establish new private investment has fallen, putting less of a strain on the public purse. Within that programme, there has been a substantial increase in special employment measures like the Action For Community Employment scheme. As for the other leading sectors, Health, Education, and the Environment attracted funding at a lesser rate than previously while Housing and Transport both saw substantial declines.

In general, the Conservatives have been less generous in the public expenditure commitment to Northern Ireland than were Labour. Nevertheless, comparison with public expenditure in Britain continues to show that Northern Ireland has been relatively advantaged in some areas. Again, comparison is made more difficult by differences in the definitions of expenditure categories. For example, in Northern Ireland, Health and Personal Social Services comes under a single budget, in Britain they are separate. But, whatever the crudeness of the comparison, certain trends do stand out. Housing has been much more protected in Northern Ireland's expenditure programme, suffering only marginal decline compared to that in Britain. Similarly, the growth of Education expenditure in the region has on average been greater than in Britain. As for the improvement in Social Security, this relates to the demands made by greater unemployment. As such, this can hardly be seen as an advantage. On the other hand some categories stand out as being relatively disadvantaged. It would appear that expenditure on both Health and Transport grew much more slowly in Northern Ireland. However, in the case of the former, it was already substantially advantaged

These figures suggest that, no matter how problematic the comparison, Northern Ireland has been protected in key programmes. Indeed the role of public spending in the local economy has been pivotal. This is reflected in the comment by the *Economist*:

> "Northern Ireland's economy resembles more closely that of an Eastern European country than Margaret Thatcher's privatising Britain. The ratio of public spending to GDP has been rising inexorably to 78% even while it has been falling for Britain as a whole."[5]

Since public expenditure accounts for such a significant proportion of GDP, the latter has actually held up better than in other regions. By 1987, GDP in Northern Ireland had increased by 109.3% from its 1979 level, compared to 98% in the North and 100% in Wales. While this was less than in the faster growing regions, like the South East with 114%, it nevertheless produced a real improvement in Northern Ireland's relative position. Certainly, the GDP figures are better than those for the index of the region's industrial production which has steadily fallen behind the British trend.

However, Northern Ireland's GDP remains low in UK terms. In 1987, GDP per head was only 77.4% of the UK average. This was the lowest in the UK, five percentage points behind Wales and eleven behind the North of England. This pessimistic assessment, however, must be qualified by two factors. First, because Northern Ireland has a high proportion of its population under 15 which makes virtually no contribution to GDP, the figure for GDP per head is artificially low. Adjusting for this fact would give Northern Ireland a figure of 85%. Second, despite the low figure for GDP, consumer expenditure per head is higher than in both the North and Wales.[6] It is unlikely that this can be accounted for by the high costs of basic commodities in Northern

Ireland which are offset by lower housing prices. One conclusion is that the inhabitants of Northern Ireland tend to consume at least as much as in other poor regions. The cost they have to bear for doing so, is a lower savings ratio.

Thus, although public expenditure trends over the past decade tended to fall below their 1974-79 levels, the evidence suggests that most of Northern Ireland's social programmes have not been as hard hit as in Britain. Even, in 1980-81, public expenditure per head in Northern Ireland was about 33% greater than in Britain. By 1986, this had increased to 42%,[7] a further confirmation of the region's relative public expenditure advantage. Figures released in February 1990 show that identifiable public spending per head for the four countries of the UK were as follows: Northern Ireland, £3,626; Scotland, £2,805; Wales, £2,489; and England, £2,161. The average for the UK was £2,275.[8] However, its fiscal base cannot sustain this level of expenditure and so the deficit is made up by a subsidy known as the British Subvention. In 1972 at the beginning of Direct Rule, the Subvention was less than £100 million. By 1988-89, it had increased to £1.6 billion (£1.9 billion if the cost of maintaining the British Army and European Community receipts are included). Consideration of this differential expenditure must be qualified by the recognition that the region's greater needs require greater resources simply to provide services at the same level. While richer regions normally subsidise poorer ones, this essential Subvention presents a problem for those who would argue that Northern Ireland should go it alone. At the same time, the most sustained increase in expenditure has been on the Law and Order programme which is under the direction of the Northern Ireland Office and does not appear under departmental budgets. This was made explicit by the then Secretary of State, Tom King, in November 1988:

> "Our first priority continues to be combatting terrorism and providing for effective law and order enforcement: this is fully reflected in today's allocations. I am particularly concerned to ensure that, against the background of the continuing terrorist campaign, the RUC has adequate resources and to that end I have allocated £30m more next year than this year — totalling a 30% increase in the past three years."[9]

Equally, since the costs of maintaining the British Army in Northern Ireland are met out of the Ministry of Defence budget, it is likely that they have also risen in line with the substantial increases in defence spending. Security has been the major beneficiary of Northern Ireland's public expenditure protection.

## Household Income and Expenditure

To what extent has this insulation from the worst of social expenditure cuts been reflected in incomes? Table 4 provides information on average weekly household incomes for selected regions.

| Table 4 | Average Weekly Household Incomes by Region (£) | | |
|---|---|---|---|
| | **1974-75** | **1978-79** | **1986-87** |
| **North** | 65.87 | 102.34 | 197.60 |
| **South East** | 74.37 | 126.67 | 302.70 |
| **South West** | 63.39 | 104.39 | 250.90 |
| **Wales** | 60.27 | 106.44 | 207.20 |
| **N.Ireland** | 53.40 | 92.30 | 207.80 |
| *Sources: Regional Trends 1976, 1981, 1989.* | | | |

The improvement in household incomes in Northern Ireland was both real and relative. The increase over the period was greater than the rate of inflation, while the figure for the most recent year available is marginally higher than in Wales and the North. In the latter regions, household incomes did not keep up with general price rises. This is in stark contrast to the remarkable growth in household income in the two southern regions of Britain. There the increase was fourfold. This not merely established a much larger gap between incomes in the South East and other regions, but brought up the South West, which in 1974 had a lower income than the North, to second place by 1987.

Such transformations are a product of more, and better paid, jobs, as well as regional migrations of population to the South, contrasted with deindustrialisation and decay in the North. This relates to the much debated North-South divide, which has significant implications for the position of Northern Ireland. In 1974, average household income in the region was £7.00 per week below Wales. The difference between Wales and the South East was £14.00. Households in Northern Ireland were, therefore, on average 50% worse off than those in the poorest British region compared to those in the richest. In 1979, a similar position prevailed. Northern Ireland households were £10.00 a week worse off than those in the poorest British region. The biggest gap between the regions in Britain was £24.00, which, in real terms, was about the same as in 1974. Yet, eight years later, Northern Ireland had caught up with both the North and Wales, which, however, had both been left far behind their richer neighbours. The gap between the British regions was then £105, reflecting a startling growth in regional income inequality. Relative to the

South East, Northern Ireland households similarly had made no gains. In 1986-87, they had a lower proportion of the former's income than in 1974.

Thus, the improvement in Northern Ireland's position is as much to do with income divergences among British regions as with real gains in its income. Paradoxically, Northern Ireland seems to have improved its position in the process whereby regional inequalities have grown in Britain. Rather than being a region which stands out uniquely in its deprivation, it looks more like a whole group of ailing regions which have suffered under the Thatcher revolution. And, given its high levels of public expenditure, which support a very large number of public sector jobs, where pay levels are determined nationally, it has even emerged with household incomes higher than in some other regions.

Nevertheless, Northern Ireland households suffer in one crucial respect: on average they contain more individuals. In 1986, household size in the other regions averaged 2.5-2.6 compared to 3.07 in Northern Ireland. Thus household income per individual is still smaller in Northern Ireland than elsewhere. However, a similar size differential existed during the 1970s, when household income per individual in the region diverged even more sharply from its British counterparts.

An indication of the proportion of households on very low incomes is given in the Table 5.

| Table 5 | The Proportion of Households on Low Incomes by Region | | |
|---|---|---|---|
| | **1974-75** | **1978-79** | **1986/87** |
| **Percentage with average weekly incomes less than** | £40.00 (£38.69) | £80.00 (£66.78) | £125.00 |
| **North** | 44.0 | 41.4 | 43.2 |
| **South East** | 34.1 | 32.9 | 25.2 |
| **South West** | 40.5 | 41.1 | 29.6 |
| **Wales** | 46.9 | 43.2 | 35.3 |
| **N.Ireland** | 51.5 | 53.7 | 42.3 |
| *Sources: Regional Trends 1976, 1981, 1989.* | | | |

The figures in brackets represent the real value of £125 in 1974 and 1978. The categories for these years were chosen to correspond with that for 1986-87. The degree of correspondence is least exact for 1978-79. The figure of £125 was chosen because it is closest to the European 'decency threshold', which is defined as 68% of average earnings, applied to Northern Ireland.

In some respects, these trends display similarities with those for average household income. In the two earlier years, Northern Ireland stands out as having a higher percentage of households with low incomes than any of the British regions. Again, the percentage difference between Northern Ireland and Wales is about 50% worse than the difference between Wales and the South East. In these years the percentages for the South West are little different from Wales and the North. Yet, by 1986-87, Wales' rate of improvement — a reduction of nearly 12% in the low income category — has outpaced the other two. In this year, Northern Ireland's proportion is actually slightly less than the North, though still greater than Wales. These changes at the bottom end of the income distribution also show the improvement in Northern Ireland's position relative to the North — though not Wales. Nevertheless, the reduction in the proportion of households on lower incomes in the Southern regions occurred at a greater rate than in any of the other three.

| Table 6 | Average Weekly Household Expenditure by Region (£) | | |
|---|---|---|---|
| | **1974-75** | **1978-79** | **1986-87** |
| **North** | 46.52 | 81.01 | 150.2 |
| **South East** | 56.09 | 96.05 | 219.2 |
| **South West** | 48.40 | 79.92 | 189.5 |
| **Wales** | 48.24 | 85.05 | 163.6 |
| **N.Ireland** | 49.36 | 83.40 | 178.5 |
| *Sources: Regional Trends 1976, 1981, 1989.* | | | |

When we turn to household expenditure (as opposed to income), the trends are very different as Table 6 shows. Average household expenditure in Northern Ireland has always been relatively high. In 1974-75 only the South East had a higher figure, although by the most recent year, the South West was also higher. The principal explanation for this continuing higher expenditure seems to be the greater average household size in Northern Ireland. As a consequence of the extra spending, the region's households have consistently had lower savings ratios (the proportion of income that does not go on consumption) than in other regions. In 1974-75, while the savings ratios of the other regions were all above 20%, the figure for Northern Ireland was 7.6%. Admittedly, this saw a relative improvement until, by 1986-87, its ratio reached 14.2% which was about equal to East Anglia's but still remained substantially lower than in other regions.

The low savings ratios in Northern Ireland have implications for the level of poverty in the region. With low savings, households have little to fall back on during periods when income is interrupted. This creates a vulnerability whenever sickness or unemployment affects household members. To sum up, while the income situation has improved relative to other regions at the lower end of the scale, this does not automatically mean that the quality of life is also similar. Northern Ireland households still occupy the bottom end of the UK's income distribution. However, as a result of the processes at work under the Thatcher government, households in other poorer regions are increasingly joining them. A further set of regularly published data on income refers to personal incomes before tax (see Table 7).

| Table 7 | Personal Incomes Before Tax by Region | | |
|---|---|---|---|
| | Percentages with incomes less than: | | |
| | £1,000 (£1,373) | £3,000 (£2,777) | £5,000 |
| Period | 1973-74 | 1978-79 | 1985-86 |
| North | 22.3 | 33.0 | 25.5 |
| South East | 21.7 | 31.5 | 20.4 |
| South West | 21.1 | 37.4 | 24.2 |
| Wales | 24.0 | 36.0 | 25.2 |
| N.Ireland | 32.2 | 41.1 | 26.2 |

Note: The figures in brackets represent the real value of £5,000 in the other years.

*Sources: Regional Trends 1976, 1982, 1989.*

In so far as Northern Ireland had greater percentages of individuals in the low income band in the first two periods and a similar percentage to other regions in the most recent year, there is considerable correspondence between these and the household income figures. Comparison with other regions confirms the point that relative incomes in Northern Ireland improved in the 1980s. By 1985-86 personal income before tax is easily on a par with Wales and the North.

Beyond that, real differences between household and personal income figures can be seen. There is less inequality in the range at the bottom end of the scale. In 1986-87, the percentage with an income less than £5,000 in the South East was only five points less than the North. For the South West it was four points. The very substantial inequalities in household incomes have not been reproduced here.

The difference between the two sets of figures may be explained by the fact that households may be recipients of multiple incomes. This is most probable where both partners are in employment. Regions with higher proportions of households with both partners employed will see the average household income for the region as a whole raised. Thus, it may well be the case

53

that the higher averages in household income for the Southern regions reflect not merely higher earnings levels, but more significantly, better opportunities for employment, in particular for women.

In summary, this survey of incomes also suggests that the relative protection enjoyed by Northern Ireland in the field of public expenditure has affected not merely its GDP, but its place in the UK income league table. Since 1979, the Conservatives have made certain regions more like Northern Ireland, while insulating that particular region from the full rigours of social market policies.

## Employment, Unemployment and Earnings

Like in other regions, the structure of employment in Northern Ireland has dramatically changed in the last two decades. Manufacturing has ceased to dominate employment, ending a process that began when the area first industrialised in the middle of the 19th Century. Women have steadily increased as a proportion of the workforce partly due to the decline of traditional male occupations, and to the fact that many of the new jobs in the service sector have gone to women. These changes are a reflection of the transformation of the region's economic base, whereby there has been not merely a steady erosion of traditional industries but in many cases after 1979 the collapse even of newer ones. A detailed account of these processes will be presented in the next chapter.

The basic changes in employment over the period are presented in Table 8.

| Table 8 | Civilian Working Population, 1974-1988 | | | | | |
|---|---|---|---|---|---|---|
| | Males | | | Females | | |
| | 1974 | 1979 | 1988 | 1974 | 1979 | 1988 |
| **Employees** | 296,600 | 303,800 | 261,800 | 196,100 | 230,800 | 235,000 |
| **Self-Employed** | 73,900 | 55,500 | 52,300 | 9,700 | 8,200 | 7,300 |
| **Unemployed** (claimant based) | 19,800 | 41,600 | 84,300 | 5,700 | 18,000 | 31,000 |

*Sources: Northern Ireland Annual Abstract of Statistics 1984, 1989.*

Male employees grew by about 2% between 1974 and 1979, only to fall back again by nearly 14% up to 1988. On the other hand, the number of female employees continued to increase during both the period of Labour rule and the Thatcher decade-by nearly 18% in the first, but less than 2% in the latter. As a consequence, the gender composition of employees changed significantly. Females employees became 47% of all employees in 1988 compared to 39%

in 1974. For both men and women, self-employment consistently declined. Whether this means that Northern Ireland lacks an entrepreneurial spirit, is an issue taken up in the next chapter.

The claimant based unemployment figures provide an opportunity to examine trends in unemployment. This is not possible with regularly published unemployment figures because since 1979 there have been 29 changes in the definition of the unemployed and the calculation of the unemployment rate. The claimant basis for calculating the numbers of jobless underestimates unemployment among particular groups, women being the largest. Nevertheless, these figures, calculated back to 1974, give an indication of the dramatically different levels of unemployment in the 1980s compared to the previous decade. Between 1974 and 1979 unemployment for males more than doubled and for females more than trebled. From then to 1988 the number of unemployed males again doubled while the number of females increased by three-quarters. Calculated in percentage terms, the annual rate of increase of unemployment was greater in the former than the latter period. However, since the numbers of unemployed in 1979 were that much greater, even large subsequent increases in the numbers of unemployed people can result in more modest increases in the rate of unemployment growth. The changes in employment are presented in more detail in Table 9.

| Table 9 | Employment By Industrial Sector, 1971-1989 | | | | | | |
|---|---|---|---|---|---|---|---|
| | 1971 | 1975 | 1979 | 1983 | 1987 | 1988 | 1989 (March) |
| Agriculture Forest/Fish. | 28,720 | 23,180 | 21,050 | 19,870 | 19,510 | 19,530 | 19,560 |
| Indexed | 100 | 81 | 73 | 69 | 68 | 68 | 68 |
| Energy | 8,380 | 10,400 | 10,140 | 9,260 | 8,600 | 8,340 | 7,970 |
| Indexed | 100 | 124 | 121 | 111 | 103 | 100 | 95 |
| Manufacturing | 174,840 | 159,060 | 145,520 | 106,900 | 101,310 | 102,310 | 102,190 |
| Indexed | 100 | 91 | 83 | 61 | 57 | 58 | 58 |
| Construction | 39,480 | 39,820 | 37,740 | 28,270 | 25,140 | 25,590 | 24,760 |
| Indexed | 100 | 100 | 96 | 72 | 64 | 65 | 63 |
| Services | 238,970 | 278,090 | 320,150 | 331,060 | 336,500 | 340,760 | 342,470 |
| Indexed | 100 | 116 | 134 | 139 | 141 | 143 | 143 |
| *Source: NI Annual Abstract 1979, 1984, 1989, PPRU 1989.* | | | | | | | |

The increase in unemployment in the 1980s can be partly related to the increase in male and female activity rates and the rise in the working population due to the 'baby boom' years of the 1960s. From 1979 to 1985 the working population increased by 3.58%. Since the mid 1980s the working population has dropped again slightly. Nevertheless, the population of working age in Northern Ireland is set to rise at over twice the rate in Britain, and the number of those aged under 25 will drop at half the rate in Britain. This may appear to offer an incentive to new investment since the supply of young workers in Britain and in many other parts of the European Community will decrease. More likely, however, young people in Northern Ireland, particularly those with marketable qualifications, will be attracted to where the jobs are, in the context of the greater labour mobility which will be possible after 1992. While such an outcome would reduce local unemployment , it would reflect a loss of skills not in the long-term interests of the economy. Graham Gudgin has noted:

"The essence of the economic problem of Northern Ireland is that it is an economy with a rapidly growing labour force tied to a slow growing national economy....Equally worrying is the fact that recovery in the national economy since 1982 has largely excluded Northern Ireland."[10]

While the relatively high public expenditure levels may have cushioned incomes in Northern Ireland, its unemployment problem has remained the worst in the UK. The causes lie not only in the fragility of the regional economy, but in the higher birth rate so that proportionately greater numbers are entering the labour market. Moreover, while female activity rates in Northern Ireland continue to be lower than in British regions, there has been a substantial increase over the past two decades, so that more women are employed and looking for jobs. In short, the Northern Ireland labour force is continuing to grow while the labour forces of other regions have stabilised.

| Table 10 | Rates of Unemployment by Region (%) | | |
|---|---|---|---|
| | 1974 | 1979 | 1988 |
| North | 5.9 | 8.6 | 11.9 |
| South East | 2.8 | 3.7 | 5.2 |
| South West | 4.7 | 5.7 | 6.3 |
| Wales | 5.6 | 8.0 | 10.5 |
| N.Ireland | 7.9 | 11.3 | 16.4 |
| *Sources: Regional Trends 1976, 1981, 1989.* | | | |

Because the basis on which unemployment rates are calculated has been altered so substantially since 1979, the figures for 1988 are lower than they would otherwise have been, compared to other years (see Table 10). Also, the most dramatic rise in unemployment occurred between 1979 and 1982. By 1988, unemployment had been falling in all regions, so the figures for that year do not represent the full depth of the earlier recession. Nevertheless, they do convey the seriousness of the problem in Northern Ireland.

In each of the three periods, Northern Ireland's rate of unemployment has remained reasonably constant, relative to the other regions. It is about 50% worse than in Wales or the North, twice the South West's rate and around three times the South East's. Thus, over a fourteen year period and despite many changes in the measurement of unemployment, the level of unemployment in Northern Ireland has remained consistently higher than in other regions. Further, the region's unemployed experience much greater durations of worklessness. In October 1988, 46% of unemployed males and 23% of unemployed females had been out of work for two years or more. The next worst case was the North with 33% and 20%. The higher duration of unemployment affects all ages in Northern Ireland. Although long-term unemployment among the young is less of a problem because of the impact of government training schemes, in July 1988 38.4% of under 25 year olds in Northern Ireland had been unemployed for more than a year compared to 23.9% in Britain. Long-term unemployment (meaning one year or longer) is concentrated in the older age groups. Over 70% of the unemployed aged 55 or more in Northern Ireland had been out of work for more than a year compared to 60% in Britain.[11]

In terms of official statistics, the burden of unemployment is disproportionately concentrated on men. The ratio of male to female unemployed is higher in Northern Ireland than in any of the other selected regions — 2.7:1 in 1988 — while a higher proportion of men, also, are in the long-term jobless category. This is partly explained by the gender bias in how official statistics count the unemployed, but is also a result of the changing industrial composition and greater opportunities for female employment than in the past. The extent to which the official statistics continue to under represent the unemployed is given in Table 11.

| Table 11 Unemployment: Department of Employment (DE) Count and Unemployment Unit (UU) Index June 1989 (Seasonally Adjusted) | | |
|---|---|---|
| | **DE** | **UU** |
| **North** | 143,600 (9.8%) | 191,300 (12.7%) |
| **South East** | 370,100 (3.9%) | 482,700 ( 5.1%) |
| **South West** | 100,100 (4.7%) | 134,400 ( 6.3%) |
| **Wales** | 98,500 (8.2%) | 132,800 (10.8%) |
| **N.Ireland** | 105,800 (15.3%) | 139,400 (19.9%) |
| *Source: Unemployment Unit & Youthaid, July/August 1989.* | | |

For the UK as a whole the Unemployment Unit's count is over 500,000 greater than Department of Employment statistics. For Northern Ireland the Unemployment Unit's figures for seasonally adjusted unemployment are about 30% higher. Only these figures enable appropriate comparison with official unemployment statistics produced before 1979. Then Northern Ireland's unemployed numbered 64,000. Thus, by 1988, despite some reduction in the joblessness figures in the immediately preceding years, the number of unemployed was still more than twice its 1979 level.

Just as unemployment in Northern Ireland is worse than in the rest of the UK, so too are earnings levels. There are, however, differences in the relative positions of men and women (see Tables 12 and 13).

| Table 12 | Average Weekly Earnings, Full Time Adult Men, 1979 and 1988 by Region | | | |
|---|---|---|---|---|
| | 1979 | | 1988 | |
| | Average Weekly Earnings £s | % Earning Less than £50 (£69) | Average Weekly Earnings £s | % Earning Less than £130 |
| **North** | 99.7 | 2.4 | 223.8 | 11.4 |
| **South East** | 108.5 | 2.1 | 283.0 | 7.4 |
| **South West** | 92.7 | 3.3 | 227.6 | 13.2 |
| **Wales** | 97.6 | 3.2 | 217.8 | 15.8 |
| **N.Ireland** | 93.4 | 5.3 | 215.2 | 20.8 |
| Note: The figure of £69 in brackets represents 1988's £130 in 1979 prices. | | | | |
| *Sources: New Earnings Surveys GB Part E, NI, 1979,1988.* | | | | |

Interestingly, the South West at the beginning of the Thatcher period had the lowest average earnings and, after Northern Ireland, the highest percentage in the low earning band. While average earnings in Northern Ireland were only marginally lower than in three of the four other regions, the percentage of workers earning under £50 was twice that in the North and nearly 70% greater than in Wales and the South East. Thus, even where average earnings are comparable, Northern Ireland's earnings distribution has a long low tail with relatively more people with very low earnings indeed.

By 1988, there had been little change in the situation. Average earnings had slightly improved relative to Wales and the North, but had deteriorated in relation to the South East and South West. At the same time, the percentage in the low earning category remained substantially above all other regions.

The processes which produce such trends again relate to the improving position of the southern regions in contrast to the northern. However, in this case, while average earnings in Northern Ireland have moved closer to Wales and the North, they have by no means caught up and the long tail of low earners remains as prominent as before. Given that the differences in average earnings between Northern Ireland and the two weak British regions are small, while the differences in the proportion of low earners remains large, the higher earning groups in the region must have comparable earnings to elsewhere. The picture for female earnings is substantially the same.

| Table 13 | Average Weekly Earnings, Full Time Adult Females, 1979 and 1988 by Region | | | |
|---|---|---|---|---|
| | 1979 | | 1988 | |
| | Average Weekly Earnings (£s) | % Earning Less than £40 (£53) | Average Weekly Earnings (£s) | % Earning Less than £100 |
| North | 60.6 | 11.4 | 148.8 | 20.3 |
| South East | 68.4 | 6.1 | 188.1 | 8.4 |
| South West | 60.0 | 10.9 | 152.2 | 18.3 |
| Wales | 61.4 | 10.3 | 150.3 | 19.8 |
| N.Ireland | 61.8 | 12.4 | 147.8 | 27.8 |

Note: The figure £53 in brackets represents 1988's £100 in 1979

*Sources: New Earnings Surveys, GB Part E, NI, 1979, 1988.*

In 1979, female earners in Northern Ireland actually had the second highest average weekly earnings in the group, although their advantage over the other three regions was very small. However, even then, the percentage in the low earning category was greater than elsewhere. Again, this implies a high degree of earnings inequality. By 1988, their position had been undermined to the point where they had the lowest average earnings. Also, by then, the percentage in the low earning category was substantially higher than in the other regions. One important conclusion emerges from this analysis. Since earnings in the upper quartile and above were still better than in Wales, the North and the South West, it becomes likely that the decline in average female earnings was a function of a growth of very low paying jobs for women. Sharp differences also emerge between manual and non-manual women's earnings in Northern Ireland. Research has demonstrated that earnings for manual women actually fell in real terms during the 1980s.[12] Since these developments affected the place of Northern Ireland in the earnings league, it is also likely that they were more extensive than in other regions.

In short, the positive features of income change which improved the situation of Northern Ireland households relative to other weak regions, have not been matched by labour market data. The decline of the region's economic base has resulted in a substantial fall in manufacturing employment. Remaining manufacturing continues to be dependent on subsidy from public expenditure which also sustains the high degree of public sector employment. Average gross value added per employee in manufacturing was only 82.7% of the UK level in 1986. Unemployment has been consistently worse than even in the most depressed region with higher levels and more long-term jobless . The information on earnings reveals not only low averages for both men and women, particularly at the end of the 1980s, but a higher proportion of the workforce in the low earning band. These weaknesses in production and the labour market remain at the core of Northern Ireland's problems.

## Social Services

Relative to Britain, Northern Ireland's social services consume proportionately more resources. For example, almost 10% of the region's GDP goes on health expenditure compared to 6% in England. It has 11 hospital beds per 10,000 population compared to England's 7; and employs 39 doctors, dentists and nurses more per 10,000 people than in England. If expenditure was provided on the same basis as in England and Wales, Northern Ireland's health care expenditure would decline by about 15%. Equally, the Tory government's decision not to slash housing expenditure in the region enabled the Northern Ireland Housing Executive to continue to tackle unfitness at a time when English local authorities were facing a resources famine. Consequently, there has been a convergence in rates of housing unfitness. The latest Northern Ireland House Condition Survey[13] indicates that the major housing unfitness problem is now in rural areas. In 1987 there were 42,900 unfit dwellings compared to 51,000 in 1984 and 89,000 in 1974. Only 5.5% of dwellings lacked one amenity in 1987 compared to 26.2% in 1974. Three-quarters of currently unfit dwellings were built before 1919 and more than one-third of these were vacant when the survey was conducted. The Northern Ireland Housing Executive believes that steady progress has been achieved in terms of the physical state of the housing stock. The *Economist* claimed that:

"Mr. Needham, who used to escort parties of English MPs round the province to show them its problems, found them so envious of his bailiwick's housing and health that he stopped inviting them."[14]

Official sources have also been anxious to emphasise that violence in the region remains on a relatively low scale. Such attempts to highlight the positive features of Northern Ireland are considered crucial to the image building required to attract industry to the region. In a speech at the Institute of Public

Relations, the former chief executive of the Industrial Development Board declared:

> "In San Francisco, there are 18 violent deaths per 100,000 inhabitants each year, whereas the figure for Northern Ireland is 5. We would prefer it to be nil, but the reality is that human society is far from perfect. In the pecking order of desirability, a Northern Ireland lifestyle ranks very highly."[15]

However, this rosy picture must be qualified in a number of ways. In the field of health, Northern Ireland has higher infant mortality and morbidity levels than other regions. Principally because of its excessive levels of unemployment, Northern Ireland's households depend to a greater degree on social security than in other regions. The proportion of average household income made up of social security benefits increased by 2% from 1979 to 1987. In 1986-87, payments of sickness and invalidity benefits per head in Northern Ireland were 58% higher than the UK average, unemployment benefit 10% higher and supplementary benefits 48% higher.

Such levels of dependency have meant that a greater proportion of Northern Ireland citizens are vulnerable to changes in the social security system which lower the real value of benefits. For instance, supplementary benefits levels just about kept up with prices for the period 1978-87.[16] But they were 41% behind the increase in average gross earnings. Thus, had benefits remained indexed to earnings, most claimants would have been at least 40% better off. Clearly this affects claimants everywhere in the UK, but having such a high social security dependency ratio, Northern Ireland suffers that much more.

In other areas like education, while there have been distinct improvements since the end of the 1970s, the level of provision in Northern Ireland still lags behind. The number of day nursery places has increased threefold since 1979, but Northern Ireland only offers 2.2 places per 1,000 population under 5, compared to 13.6 in the North and 24.2 in the South East. The next closest figure is for Wales at 8.2, which is nearly four times better provided. While 45% of children under 5 in Northern Ireland are in education, this compares with 67% and 69% respectively in the North and Wales. At the other end of the education spectrum, the proportion of school leavers with one or more A-levels in Northern Ireland (23.5%) is second highest of the five selected regions, but the percentage leaving with no graded result is greater than in any other region — 20.4% compared, for example, to the North's 11.0% in 1987.[17]

Thus, even if insulated from the most extreme aspects of public expenditure cuts, Northern Ireland continues to experience a range of acute social problems. The degree of convergence described here has only been with some of the most deprived areas in Britain which have borne the brunt of Thatcherism. However, rather than standing out significantly below the even worst British region on a range of social indicators, as was the case in the 1970s, Northern Ireland has now become firmly part of the deprived half of the

North-South divide. Curiously, this does represent a measure of progress, even if only in terms of a greater harmonisation of regional misery.

This chapter has demonstrated some of the key economic and social changes over the past decade. Northern Ireland, for much of the 1980s, was relatively insulated from one crucial dimension of Conservative policy — the desire to restrain public expenditure. Under Labour, Northern Ireland had been even more favoured. The Labour government did not positively embrace public expenditure restraint until at least 1976. For the Conservatives, this has been a central plank of economic policy which has been applied to most areas of social expenditure. Nevertheless, the other side of the fiscal coin relates to changes in taxation policy. In the decade up to 1988-89 tax as a proportion of GDP actually rose from about 34% to 38%. While the contribution of income tax to total revenue fell from 34.6% to 28.1%, the shortfall was more than made up by VAT whose share rose from 8.3% to 15.1%.[19] Indirect taxation tends to be regressive and thus falls proportionately harder on regions with lower incomes. Northern Ireland has thus suffered substantially from this recomposition of tax.

Other dimensions of Conservative policy have also been much delayed, as we shall see, in their application to Northern Ireland: legislation on trade unions and privatisation, to name but two. The whole profile of Conservative social and economic policy in the region suggests it has been relatively favoured.

One of the key reasons for this 'soft' approach in the economic and social fields has been the nature of the political challenge posed by Republicans, especially their use of violence. After two decades, the administration in Northern Ireland has developed a very specific response: the maintenance of a high security profile buttressed by emergency legislation and juryless courts; the quest for an internal political settlement, recently linked to an external accommodation with the Irish Republic, in order to isolate 'terrorists'; and the development of relatively generous social provision. The last has been based, not merely on the need to make up for the backlog of neglect under Unionist administrations, but also in the belief that deprivation and despair are important recruiting factors for paramilitaries. In a speech to the Institute of Directors Tom King said:

> "We all know that better security and economic policies are interlinked. There is no future for Northern Ireland as an economic wasteland, no future for Northern Ireland through terrorism and no future in a political vacuum, we need action on all fronts."[18]

In short, in a region where Thatcherism is faced with an unusual political challenge, it has proved more flexible and more pragmatic in its social and economic agenda.

# 3. The Economy: Accounting for Change

As the most critical testament to its tenure, the Thatcher government has claimed the achievement of a miracle turn-around in the UK economy. To sustain this, the economy would need to have developed in certain key directions. Significant improvement in economic growth, without high levels of inflation, unemployment, government borrowing and a balance of payments deficits, would be one factor. There would also have to be a considerable improvement in rates of output, productivity, profitability and investment, which would augur well for a long-term transformation.

The purpose of this chapter is to assess the credibility of the Thatcher 'miracle', examine the theories and policies which contributed to the main economic developments , and identify the extent to which these were similarly evident in Northern Ireland as in Britain.

For the three decades after 1945, the UK economy averaged annual growth rates of 2.5% — the lowest rate for any leading industrial country. In many ways the economy was in persistent decline — in particular, its competitiveness in world trade. Certainly, the Labour years preceding the first Thatcher government in 1979 were hardly auspicious ones for the economy, which experienced not only high inflation but also stagnation and mounting unemployment, following the recessionary pressures in the mid 1970s.

To counteract this, the Labour government adopted a conventional Keynesian response of increasing public expenditure. However, it was a policy which, in 1976, culminated in the IMF forcing the government to reduce public borrowing and spending, and the growth in the money supply, in return for its financial rescue of the run on sterling. Under Mrs Thatcher this same strategy was to be strengthened and pursued with conviction rather than apology.

The thinking behind this strategy has been elaborated earlier, so we need only recite its key tenets here. A tight fiscal and monetary policy was to provide the long-term basis for low inflation and low interest rates, and so higher profitability as the basis for increased employment, investment and output. This approach was to be operated in tandem with a new emphasis on the supply side of the economy. For example, unemployment, once considered a macro-economic problem related to aggregate demand, was now deemed to be a micro-economic difficulty determined mostly by costs and rigidities in local labour markets. Those without work could best resolve their predicament by being prepared to 'price themselves' into a job in which their efficiency and flexibility assured employers of an appropriate profit. In this sense, unemployment could be seen as a just retribution on the indigent and unenterprising.

Government intervention in general, and industrial planning in particular, were predicated, in this view, on delusory assumptions about the capacity of politicians and bureaucrats to second guess the market. In Thatcherite rhetoric, the market could not be 'bucked'. Its regulatory and disciplinary power was an indispensable precursor to the 'real' jobs that derived ultimately from profitable private sector activity. The government would not bail out firms or industries which transgressed these nostrums, but rather it would restore to management its responsibility and capacity to manage, partly through a series of new legislative constraints on the operation of trade unions. In addition, privatisation of the economy would be pursued, as would greater deregulation, including the removal of controls on prices, incomes and the movement of capital.

The immediate effects of this strategy were calamitous. In the period 1979-81, adherence to tight fiscal and monetary restraint amid the deflationary pressures of a global recession saw many areas of the economy nose dive into unprecedented depths of depression. Following that, the years 1982-87 saw very creditable levels of growth and much lower inflation. The period also marked a change in the government's monetarist credo, formally acknowledged by the then Chancellor of the Exchequer Nigel Lawson in his Mansion House speech in late 1985 when he announced the abandonment of broad money targets. Since 1987, however, the durability of this economic improvement has looked very dubious. Though represented by the government as the normal over-heating problems of a fundamentally sound economy, recent events bear many of the hallmarks of the traditional UK economic 'stop-go' pattern. However, a more detailed assessment of what happened economically is necessary before making a comprehensive appraisal of the Thatcher decade and its impact on Northern Ireland in particular.

## Economic Performance: Key Indicators

### Employment and Unemployment

In the period of the fastest job shake-out, 1979-83, there was a loss of nearly two million jobs, the majority in full-time manufacturing. The 1984 Census of Employment showed that this process was experienced unevenly across the regions — 94% of job losses were outside the South. Since 1983 there has been employment growth, with the total number in jobs in 1987 surpassing the previous 24.2 million peak of 1979. However, around 60% of job creation since 1983 has been in part-time employment, so that whereas in 1979 the workforce comprised 15% part-time employees, by 1989 the figure was close to 22%. If the changes made since 1982 in the calculation of unemployment figures are ignored, unemployment was over three million for six years, representing over double the 1979 figure.[1] The growth and persistence of the problem is most obvious in the figures for the long-term unemployed. In 1979 the percentage of the total unemployed who were jobless for more than a year was 25%; by 1988 it had increased to 41%.[2] As for the future, the Treasury is projecting that unemployment will rise again from an official average level in 1989 of 1.6 million to 1.75 million in 1990.

## Growth

The government has claimed that the recent years of economic growth compare very favourably with both historic performance in the UK and also with its international competitors. Certainly, the recent five-year period, 1983 to 1988, showed the fastest UK growth since the War. Moreover, from 1981, the UK has experienced higher annual growth rates than the OECD average, surpassing all the main industrial countries with the exception of Japan and the United States. However, choosing those particular years is conveniently selective. If, instead, the starting point is taken as 1979, when Mrs Thatcher came to power, a less creditable picture emerges.

This becomes starkly clear if we take a longer perspective and go back thirty years, and sub-divide the period into the 'peak to peak' years of growth: 1960-64; 1965-68; 1969-73; 1974-79 and 1980-88. GDP growth in the peak Thatcher years at under 2.5% in fact only surpasses the lean years of 1974-79 when the figure was 1.3%. An international comparison also indicates the dismal performance over most of the Thatcher decade.[3] Between the second quarter of 1979 and the first quarter of 1989, the annual growth rate of total output was 1.9%, and that of manufacturing output 0.9%, a performance which relegates the UK below the OECD average.

What is more, in 1989, the Chancellor was compelled to slam the brakes on the economy in order to counteract serious inflationary pressure. The Treasury prediction for 1990 is that growth will plummet to its lowest level since 1981—only 0.75%, if North Sea oil output is excluded. It is also important to record that the UK's regional pattern of growth has been significantly biased towards the South East.

## Productivity

In the 15 years prior to 1979, growth in productivity in manufacturing and the economy as a whole, relative to other industrial countries, puts the UK near the bottom. Since 1979 labour productivity in manufacturing has risen faster than in any other principal competitor; and in the whole economy, at an annual average of 5.5%, which is lower only than Japan.[4]

But even such a notable achievement needs to be put into perspective. The UK remains 25% behind most other European countries in terms of productivity. Of the 21 European countries, it ranks only 16th. As Smyth and Sentance comment:

"....Britain has recently surpassed the productivity growth rate of all our major competitors. But we may still be nearly ten years from equalling productivity levels in West Germany and France, some twenty years off Japan and may never catch up with the Americans."[5]

**Profitability and Investment**

Whereas in 1979 the UK economy's profit share was just under 32% — ranking amongst the lowest of its main competitors; by 1987 it stood at 42.5%, making it just the highest. Return on capital for UK companies was at its best for a quarter of a century:

"Excluding North Sea oil, the real net rate of return achieved by industrial and commercial companies soared to 11% by 1988, far higher than during the peak of the last economic cycle in 1978-79 and, indeed, a level not seen since the early 1960s."[6]

In recent years investment has been growing. In 1989 total investment was up by 6% and manufacturing investment showed a 4% rise. However, this boost has to be seen against overall investment trends in the Thatcher years. Between 1979 and 1987 investment increased by only 9% or less than half the growth in consumer spending.[7] Wynne Godley makes the point:

"If we take the last nine years as a whole, net fixed investment by manufacturing (including leased assets) was astonishingly low, about two-thirds down on 1971-79, which had itself been a pretty dismal period — and these figures almost certainly flatter the true position because they take no account of the plant which was scrapped during the initial Thatcher-Howe slump".[8]

Mr Lawson's prediction, just before his resignation, of a 3% increase in investment in 1990 is challenged by a recent CBI survey which suggests that while manufacturing investment will remain fairly constant, overall investment will rise by only 1% in the year.[9] Even this is regarded as optimistic by city experts such as Goldman Sachs, the Midland Bank and the National Institute of Economic and Social Research, which anticipate an actual drop in investment of 2% or more.

**Trade**

In 1988 the trade deficit totalled £14.3 billion, or 3% of Gross Domestic Product. The current account deficit for 1989 was estimated at £20 billion, with a reduction to £15 billion in 1990. The long-term trend in the country's export performance does not bode well. A recent report notes that a: "majority of product groups still recorded losses in world market share in the 1980s and many of them in strongly expanding markets".[10]

A persistent and very large trade deficit is an ill harbinger of any immediate prospects of permanently improved economic performance. It risks triggering a run on sterling and/or prompting a renewed bout of even more severe deflationary strategy than at present, which will see output more stagnant and unemployment more rampant as high interest rates are maintained. Some critics of Thatcherite economics, such as Wynne Godley, see long-term problems in a high interest rate policy attracting 'hot money' to forestall a crash in sterling. However, government sympathisers, such as Samuel Brittan, argue that concern about the current balance of payments deficit is overstated. He is confident that the international financial markets are taking a considered commercial view of Britain's underlying economic health, including the fact that its net overseas assets now total around £100 billion, a hugely increased level which was encouraged by the abolition of exchange controls in 1979.

**Inflation**

Inflation, by the government's own admission, is the judge and jury of its whole economic policy. When Mrs Thatcher assumed office in 1979 it was dipping to 10% from a peak of 26% reached under Labour. Yet, by 1980, inflation had once more sharply risen to 16%, due mostly to government decisions to hike up VAT rates and prices of nationalised services. After that, the inflation rate dropped to a low of 3.5% in 1987, a reduction assisted considerably by the fall in world commodity prices. But in 1989 it was on the climb again, peaking at 8.5%, compared to the European Community's average of 5.5%.

This indicates that, previously, the inflation problem was only being temporarily contained rather than conquered. The cause of the recent rise is attributable to the private consumer boom, which the government deliberately facilitated preceding the 1987 General Election. To reduce this higher inflation, interest rates were raised no less than ten times in the period June 1988 to October 1989 to stand at 15%. As in the early monetarist period, high interest rates were employed to increase the cost of domestic credit, thereby pressuring employers to resist high wage demands. Since they also attracted footloose international capital, appreciating the value of sterling in the process, they should also help to lower import costs and stimulate companies to greater competitiveness in order to maintain their exports. But this resort to a monetary policy which creates an exchange rate conducive to higher imports takes further risks with the trading deficit, itself partly a result of the relaxed fiscal policy in the form of income tax cuts in 1987 and 1988.

Certain features of the Thatcher record on inflation are apparent. Though the average rate since 1979 has been lower than the average rate of 15% under the last Labour government, the improvement achieved over this period has not been as great as that in other leading industrial countries. In fact, the current

UK rate remains significantly higher and sustained non-inflationary growth remains elusive.

## Public Spending

As noted earlier, the goal of reduced public spending in real terms was also seen as central to the whole Thatcherite project. But as its achievement proved problematic, the objective became the more modest one of cutting it as a proportion of GDP. Yet for much of the period even this ratio increased, reaching a peak of 47.7% in 1984, and only falling below the 1979 point by 1986.

In the government's first two terms the spending over-runs were attributable largely to the consequences of unemployment. Indeed, the more or less involuntary expenditure increases in this area were accompanied by major cuts in certain other crucial public sector categories. For example, between 1979 and 1987 across Britain as a whole there was a 60% reduction in housing expenditure in real terms, and a similar drop in Department of Industry spending, in a period of manufacturing decline and high unemployment.

After 1986 the government set about an expansionary programme which effectively amounted to a U-turn. Actual public spending for 1988/89 amounted to an extra £8 billion compared to the 1986 plans for that year's expenditure. Interestingly, the government remained ambivalent about public expenditure. When criticised about public sector programme under-funding, it would boast about its record levels of spending. Yet, it persisted in its rhetoric about the need to trim public finances. In reality, this increase in public spending, together with the £6.5 billion of the 1987 and 1988 budget tax cuts, added up to a substantial reflationary package of £14.5 billion in 1988-89.

## Borrowing and Debt

In 1979 the Public Sector Borrowing Requirement (PSBR) represented 6.4% of GDP. By 1987 it stood at -0.3%. In other words, government was no longer having to borrow but was instead repaying public debt. In the 1989 budget, Mr Lawson announced that the Public Sector Debt Repayment (PSDR) in 1988-89 was £14 billion. He insisted that this had been only made possible by the financial prudence shown in achieving a budget surplus of £14 billion. However, some critics charged that this neat balance sheet was only the result of some highly dubious accounting practices.

The PSDR in 1988-89 may have been largely financed by public sector asset sales, reductions in social security benefits and increases in tax receipts resulting from the credit-based boom. Table 14 illustrates some of these 'savings' and unanticipated extra income.

| Table 14 | Mis-estimates in Recent Government Income and Expenditure (£billion) | | |
|---|---|---|---|
| | Est.1988 | Est.1989 | Difference |
| **Income Tax & NI Contributions** | 73.7 | 76.6 | 2.9 |
| **Privatisation** | 5.0 | 7.0 | 2.0 |
| **VAT** | 26.2 | 27.5 | 1.3 |
| **Social Security** | -48.5 | -47.4 | 1.1 |
| **Capital Taxes** | 5.0 | 5.8 | 0.8 |
| **Transport** | -5.1 | -4.8 | 0.3 |
| **Total** | | | 8.4 |
| *Source: HMSO, 1988.* | | | |

At its height in 1987, the credit explosion expanded the money supply by 22% and clearly contained the seeds of inflationary pressure. According to *Social Trends 1990*, consumer debt (excluding mortgages) in 1989 totalled £45.4 billion — representing over 15.5% of annual household disposable income, nearly double the 1981 figure of 8%, and amounting to a real increase of 130%. For this growth to cease: "....we could see a fall in personal consumption of as much as 10%. The balance of payments would improve but there would be a recession comparable in magnitude with what occurred in 1979-81."[11]

Yet, while presiding over this massive boom in consumer credit, the government has persisted in its strictures against public borrowing:

"Just why Mrs Thatcher should think it is economically sound to allow people to borrow at penal rates of interest of up to 20% to purchase (say) depreciating Japanese videos, while unsound to allow the public sector to borrow at barely half that rate to finance profitable capital projects is a mystery which time is unlikely to solve."[12]

It is this vast 'Private Sector Borrowing Requirement' which is causing interest rates to be held so high. This is an intriguing private sector parallel to, and contradiction of, the government's own analysis of the Public Sector Borrowing Requirement in its first Medium-Term Financial Strategy in 1981: "The Public Sector Borrowing Requirement as a proportion of GDP will be brought down substantially over the medium-term so as to create conditions in which interest rates can fall."[13]

Figures released by the Central Statistical Office in January 1990 showed that the UK corporate sector was in its largest ever financial deficit. In 1988 the deficit amounted to just over £6 billion. But in the first nine months of 1989, it zoomed to £15 billion. The scale of private sector borrowing — to help finance dividends, takeovers and investment — at penal interest rates, could exert recessionary pressures in the early years of the 1990s.

**Privatisation**

Promoted in recent years as popular capitalism, privatisation has provided a significant boost to government revenue, contributing nearly £20 billion in total. By mid 1989 almost 40% of the nationalised industrial sector had been sold on the private market. Whereas in 1979 some 7% of the adult population were share holders, a decade later the figure had reached 20%, with the government claiming that in the 1990s share owners would well outnumber trade unionists. Two major sell-offs were poised to net a further £25 billion — namely water and electricity. But, in the case of water, the need for a political success, in the face of the electorally unpopular decision to sell off a basic natural asset, has prompted the government to sweeten the sale:

"....because the government has already written off all the industry's debts of £5 billion and given it a 'green' dowry of almost £1.6 billion, this means that a monopoly industry with considerable potential for increased profits and dividends is being sold for minus anything up to £1 billion simply to avoid a politically embarrassing failure."[14]

The sell-off of the electricity industry was similarly blighted when financial institutions advised the government that the nuclear sector was not commercially viable.

While the sale of public assets has lent a favourable gloss to the state of public finances in recent years, there remains the problem that the state income will no longer be able to draw so much income from these profitable enterprises once privatised. In this transition from public to private monopolies, designated by some as "selling off the family silver", the supposed gains in terms of efficiency and competitiveness are difficult to perceive.

# What Has Happened to Manufacturing?

Perhaps the most significant measure of how the economy has fared under Mrs Thatcher is the extent to which manufacturing has been revitalised. The sector's decline has been a consistent and notable feature since at least the mid 1960s. It can be said that this is no more than a trend that the UK shares with most other advanced industrial countries. However, the UK's rate of decline has been more pronounced. Whereas in 1960, 36% of the UK work force was in manufacturing, by 1980 this share had dropped to 28% and by 1986 to 22.5%. No other major competitor suffered this rate of collapse. West Germany, for example, went from 37% in 1960 to just below one-third in 1986. Over the same period, Japan actually increased from over one-fifth to just under one-quarter[15].

The decline in manufacturing jobs was not simply the result of better productivity allowing fewer workers to contribute the same or increased levels of output. In 1960 nearly one-third of total UK output came from manufacturing, but by 1986 this had dropped to just over one fifth.[16] While again this reduced share of output is true of all the main industrialised countries the decline in the UK is above the average. It is also interesting that by 1986 manufacturing in West Germany and Japan — the two strongest economies — held a considerably larger share of total GDP than in the others, 33% and 29% respectively. The most decisive evidence, which confirms the particularly severe deterioration in UK manufacturing, comes from the country's balance of trade in manufactured goods and its share of world manufacturing trade. In 1983 the UK had its first peace time deficit in manufacturing trade since the Industrial Revolution, a pattern which has since persisted. The UK share of world trade in manufactures dropped from 9.1% in 1979 to 7.6% in 1986, since when it has made some recovery.

The trend in some of the key indicators for manufacturing over much of the Thatcher period is shown in Table 15.

| Table 15    UK Manufacturing Performance 1979-1987 | | | | | | |
|---|---|---|---|---|---|---|
| | 1979 | 1981 | 1983 | 1985 | 1986 | 1987 |
| **Manufacturing Output: % change in each year** | -0.1 | -6.0 | 2.9 | 2.9 | 0.2 | 5.4 |
| **Manufacturing Productivity: % change in each year** | 0.4 | 3.5 | 8.5 | 3.2 | 2.3 | 6.8 |
| **Manufacturing Employment (millions)** | 7.2 | 6.2 | 5.5 | 5.4 | 5.3 | 5.2 |
| **% Share of World Trade of Manufactures** | 9.1 | 8.5 | 7.9 | 7.9 | 7.6 | 8.0 |
| *Source: Ball, 1989.* | | | | | | |

A significant determinant of the loss in UK competitiveness was the appreciation of sterling:

"Between early 1977 and early 1981 the loss of competitiveness exceeded 50%, described by the IMF as the biggest single loss of competitiveness ever recorded. In the four years following 1981 the fall in the exchange rate was sufficient to restore the level of competitiveness to the level of 1977."[17]

Since the Thatcher government's primary concern upon taking office was the control of inflation, it applied a rigid monetary policy supported by high interest rates. Together with the North Sea oil effect, this in turn promoted an increase in the value of sterling of over 20%. While this rise may have had beneficial effects on inflation in terms of falling import prices, it had a detrimental impact on competitiveness and on export performance.

Accordingly, in the critical years 1979-81, when the government persisted in tight fiscal restraint amid the deflationary pressures of a global recession, manufacturing was dealt a particularly debilitating blow. Output dropped 14%, around one million jobs were shed and about one fifth of capacity was lost. This represented the largest fall in output and the biggest rise in unemployment since the war. While the government presented this in terms of slimming down a flabby economy to a leaner and fitter state, critics saw it more in terms of starving an already anorexic industrial base.

It wasn't until seven years later, 1986, that manufacturing output regained its 1979 level, though by this stage it was being produced by 30% fewer workers. This reflected a significant improvement in the sector's productivity — up by 39% in the period 1979-87. However, it remains much in dispute whether this reflects a really new trend or is largely a one-off result of shedding less productive labour, together with the effects of a cyclical upturn in the sector.

The argument that trade in services will compensate for any manufacturing decline is hardly supported by current evidence. In any case, between 1985 and 1988, the surplus on trade in services dropped by about 40% from almost £6 billion to £3.5 billion, a tiny figure compared to the £14.3 billion trade deficit in that year. Similarly, the notion that service sector employment can compensate for manufacturing job losses is invalid if the historic trend is examined:

> "Private service employment rose by only one million over the two decades 1960-1980, compared with a loss of three million jobs in manufacturing, and there are many signs of substantial overmanning which will tend to lead to stagnation or decline in service sector employment as productivity increases."[18]

## The Thatcher Economic Record: A Summary

With an average annual growth rate of national income over the Thatcher decade of around 2%, unemployment still nearly double its 1979 level, investment only now back to where it was ten years ago, a current account deficit of £20 billion, inflation peaking at 8%, and interest rates at 15%, the government persists in self flattering accolades about its economic performance. In this assessment it does have some support. For example, Geoffrey Maynard[19] has contended that though high in cost and sacrifice, the Thatcher experiment will deliver enduring benefits. He infers that the 1979-81 deflation was necessary and helpful insofar as it proved cathartic to the economic sclerosis which had afflicted the UK for so long.

In this he is supported by a recent OECD report on the UK economy, which noted that: "the persistence of high rates of output and productivity growth throughout an exceptionally long recovery phase, judged by past performance and that of other countries, suggests that the improvement on supply side performance is more than a transitory cyclical phenomenon."[20]

But even sympathetic reviews of the Thatcher years are notably circumspect about extravagant claims of an economic miracle:

"....progress on a number of fronts has simply put us on a par with some of our international competitors. Having been at the bottom of the class we have become more of an average performer.... in other key respects, of which the most important is productivity, despite the improvement we are still well behind."[21]

The National Institute Economic Review, identifying the factors behind the relative upturn in the UK economy from the early Eighties, has been even more sceptical of government claims for the efficacy of its market ideology:

"The strength of the recovery in output owes little to the success of the macro-economic strategy as originally conceived. It owes more to its failures and subsequent modification. It was helped by the retreat from monetarism and it was helped by the failure of employers and unions to heed the exhortations in favour of a 'low wage' and 'low technology' solution."[22]

Certainly, by 1987 strict application of monetarism had been jettisoned, public spending restraint relaxed, and the strong pound policy of the early 1980s replaced by a gradual reduction in the value of sterling. The economic boost which accompanied these changes was quasi-Keynesian in nature, although it was oriented towards private consumerism and an attendant penchant for imports rather than a strategic investment in the capital base of industry and the enhancement of physical and social infrastructure.

Nevertheless, despite its long tenure in office, its fortunate bonanza of North Sea oil, and the new policies adopted, the government's claim to unique success in restructuring the economy has ultimately to be judged as spurious. This is evident from Table 16, which examines some key indicators, like growth, inflation and employment under different political administrations over the last four decades.

After 10 years of Thatcherite economics, according to OECD forecasts, Britain appears set in 1989 and 1990 to have the most sluggish growth of the top seven industrial powers, together with the highest inflation rate and the biggest current account deficit as a proportion of GDP. Moreover, the OECD half-yearly Economic Outlook in July 1989 relegated the UK economy below that of Italy, thus ranking it sixth in the league table of the top seven industrial countries.[23] In the first quarter of 1990, declining growth rates in output and productivity, together with rising unit labour costs held a real prospect of a hard landing for the economy.

| Table 16 | Macro Economic Indicators by Party in Power 1951-1988 (annual average) | | |
|---|---|---|---|
| | Growth GDP (%) | Inflation Rate (%) | Unemployment (%) |
| Conservatives 1951-64 | 3.2 | 3.5 | 1.7 |
| Labour 1964-70 | 2.4 | 5.2 | 2.0 |
| Conservatives 1970-74 | 2.4 | 11.7 | 3.1 |
| Labour 1974-79 | 1.8 | 21.2 | 4.7 |
| Conservatives 1979-88 | 2.0 | 8.4 | 9.5 |
| *Source: T. Thirlwall, Guardian, 26th April 1989.* | | | |

Looked at from outside the insular shores of Mrs Thatcher's Britain, the economic turn around of the British economy is viewed with increasing scepticism. Even the Wall Street Journal, previously an ardent supporter of the Thatcher revolution, has recently remarked how the international financial markets are more and more 'reflecting the gloom' of Britain's economic prospects.[24]

## What Has Happened in Northern Ireland?

Comparing the economies of Northern Ireland and Britain, or indeed the UK as a whole, is a difficult exercise. For one thing, comparison is being drawn between a large market and a small region, containing only 2% of the UK population. We have already drawn attention to this problem and have argued instead for comparison with other weak British regions. However, there are further problems in the analysis of any regional economy. For example, it can hardly be considered a discrete entity. And there is less detailed, accurate data on such matters as investment and export performance. Nevertheless, using some indicators such as employment, output, growth and public spending, some comparative insight is possible into the respective performance of both 'economies' in the 1980s.

What emerges clearly in such a review is that Northern Ireland's manufacturing industry suffers the frailties of its counterpart in Britain in an even more acute form. Because of the small size of the region's economy, the role played by a few large industrial firms can, of course, make a disproportionate impact. Nevertheless, this cannot be apportioned the main responsibility for the recent decline. The fact is that about half of Northern Ireland's total manufacturing jobs are in traditional sectors — shipbuilding, textiles and tobacco. Development of modern industries with good growth potential has been disappointing. Again, the fault cannot be simply attributed to the Thatcher years. The rot had set in long before. However, the pertinent question is to what extent has the Thatcher medicine proved to be an effective remedy?

## Employment and Unemployment

For much of the Thatcher period the trends in the key economic indicators between Northern Ireland and the rest of the UK have been divergent. This is very evident in the case of employment. In the period 1979-86 when manufacturing faced a severe squeeze, employment in that sector dropped by a quarter in the UK but by one-third in Northern Ireland. Moreover, when employment started to rise in the UK after 1983, Northern Ireland continued to experience a jobs decline.

| Table 17   Changes in Employment: Northern Ireland and the UK, 1979-1988 (%) | Northern Ireland | UK |
|---|---|---|
| **All Industries** | | |
| 1979-1983 | -10.3 | -9.1 |
| 1983-1985 | -0.6 | +1.9 |
| 1985-1986 | -1.6 | +0.4 |
| 1986-1988 | +0.7 | +4.5 |
| **Manufacturing** | | |
| 1979-1986 | -33.1 | -25.0 |
| 1985-1986 | -4.0 | -1.7 |
| 1986-1988 | -1.3 | +0.1 |
| *Source: Coopers & Lybrand, PPRU, 1989.* | | |

It was not until 1986 that Northern Ireland's growth in unemployment was arrested and began to be modestly reversed. In the decade since 1979, over 40,000 manufacturing jobs were lost. Even since the mid 1980s there has been a net loss of over 5,000 manufacturing and 3,000 construction jobs. This drain was only partially offset by a steady rise in service employment, around half of which was in the public services. Growth of jobs in private sector areas such as banking, insurance and business services has been extremely modest. Whereas between 1981 and 1989 employment in this sector increased by 52% in Britain, in Northern Ireland it rose by only 32%.[25] The sectoral composition of employment also underwent change, as Table 18 shows.

| Table 18 | Civil Employment, by Sector 1974-1988 | | | | | |
|---|---|---|---|---|---|---|
| | Males | | | Females | | |
| | 1974 | 1979 | 1988 | 1974 | 1979 | 1988 |
| Agriculture | 52,950 | 42,250 | 38,900 | 5,250 | 7,450 | 5,500 |
| Energy etc | 8,650 | 8,800 | 7,200 | 1,050 | 1,350 | 1,150 |
| Manufacturing | 111,250 | 96,100 | 67,200 | 60,800 | 51,500 | 37,400 |
| Construction | 45,200 | 43,900 | 31,450 | 1,750 | 2,150 | 2,500 |
| Services | 152,400 | 168,300 | 169,400 | 136,950 | 176,550 | 195,400 |
| Total | 370,450 | 359,350 | 314,150 | 205,800 | 239,000 | 241,950 |

*Sources: Northern Ireland Annual Abstract of Statistics 1984, 1989.*

The most obvious trend is the decline in manufacturing employment for both males and females. For each, employment in manufacturing in 1988 was only about 60% of what it had been in 1974. For males, manufacturing fell from 30% to 18.7% of total employment. The decline for females was greater, from 29% to 15%, reflecting the greater degree of compensation in new female service jobs.

There was a substantial increase in service employment, but, whereas males gained about 24,000 service jobs, the gain for females was about 60,000. Males also experienced a large fall in construction jobs of about 30% over the period.

By 1988, in terms of employment, Northern Ireland was quite definitely a service economy. The decline in private sector jobs has been partly compensated for by the growth in the public sector. But public sector jobs are no longer on the increase. In the last decade there was an overall 4% decline in public sector employment, including a 25% decrease in jobs in public corporations though with an 18% increase in the Police and Prison Services. Since 1979, manufacturing employment has fallen by 40%, so that by 1990 manufacturing employment represented just over 20% of all jobs compared to over 30% ten years previously. Nearly 90% of the remaining manufacturing jobs are directly or indirectly subsidised by the state. Public support for manufacturing jobs averages about £39 per employee per week. Despite this degree of public support, manufacturing jobs have continued to haemorrhage. There was for a short time a small sign of a reversal of this trend. While, as recently as 1986-87, there was a net job loss in manufacturing of 8,240 jobs, the following year, 1987-88, saw a net gain of 4,470 jobs. However, in 1988-89 there was a loss of 3,280 jobs. It is thus likely that services will continue to dominate employment, having grown from 50% to 65% of all jobs over the period. This probability is reinforced by the fact that 50% of remaining manufacturing employment is still concentrated in traditional sectors which are likely to continue to shed jobs. Harland & Wolff and Shorts Brothers & Harland accounted for 10% of manufacturing employment and certainly the former has suffered serious redundancies. The gloomy condition of the economy has been summarised as follows:

"Northern Ireland's manufacturing sector, together with agriculture, is probably capable of supporting a regional income at only half to two-thirds of the current level. As a result of the contraction of manufacturing, without replacement by other sectors producing externally tradable goods, the Province has become dependent on the public sector, much of it externally financed to support current levels of employment and income."[26]

Between 1978 and 1988 male unemployment as a proportion of the workforce more than doubled from 9.4% to 20%. Female unemployment nearly doubled from 6.1% to 11% in the same period. The deep recession of the early 1980s hit the Northern Ireland economy particularly hard. Between 1979 and 1981 alone, unemployment increased by over 60%. Not until late 1986 did the trend start to decline. A decade after Thatcher, official unemployment still stood at 104,000, representing 15.1% of the workforce, nearly two and a half times the UK rate of 6.3%. As noted in a recent economic review:

"The gap between Northern Ireland and the next worst region, the North of England, remains a wide one. If Northern Ireland had the same rate as the North of England (9.8%), total unemployment would be 68,000 — 36,000 less than it is at present."[27]

Despite demographic changes which reduce the number of 16-18 year olds in the labour market, the growth of jobs cannot match the number of people in the labour market. The gap would be considerably worse but for:

☆ Net migration, estimated in 1990 to be nearly 10,000 people, almost double the 1979 figure;

☆ The expansion of government employment schemes, which by the end of the 1980s was over double the 1979 figure, and, amounting to 25,600 places, was equal to 25% of all manufacturing jobs;

☆ And the relatively low participation rates in the region, itself an indicator of low demand in the labour market. The severity of Northern Ireland's jobless problem remains very evident. One particularly illuminating dimension is that of long-term unemployment. In July 1988, the share of long-term male unemployment in Northern Ireland was 59.2% compared to Britain's 44.6%. Indeed, since 1979 the percentage of the total unemployed in Northern Ireland in the long-term category has doubled and for those out of work five years or more, it has trebled — from 26% to 55%, and 5% to 15%, respectively.

## Output and Growth

Both Northern Ireland and the UK as a whole suffered a similar rate of decline in manufacturing output in the period 1979-81: 14.2% in the case of Northern Ireland and 14.3% in the UK. However, while there has appeared to be significant improvement since this time in the UK as a whole, Northern Ireland has not shown a similar pattern. For example, between 1983 and 1986 production and construction output in the UK rose by 7.8% whereas the figure for Northern Ireland was a mere 1%. This disparity was mirrored in the patterns of employment change in the same period. While the UK experienced a growth of 2.6%, Northern Ireland continued to endure a decline of 1.2%. It wasn't until the late 1980s that an improvement in Northern Ireland's industrial output reflected the UK's economic growth.

| Table 19 | Industrial Output: The UK and Northern Ireland, 1983-89 (1985=100) | | | |
|---|---|---|---|---|
| | United Kingdom | | Northern Ireland | |
| | Production Industries | Manufacturing Industries | Production Industries | Manufacturing Industries |
| 1983 | 94.7 | 93.7 | 94 | 94 |
| 1984 | 94.9 | 97.6 | 97 | 97 |
| 1985 | 100.0 | 100.0 | 100 | 100 |
| 1986 | 102.2 | 101.0 | 100 | 100 |
| 1987 | 105.8 | 106.6 | 99 | 99 |
| 1988 | 109.5 | 114.0 | 102 | 102 |
| 1989 (First Quarter) | 108.9 | 117.7 | 104 | 105 |
| *Sources: NIEC 1989, PPRU 1989.* | | | | |

While Northern Ireland shows some improvement, it remains behind the growth rate for the UK as a whole, particularly in the last two years. Output in UK manufacturing increased more than three times as fast as Northern Ireland over the same period. Manufacturing continues to be the weakest sector of the region's economy.

While the UK's GDP grew on average by over 3% per annum between 1981 and 1986, Northern Ireland's rate was just over 1%, well below the next worst UK region, Scotland, at 2.4%. However, in March 1988 the government declared that the figures had been subject to error, and suggested that by 1986 the figures were under stated by between 10 and 15%. This adjustment, if correct, would mean that Northern Ireland was in fact one of the fastest growing regions![28] On the other hand, the initial figure given for 1988 was also in error. The original figure of 5.9% was later revised to 3.3%. Whatever of this argument, the major component of growth in the 1980s was consumer expenditure.

The up-beat calculations for the earlier years have to be treated with some scepticism since they are at variance with evidence from other key economic indicators. For example, unemployment in Northern Ireland was growing faster than the UK average during this period. Moreover, while the revised figures computed a near 5% growth in manufacturing output between 1985 and 1986, the index of manufacturing output in Northern Ireland remained constant. As indicated earlier, the discrepancies between output and employment figures on the one hand and GDP statistics on the other, are most likely accounted for by the relatively favourable treatment of Northern Ireland's public expenditure which makes up a significantly greater proportion of the region's GDP.

Nevertheless, if the revised figures for growth rates are accepted, between 1981 and 1987 GDP per capita in Northern Ireland increased at a rate of 3.2% per annum in real terms.[29] Over the decade, there was a marginal decline in performance relative to the UK as a whole since GDP per head in Northern Ireland was 78.3% of the UK average in 1979 and 78.0% in 1989.[30] At the same time, the higher dependency ratio in Northern Ireland reduces its per capita GDP. The dependent section of the population is less likely to contribute to GDP.

## The Public Sector

As already emphasised, the public sector is the dominant influence in the region's economy. In 1978 the public sector share of total GDP was 39% in Northern Ireland compared to only 32% in the UK. By 1986 it had increased to 43% in Northern Ireland and 34% in the UK. However, "the faster rate of growth in Northern Ireland....is due to a more modest increase in GDP rather than a more rapid growth in the public sector component."[31] In other words, it has been the relatively poor performance of the private sector in the region which makes the growth in the contribution of the public sector appear large. According to Thatcherism, of course, this poor showing by private business is significantly due to its being 'crowded out' by the public sector.

Taking public spending as a percentage of GDP, in 1979-80 in Northern Ireland it was 70%, rising by the mid 1980s to 75%. This is higher than the public sector's share of GDP since transfers are not excluded from the calculation. In Britain, on the other hand, public spending fell as a proportion of GDP from 44% to 40% over the same period.[32] Coopers & Lybrand Deloitte argue that in 1989-90 the share was just over 60% in Northern Ireland compared to 39% for the UK as a whole.[33] This would appear to be at variance with other indicators. For instance, public expenditure change was positive over the period — 9.1% growth in real terms — while the highly optimistic interpretations of GDP data have been since revised. Accordingly, it is hard to credit a fall in the ratio from 70% to 60%.

The apparent relative generosity shown to Northern Ireland by the government has earlier been related to its particular circumstances. Amongst other factors, security demands, demographic patterns, the significant role of agriculture, the decline in private sector employment and a backlog of unmet social need compared to Britain, all influenced higher spending. When these differences are allowed for, the 'extra' public spending experienced by Northern Ireland has been more modest, as Table 20 indicates:

| Table 20 | Public Spending Per Capita in Northern Ireland as a % of Britain, 1980-1986 | |
|---|---|---|
| Year | Unadjusted | Adjusted to allow for special features of Northern Ireland |
| 1980-81 | +33.4 | +2.6 |
| 1981-82 | +33.6 | -1.6 |
| 1982-83 | +35.8 | -0.5 |
| 1983-84 | +37.8 | +1.1 |
| 1984-85 | +37.6 | +0.6 |
| 1985-86 | +41.9 | +1.7 |
| *Source: NIEC, 1989.* | | |

The Northern Ireland Economic Council has argued that: "the residual differential in per capita public expenditure compared with GB has generally been insufficient to meet other special needs in the Province such as the requirement to greatly enhance the effectiveness of the industrial development programme."[34]

The issue of how much public spending is merited by need is the subject of much dispute. A Needs Assessment Study undertaken by the UK Treasury in 1979, using various indicators, concluded that the appropriate level of expenditure for each country in 1976-77 was represented by the following indices:

| England | Scotland | Wales | Northern Ireland |
|---|---|---|---|
| 100 | 115 | 108 | 130 |

The actual expenditure in that year was as follows:

| England | Scotland | Wales | Northern Ireland |
|:---:|:---:|:---:|:---:|
| 100 | 123 | 101 | 136 |

It is, of course, a question of not only the volume of spending, but the use to which it is put. For example, of the estimated total expenditure of £5.5 billion in Northern Ireland in 1989-90, law and order increased to £630 million, representing over two-thirds of what was to be spent on education or health. On the other hand, the sum to be allocated to industrial development amounted to £242 million, a mere £12 million more than four years previously. Government argues that it is not being deliberately tight with the budgets of the development agencies, but that the apparent modesty of funding reflects the difficulty of attracting viable projects for support.

## Recent Developments

Recent developments in the economy again demonstrate how Northern Ireland is slow to pick up the benefits of an upturn in the UK economy yet quick to experience the fall-out of depressed demand. Table 21 illustrates some aspects of this experience:

| Table 21 | Indicators of Recent Economic Performance, Northern Ireland | | |
|---|:---:|:---:|:---:|
| **Indicator** | **Period** | | |
| | 1988 | 1989 (2nd half) | 1990 (1st half) |
| **Industrial Output/Growth** | 3% | 2% | 1% |
| **Employment** | +5,400 | -2,000 | -3,000 |
| **Unemployment** | -8,800 | 0 | +5,000 |
| Note: Figures for 1989 and 1990 are projections. | | | |
| *Source: Coopers & Lybrand, 1989.* | | | |

Though 1988 was a significantly buoyant year for the Northern Ireland economy, some of the statistics may overestimate the improvement. In particular, the rise in employment and related fall in unemployment have to be seen in terms of the 3,500 extra one-year jobs for the long-term unemployed provided by the government's Action for Community Employment (ACE) scheme, and the impact on the local labour market of increased emigration amongst those of working age. Nevertheless, growth in output of 3% in 1988 did represent the first indication of Northern Ireland being influenced by the reflationary experience in Britain, even if it was still less than half the 7% industrial output growth in the UK as a whole.

In 1990-91 Northern Ireland is expected to endure the negative impact of Britain's recent poor economic performance and the government's deflationary policy. However, the effect of the high interest rates is somewhat different in Northern Ireland. Because of the region's low level of house prices, high interest rates do not decrease personal disposable income nor dampen consumer demand as much as elsewhere in the UK. However, because of the high gearing in the corporate sector manufacturing investment is particularly hard hit. One indication of this is that Dun and Bradstreet recorded the business failure rate in 1989 at 22% in Northern Ireland compared to 9.7% in England and Wales. Nevertheless, growth in the region's industrial output is expected to be around only 2% in 1989 and 1% in 1990 compared to the 3% rate in 1988. Employment during 1990-91 is expected to fall by around 2,000 and unemployment to increase by a similar figure.[35] To sum up, at the end of the Thatcher decade, Northern Ireland has the lowest proportion of employees in employment in the UK, a level of vacancies at about a quarter of that in Britain, and the fall in unemployment has followed later than that in Britain and at a slower rate.

## Northern Ireland: The Economic Problem

For many decades Northern Ireland's weak economic performance has been attributed to its location on the margins of the UK and its restricted domestic markets.[36] Similarly, the Hall Report referred to: "Northern Ireland's disadvantages of remoteness, a small domestic market and lack of home supplies of raw materials and fuel...."[37] In response to these perceived defects, a regional development strategy was adopted as long ago as the 1960s to improve physical infrastructure, to enhance the incentives package, and to sell to potential external investors the particular resources which the local economy could offer, such as good water supplies and a surplus of labour accustomed to low pay. The objective was to attract transnational capital, which could help diversify the industrial base away from its traditional specialised dependence on shipbuilding, natural textiles and engineering. This strategy was typical of the regional policy approach adopted by depressed regions in Britain since 1945, even if Northern Ireland caught up with this form of indicative planning much later. In Northern Ireland this development plan met with some success. Up to 1971 around 34,000 jobs were created in the manufacturing sector. As noted by Canning, Moore and Rhodes:

> "The dominant feature of the period (1961-1971) is the large differential growth in Northern Ireland's manufacturing employment after allowing for its industrial structure. We attribute this primarily to the greatly strengthened regional policies."[38]

In these years Northern Ireland was one of the best regions in the UK for employment growth. However, this reindustrialisation process grew stagnant and then went into reverse in the 1970s. International capital, upon which the drive to rejuvenate depended, was both scarcer and being more widely sought by other parts of the world, given the whole process of the internationalisation of production and the related reorganisation of the global division of labour. In this changing world economy, Northern Ireland's comparative advantages were being eroded.[39]

Thus in the 1970s, under Direct Rule from Westminster, Northern Ireland's ailing economy had to be supported by greater public expenditure. This was perhaps most noticeable in the allowances made by the last Labour government which, while imposing greater fiscal restraint in Britain from 1976, treated Northern Ireland with a certain latitude. For example, in 1977 Selective Financial Assistance for industry was improved alongside other reliefs and concessions. The impact was evident in the number of jobs promoted which in 1976 had dropped to a low point of 3,678 but which by 1978 had climbed to over twice that level.

This Labour approach was characterised by some commentators as combining a tough military offensive against the IRA with a tender 'hearts and minds' campaign based on greater support for social and economic improvement. However, the interventionism adopted was also in response to pressure from organisations such as trade unions as well as sections within the local Civil Service. For example, the Quigley Report,[40] which argued for greater public sector-led development, helped to generate a climate sympathetic to greater state expenditure.

So, while up to 1970 expansion of the public sector in Northern Ireland was about the same as in Britain, "since 1970 about 50,000 jobs have been created in the public sector over and above what would have been expected given national trends".[41] Though the absolute accuracy of this estimate may be disputed, the period did see a substantial increase in public service employment, which offered new labour market opportunities for women, thereby enhancing family income.

In contrast to the 1960s when economic regeneration was pinned on the private sector — predominantly in the form of inward investment — heavily subsidised by an interventionist state, and the 1970s which came to depend a great deal on public sector expansion, the period of Mrs Thatcher has seen a change. The Thatcher government was generally dismissive of the benefits of an active regional policy in the restructuring of declining areas, and set about diluting its contribution. The 1983 White Paper on the issue stated firmly:

"The incentives must be made much more cost effective than at present with greater emphasis on job creation and selectivity, and less discrimination against service industries. They also need to focus on encouraging new and indigenous development in the assisted areas rather than simply transferring jobs from one part to another."[42]

The current residual form of the policy in Britain has been continued partly out of some political sensitivity to the social rather than the economic dimension and partly to protect the government's financial case for European regional assistance.

Northern Ireland's industrial policy in the 1980s has been significantly influenced by similar concepts — greater selectivity and targeting, more emphasis on the service sector in particular and indigenous industry in general. In 1981 a strategy document **A Framework For Action**, aimed for a 50% improvement on the previous decade's job promotion record. This objective comprised a doubling of the achievement rate of the small business agency, the Local Economic Development Unit (LEDU), and a quadrupling of the Industrial Development Board (IDB) record in attracting inward investment. As can be seen in the analysis which follows, the target for inward investment has proved unattainable. Mainly in response to this difficulty, in the late 1980s the local Department of Economic Development (DED) undertook a new assessment in which many of the region's economic ailments were ascribed to the following debilities:

☆ lack of an enterprising tradition;

☆ training and managerial deficiencies;

☆ penalties involved with being a small local market and

☆ being distant from the main markets;

☆ dependence on public funds;

☆ and the unstable political situation.[43]

The so called **Pathfinder** initiative launched in 1987 proclaimed the need for Northern Ireland to become less dependent on external funding from both the public and private sectors, less controlled by external ownership and less reliant on external ideas and decisions. It also echoed again the well worn litanies about limited domestic markets and peripheral location.

Given its serious and deep-rooted problems, and the more acute competition for resources and investment it faces from other depressed UK regions, it is argued that Northern Ireland must shake off the dependency patterns associated with being an employee rather than an employer-oriented society.[44]

Reference to the need for an enterprise culture imitates the new emphasis accorded to this feature in the Thatcher vocabulary. However, drawing conclusions about the absence of an entrepreneurial tradition in Northern Ireland is itself facile. For one thing, the industrial dynamism behind its economic development historically testifies to the existence of such a tradition. If the argument is more that small business creation and expansion has been retarded in more recent years this would be an indictment of much of the inward investment attracted during the last thirty years. In particular, it would confirm its failure to establish better industrial linkages and to disseminate knowledge, skills and new technology.

However, the basic assumption about current indigenous entrepreneurial activity in Northern Ireland may itself be suspect. A recent study[45] contends that Northern Ireland's ability to generate new firms is more impressive than that of other depressed UK regions. In addition:

"....whereas Northern Ireland is below average in generating new firms it is well above average in maintaining them once formed. To put the same point a different way Northern Ireland apparently has a good record in generating new firms which survive in the medium term."

This relative durability contrasts with the short lifespan of some major prestigious inward investment projects in recent years — De Lorean and Learfan being two notorious examples. Whereas, for much of the 1980s the main development agency, the IDB, was most successful with job renewal and expansion of existing businesses, LEDU's role in job creation had been expanded so that by 1985-86 it was promoting jobs at five times the level it achieved a decade previous. Meanwhile, the IDB was diverting greater effort into assisting indigenous industry, so that while in 1982-83 it was allocating about 50% of its budget to attracting outside investment, by the end of 1986 it was devoting only 10%.

| Table 22    IDB and LEDU Job Promotions, 1987-1989 | | | |
|---|---|---|---|
| | 1987-88 | 1988-89 | % Increase |
| **IDB** | | | |
| New Projects-Inward | 850 | 1856 | 118% |
| New Projects — Indigenous | 183 | 424 | 131% |
| Expansions — Indigenous | 1,977 | 1,416 | -28% |
| Expansions — Non-Indigenous | 2,273 | 1,957 | -14% |
| **LEDU** | | | |
| New Projects | 2,192 | 1,996 | -9% |
| Expansions | 1,855 | 2,585 | 39% |
| *Source: NIEC, 1989.* | | | |

The consultants Coopers & Lybrand Deloitte have estimated that to reduce the unemployment rate to 10% by the year 2000, assuming net migration of 5,000 per year, a net addition of 66,000 jobs would need to be created. This would demand a doubling of present job creation performance by the development agencies. Moreover, evidence provided in February 1990 by the Northern Ireland Economic Council has raised doubts that job promotions materialise into actual jobs created — only around half of the promotions translate into real jobs.

The government has expressed itself discontented with a policy which provided private industry with an annual state subsidy of £204 million but still failed to achieve a "vibrant self-generating economy." As the recent NIERC report puts it:

> "....after three decades of intensive policy assistance and the expenditure of several billions of pounds at 1988 prices, only 109 assisted firms remained in 1986 employing 21,742 people (approximately one-fifth of total manufacturing employment)."[46]

Alongside the shifts in government conceptions of the problem, there have been local Northern Ireland variants of the supply side theories fashionable with the New Right in Britain. For example, there is the suggestion that a depressed region like Northern Ireland should delink itself from national wage negotiation since its lower costs of living — especially in relation to housing — provides it with an opportunity to establish a comparative advantage through lower wages. Appropriate adjustments to the tax and benefit structure could facilitate this move, which would help the unemployed to price themselves into jobs.[47] Evidence from Northern Ireland to support this proposition is difficult to find. If patterns of earnings and unemployment are compared, it in fact reveals that while the lowest paid groups of male workers were experiencing a rapid growth in joblessness, they were simultaneously experiencing a deterioration in their earnings position.

If a low wage economy like Northern Ireland was to be subject to further reductions in real wages it would, unless accompanied by a large growth in employment (which the earnings data suggest it would not), further depress aggregate demand in the local economy. Moreover, should significant disparities emerge between the earnings of professional and skilled workers in Northern Ireland and their counterparts in Britain, then the scene for an even greater skills drain out of the region would be set. An alternative approach which recognises the low competitiveness and poor productivity of Northern Ireland's manufacturing, emphasises instead the need for large-scale high quality training, the encouragement of more efficient management and superior systems of quality control.[48] However, despite such considerations, the Thatcher government has referred more and more frequently in its third term to the need to depart from national wage negotiation. It appears to be particularly keen to give a lead to this process by instituting regional pay bargaining in many parts of the public sector. Northern Ireland, as a region heavily dependent on public sector employment, would be acutely affected should such a policy ever be implemented.

Despite all these changes, state support for industry in the region remains considerable. But is this level of exceptional government support peculiar to Northern Ireland? Could Wales be another example? It has had a Secretary of State, Peter Walker, the only surviving original 'wet' in Cabinet, who has recently declared his intention to resign. His appointment, like Jim Prior's to Northern Ireland before him, was interpreted as a form of exile, but some commentators recognised that it could offer an opportunity to resort to the old consensus in defiance of the axioms of Thatcherite market economics:

"As with Scotland, Wales would provide a 'kingdom' within which he could conduct a policy of his own. When James Prior was in Belfast he used to greet visitors by saying that 'we are all Keynesians here'; George Younger, when Secretary of State, protected Scotland from the worst excesses of Thatcherism. Could not Walker do as much for Wales?"[49]

In fact, Walker's period in Wales has seen him reject Treasury pressure for reductions in the region's financial assistance to industry. The Welsh Office has adopted a distinctly proactive role in industrial development, and over the recent period Wales, with 5% of the UK population, has attracted around one-fifth of UK inward investment.

A more cautious, but still perceptible, distancing from Thatcherite doctrine has also been a hallmark of Malcolm Rifkind's recent tenure at the Scottish Office. Confronted with dwindling electoral support for Toryism and a revival of Scottish nationalism which has exploited the image of an uncaring and remote Southern oriented government, Rifkind has attempted to ameliorate the application of the 'free economy'.

In both Wales and Scotland the tradition of corporatist tripartism has not been completely abandoned. Both the Scottish and Welsh Development Agencies remain instruments of interventionism operating in co-operation with local authorities and trade unions. The ministerial teams in both countries have tended to align themselves more in recent years with 'caring capitalism'. Of course, the distinctiveness of their approach always represents a relative rather than an absolute departure from central government credos. Indeed, they can, like Scotland in the case of the Poll Tax, find themselves involuntarily in the vanguard of the radical march of Thatcherism. Mrs Thatcher's own response to evidence of the wayward behaviour of these Secretaries of State is ambiguous. Instinctively, she might feel that the problems of places like Wales and Scotland stem from a dilution rather than an over dose of her medicine. Yet, politically, she appears prepared to turn a blind eye to such examples of dissent, when they clearly command local electoral appeal.

## Industrial Policy: A Greater Pragmatism?

So also in Northern Ireland a policy of some latitude with respect to Thatcherite axioms appears to have been accepted. The Industrial Development Board retains a remit which allows it a high degree of support and subsidy. Even diehard free marketeers like Rhodes Boyson, when Minister for Industry in Northern Ireland, adopted a hands-on policy particularly evident in his effort to forestall the closure of the Molins plant in a job blackspot in the west of the province. A similar pragmatism has been applied to trade union legislation.

Certain key provisions of the Trade Union Act 1984 and the Employment Act 1988 have not been transferred to Northern Ireland. For example, compulsory secret ballot elections for union executive committees, the need for secret ballots before industrial action and the removal of legal immunities where a closed shop operates are all features of British legislation which do not apply in Northern Ireland. Moreover,there have been substantial time lags in the introduction of whatever trade union legislation has been transferred. The Industrial Relations (Northern Ireland) Order 1987 covers provisions implemented in Britain in 1982.[50] The orthodox view that industrial relations in the region have been more quiescent than in Britain has been challenged by a recent paper[51] which argues that if particularly strike-prone industries like mining, which have no equivalent in Northern Ireland, are removed from the British figures, then the respective rates of days lost through strikes are comparable. The Thatcher government's greater reluctance to pursue trade union legislation, despite frequent calls from the Northern Ireland CBI, is probably related more to the perception that the trade unions are actually a stabilising feature in the complex political conflict than to any acceptance of their role as necessary to good industrial relations. The Irish Congress of Trades Unions attempted to overturn the political Ulster Workers' Council strike in 1974, though without success. Similarly, it supported Roy Mason's quelling of a similar strike attempt in 1977. It is perhaps the politics of the region rather than its industrial relations which continues to allow trade unions to be treated more as social partners. Moreover, the absence of a locally elected political legislature and the related proliferation of nominated boards have created many opportunities for trade unionists to be appointed. Such institutional conditions create more favourable conditions for corporatism.

Turning to another favourite item on the Thatcherite economic agenda, privatisation of state industry, this too has been pursued more cautiously than in Britain, as illustrated in the case of Short Bros & Harland and Harland & Wolff. Given the decline in support for shipbuilding allowed under EC regulations, Harland & Wolff had been losing money, and requiring subsidy, on a long-term basis. Despite its relatively full order book, Shorts was also receiving substantial public support. These two companies, which accounted for about 10% of all manufacturing employment, received around a third of all public resources going to industrial support. Harland & Wolff was in by far the weakest position. An EC directive on shipbuilding had specifically mentioned it as one of a number of UK yards that might have to be closed. Equally, Shorts could not maintain a long-term operation, particularly in its aircraft construction division, with such high losses.

The government decided that both companies should be privatised. Considerable public resources were made available to facilitate the process — £500 million to subsidise a management/employee buy-out of the shipyard. In February 1990, the House of Commons Defence Committee drew attention to a disputed extra payment of £22.5 million to the Belfast shipyard by the MoD for a Royal Fleet auxiliary training ship, raising questions about whether 'hidden subsidies' had been given to the yard in the lead up to its privatisation. This was in contrast to yards in other parts of the UK, for example in Sunderland, which were closed even though private offers to buy were made. As for Shorts, the total public sector cost of financing its sale to Bombardier, the Canadian aircraft conglomerate, amounted to £760 million. In both cases, while privatisation was carried out in line with the dominant ethos of central government, the levels of subsidy were extraordinarily high, relative to the total size of the workforces and the nature of the industries.

Accordingly, one interpretation of government economic policy in Northern Ireland in the Thatcher decade is that its market ideology has been followed in a more tentative and qualified form. This greater pragmatism has been true, though to a lesser degree, in the depressed regions of Wales and Scotland, though not in other declining regions of England. As the Northern Ireland Industry Minister commented:

> "If therefore the forces driving economic change in the Province are common to those elsewhere we cannot be unique in the type of economy which we seek to create. It follows that government must develop here, as in the rest of the UK, the same broad policies which have been central to the renaissance of the national economy, freeing enterprise which abounds throughout the community....These policies have been applied at national level *and after careful consideration we have applied them to Northern Ireland* (authors' italics). However, our involvement in the Northern Ireland economy, as in the less advanced regions in Britain, has always been greater than the wealthier areas...."[52]

This suggests a much more pragmatic politics than customary Thatcherite rhetoric infers. But it would be mistaken to argue that Thatcherism is only an English phenomenon whose impact is challenged and effectively subdued in the Celtic fringe. Quite clearly, the Northern Ireland Office has never explicitly disowned the Thatcher logic. Despite appeals from local sources like Coopers & Lybrand, for example, to develop a strategic economic plan, the government has retorted that it is no longer in the business of constructing such blueprints. Similarly, it has been disinterested in local trade union proposals for public sector-led economic renewal.[53] The government also appears to have paid scant attention to a major review of local economic options by reputable regional economists, Canning, Moore and Rhodes. The latter suggested a strategy for long-term development which over a minimum period of ten years would see indigenous industry receive greater support, with resources devoted especially to the identification and nurturing of modern industries. Rather than measure their effectiveness in terms of the number of jobs generated, new projects should be evaluated in terms of their contribution to a sustainable modern industrial structure. This proposal agrees with recent critiques of traditional regional policy which argue that economic impact has been judged too often in terms of immediate job gains rather than the suitability and durability of the total development. In the intervening ten year period, the authors conclude that the burden of job creation would legitimately fall on the public sector which is best placed simultaneously to improve services, create jobs, and stimulate wider economic activity.

Such a strategy, involving even this modified transitional role for the public sector, seems doomed to be rejected by government. Indeed, the newly designated Ministry of the Economy has committed itself to a future programme of widespread privatisation, including the bus service, Northern Ireland airports, harbours, electricity and probably water as well. This delayed pursuit of similar objectives to those of the Westminster government has to address particular problems in Northern Ireland. For example, electricity generation faces higher local costs and accordingly imposes higher tariffs on customers. Yet, should it be privatised and established on a more profit-based footing, charges will become even more exorbitant. Moreover, it would not make commercial sense to split up such a small generating capacity; so the new privatised corporation would retain a monopoly hold on the local market. The executive of Northern Ireland Electricity has argued also that public subsidy would still be required after privatisation in order to maintain a stable price structure. Government response to such predicaments seems to be based on a hope of injecting a competitive edge by linking up connectors to Scotland and maybe the Republic of Ireland, though both options face major impediments.

A further complication for government in Northern Ireland trying to pursue policies similar to those in Britain is that the prospects for the economy also have a 'peace dividend'. That is to say, improvements in income and employment, particularly in the deprived communities from which the paramilitaries recruit volunteers, are perceived by government to have a direct bearing on the level of violence. In a recent interview, the Minister for the Economy, Mr Needham, alluded to this connection:

"With little movement anticipated on the political front, and not much beyond containment in security policy, the economy, he says, is now 'the interesting leg of the stool'. If work can be found for the idle hands of '10,000 unemployed boys in West Belfast', he says, 'that in itself will do more to impact on the political and security areas than anything else'."[54]

In a wider sense, every major economic move made by government in Northern Ireland is sensitively monitored for its political significance by the main protagonists . Some Unionists have argued that Northern Ireland's status as part of the UK is best demonstrated by its being subject to precisely the same policies as the rest of the UK. This line of argument has even prompted one Unionist MP to issue the bizarre demand that Northern Ireland should be liable, as elsewhere, to the Poll Tax!

Another example of the implications that can be drawn is the long-standing suspicion by different sides of the Northern Ireland political spectrum that government policy in relation to the region's economy amounts to economic withdrawal as a prelude to a political withdrawal. This charge has been strenuously refuted by the Northern Ireland Office. For instance, Tom King, speaking to Northern Ireland business people at a seminar organised by the Trustee Savings Bank in November 1988, said:

"One of the most fashionable and ludicrous buzzwords I have heard in my three years in Northern Ireland is the allegation of economic withdrawal.... What we are now seeing in Northern Ireland is the benefit of government's economic policies, a move away from the smokestack industries to the newer high technology industries.... our dynamic approach can also lead to the successful privatisation of those few companies which remain in public ownership."[55]

Nevertheless, while some might interpret the privatisation of the local shipyard as being in line with policy elsewhere in Britain and thereby illustrative of Unionism in practice, others see the same decision as evidence of further economic disengagement by the British state. The result is confused patterns of political opposition to government economic policy. For example, Ian Paisley's Democratic Unionist Party poses as a stalwart defender of the union with Britain. Superficially, it might seem that the party would welcome policies in Northern Ireland which achieved a greater convergence of the region with the rest of the UK. However, the party's electoral base comprises mainly lower middle and working classes, whose material circumstances would be detrimentally affected by some of the harsher repercussions of Thatcherism. Accordingly, the DUP wobbles between embracing initiatives which symbolically cement the integration of Britain and Northern Ireland, while arguing for a markedly more lenient treatment for the region.

A further example of the unique features of Northern Ireland economic policy relates to the fact that Catholics and Protestants have unequal employment opportunities. Much attention has been drawn to the persistence of such inequalities. Catholic males, for example, are over twice as likely to be unemployed as their Protestant counterparts. And figures from the Continuous Household Survey demonstrate that for 1985-87, 45% of Catholic males were recorded as working compared to 62% of Protestant males. The unemployed rates were 25% and 10% respectively. For females the respective rates of unemployment were 6% and 4%. Various arguments have been adduced to explain this wide disparity. For some it is clearly a product of sectarian discrimination.[56] For others there are certain inherent characteristics of the Catholic community which make it less employable. Paul Compton has argued that:

"....the only effective way to guarantee improvement in the relative position of Roman Catholics in Northern Ireland is through the encouragement of fundamental change in certain of the innate features of that community. Acceptance of the desirability to bring Roman Catholic family size and rate of growth closer to the national and European average would be an important step along the road to greater equality."[57]

Still others like Eversley[58] attribute a combination of these factors. For example, he accepts that perceptions of discriminatory practice have inhibited Catholic job applications and are "a central part of the total explanation of differentials". But he also considers that factors operating in the past such as high Catholic fertility rates and a tendency to concentrate on a restricted range of occupations among Catholics have played a part. More recent features of the labour market, such as the limited number of men retiring, conspire to make it "a more closed market situation".

At the same time, it is evident that the labour market in Britain also operates patterns of disadvantage, for the black community in particular. Yet the government response to these two incidences of unfair employment practices varies considerably. In Britain some Labour-controlled local authorities have attempted a 'contract compliance' approach, whereby they use their considerable buying power to exert pressure for a fair employment policy on firms with which they do regular business. But tentative moves in this direction have been aborted by the recent legislation in Britain, which seeks to ensure that all contracts are awarded on strict commercial rather than social criteria.

In contrast, Northern Ireland has fair employment legislation, and it has been recently reformed by government. The essence of the new legislation has been summarised by the Department of Economic Development:

"....it puts new duties on employers to ensure the active practice of fair employment. Employers must register, monitor their workforces and regularly review their recruitment, training and promotion practices. They must take affirmative action measures and set goals and timetables where necessary. There are both nominal fines and economic sanctions — involving loss of business and grants—for those guilty of bad practice".[59]

The legislation has been subject to considerable criticism. For example, the Northern Ireland Committee of the Irish Congress of Trade Unions has pressed for a timetable for the reduction of the unemployment differential between Catholics and Protestants. Whatever its weaknesses, the legislation goes beyond any efforts in Britain to redress the discriminatory employment prospects experienced by black people and its sanctions embrace a form of contract compliance which the same government has outlawed in Britain.

The surprising aspect of the Fair Employment Act is not that it fails to be the perfect instrument to deal with labour market inequalities. After all, it has emerged from a government determined to increase general inequality. Rather, what needs to be explained is why this government led by Mrs Thatcher has been prepared to go so much further in Northern Ireland than in Britain. The impact of persistent pressure from trade union and other organisations, a political campaign in the United States (the McBride lobby), a genuine commitment by sections of the Northern Ireland civil service and the specific pressures of the internal politics of Northern Ireland, have all had their effect.

This chapter posed the initial question of whether the medicine of Thatcherism was capable of arresting the long-term decline of the Northern Ireland economy. That was put in the context of developments in the British economy where we concluded that the evidence for a permanent transformation of the supply side is less than convincing. Some of the key problems which the government boasted had been eradicated, have re-emerged. Productivity has improved but remains behind our key European partners, not to mention the US and Japan. The price of long term high level unemployment continues to be paid by millions of people and their families.

Within Northern Ireland, the impact of UK-wide policies has been severe. This has been indicated by the loss of output between 1979 and 1983 followed by a slow recovery, and the continued growth of unemployment until the end of 1986. While the past three years have seen improvement in the major indicators, few prognoses for the regional economy — other than those issued by the government — see the improvement being continued in 1990.

Nevertheless, in certain key respects the application of Thatcherism has been more flexible and more pragmatic than elsewhere. This has been true with respect to public expenditure, the more interventionist role of government in economic development and the highly favourable terms for the privatisation of ailing industries. Further, with respect to religious discrimination and inequality in the labour market, policies have been adopted which have been explicitly outlawed in Britain.

Northern Ireland has suffered from the application of policies which are UK in scope but has been insulated from the worst excesses suffered by other regions. At the same time, there has also been a failure to develop the long-term strategic initiatives required to reverse historic decline. Another issue is whether the local economy has been adequately prepared to face the rigours of a unified European market post 1992. A recent joint publication[60] of the Northern Ireland Economic Council and the National Economic and Social Council in the Irish Republic casts doubts on the capacity of Northern Ireland to benefit from 1992. While remaining an Objective I region and thus gaining highest priority in the allocation of structural funds, it begins to look less deserving in comparison with the poorer regions of Spain, Portugal and Greece. Moreover, since its lack of competitiveness has been identified as a key failing of local industry, the wider competitive European environment may well put severe pressure on Northern Ireland's industrial base. In that situation the region would further decline.

## A Different Agenda

We have employed, in the main, conventional economic indicators. These are by no means the only method of assessing the performance of an economy or a region.[61] If we take the example of GDP (Gross Domestic Product), this is meant to be a calculation of the value of goods and services produced in the economy. But it suffers from many limitations. For one thing, it is concerned with formal production. It deals with what is accountable. Accordingly, it excludes the black economy, the household economy where women in the main provide many subsidised services for society, and the voluntary economy in which people contribute to social well-being in an unpaid capacity. In addition, some of the goods and services measured in GNP are those which are needed to redress or compensate for irresponsible forms of economic development. These may include the social costs of certain types of urban development such as congestion and crime, environmental damage, ill-health due to stress or foods produced by modern agribusiness and poverty.

Alternative indicators have been suggested to help produce a more rounded estimation of the impact of economic development. One example is the PQLI (Physical Quality of Life Indicator) which derives from a weighted average of such factors as life expectancy, infant mortality, adequate housing, education levels etc. Another is the BHN (Basic Human Needs) index which attempts to measure the success of social and economic policy in terms of the extent to which it satisfies the basic human needs — e.g. decent housing, income, education — of the poorest fifth of the population.

An alternative way forward — associated up to now with Green politics — is referred to as the Sane, Humane and Ecological (SHE) model. It allows for a more decentralised and human scale path to development. New opportunities are foreseen through the greater availability of advanced small scale technologies. It is believed that such systems could return greater control over work to the domestic and communal arenas. The related reorganisation of industry and commerce would result in a blurring of the current distinctions between work and leisure. There could be a tension in this outcome between a privatised, individualist and self reliant approach and one which adapts the technologies to promote greater social solidarity.

Judged by these criteria, which are social and ecological as well as economic, Northern Ireland could be said to have sadly deteriorated since 1979.

In short, while the region has been favoured in certain respects, these are outweighed by the general impact of Conservative strategies, and, in the final analysis, judged even by conventional criteria, the long-term development needs of the Northern Ireland economy have not been met. If we are to judge economic performance in terms of the alternative indicators outlined above, an even harsher judgement might prevail.

The future of the UK economy as a whole is perhaps reflected in the way government has been recently selling its strengths. In March 1990, the *Guardian* reported the Industry Minister, Eric Forth boasting about the low wages and lax labour protection which could provide vital incentives for inward investment:

"Britain has one of the lowest labour costs in the European Community — one half of the costs in Germany and one third of the costs in France or Italy. Only Greece, Portugal, and Spain are cheaper. The workforce is also skilled and flexible, since it is not limited by rigid labour laws."[62]

# 4. The Tories and Poverty: Privatising the Poor

An important dimension in evaluating recent Conservative strategies in Northern Ireland is the issue of poverty. It has become commonplace to argue that Northern Ireland contains greater poverty than any other UK region.[1] A crucial test of social and economic policies concerns the degree to which they either alleviate or exacerbate such conditions of poverty. Yet, a central criticism of the Thatcher government has focused on its insensitivity to the poor and on the growth of poverty during the last decade. Piachaud,[2] for example, shows that the number of homeless families nearly doubled between 1979 and 1987, while the number of supplementary benefits claimants increased by more than 50%. Similarly, in the four years after 1979, the number of people living on or below supplementary benefit levels grew by nearly three million. Average real household income increased by 12% between 1979 and 1986, but, for the top tenth of the population the increase was 31% while the bottom tenth saw their real income decline by 8%.[3] Or to take another example of increasingly unequal income distribution, in 1979 the top 20% of households received 45% of all pre-tax income: by 1986, that had risen to 51%.[4] Simultaneously, the burden of direct taxation increased for those at the bottom end of the earnings distribution but fell significantly for those at the top. Byrne[5] argues that a married person with two children, on half the average male earnings, saw their aggregate income tax and national insurance contributions increase by 163%, while those on ten times average earnings enjoyed a decrease of 21%.

According to these arguments, certain sections of the community have borne the major cost of the Thatcher revolution. Those inhabiting decaying regions with very high rates of unemployment, ethnic minorities, and women, in short those groups most vulnerable to poverty, have been bypassed by the economic growth of the past seven years and have become more dependent on state benefits.

Yet, in Chapter 2 Northern Ireland's average incomes were shown to have converged with what were previously more prosperous neighbouring regions. Has poverty increased in Northern Ireland during the Thatcher years, and if so, what have been the consequences? This chapter addresses these questions and argues that, although the Thatcher government has a poverty agenda, its essential purpose has been to reinforce the work ethic.

## The Nature of Poverty

> "Attempts to construct an objective (i.e. value-free) poverty line face a series of largely intractable problems."
> Nicholas Barr 1987

Ever since the middle of the 19th Century there has been an ongoing debate about the meaning of poverty and the numbers who experience it. The impressionistic, though highly systematic, accounts of Engels and Mayhew were superseded by the survey methods of Booth and Rowntree.[6] The latter two attempted to provide incontestable definitions of poverty through the construction of poverty lines, based on fundamental physiological needs. Rowntree attempted to establish precise dietary needs and the range of food-stuffs required to maintain them. This 'grocery basket' was then priced to provide a basic income component. The addition of amounts for clothing, shelter and a small number of sundries permitted a precise poverty line to be drawn and the numbers living on or below it could be classified as poor. This came to be known as the concept of 'absolute poverty' since it referred to an income necessary to sustain mere physical efficiency. It specified a level below which no individual or household should fall.

Rowntree admitted that certain families with incomes above this line might also not be able to achieve the entirely rational expenditures to meet these basic needs. Such families, said to be in 'secondary poverty', were in no sense less poor and Rowntree himself never regarded their expenditure patterns as wasteful. Moreover, it was also clear that an individual's life trajectory might carry him or her above the poverty line at certain points and below it at others. This idea of the 'poverty cycle' enabled the identification of groups most at risk, i.e., at particular points of vulnerability in the cycle. Hence, the special concern which developed among poverty campaigners for the old and for families with large numbers of children.

For nearly half a century this approach to deciding who and how many are the poor prevailed. The poverty lines themselves gradually rose over time, not merely to take account of inflation but in recognition of social change and the generation of new forms of need.[7] Rowntree's last poverty line in 1950 was nearly five times higher than in 1899. However, although subject to periodic increase, poverty lines were raised neither as fast as the growth of GDP nor of average incomes. After the introduction of the welfare state, it appeared that poverty was being eliminated. Not merely was general social progress creating an increased prosperity for the majority, but the application of minimum income levels, principally through the use of national assistance, ensured that even those at the bottom of the scale received a nationally agreed minimum. Indeed, Rowntree's final survey seemed to confirm that poverty was now confined to a relatively small number of marginalised individuals and families.

Nonetheless, new approaches to the definition of poverty were presenting considerably more pessimistic conclusions. For example, Abel-Smith and Townsend[8] contended that the notion of poverty only made sense if put in the context of the social environment in which it occurred. Since the living standards and what were regarded as acceptable lifestyles of affluent societies were considerably above those of less rich societies, individuals in the former, even if they had sufficient for food, clothing and shelter, might still be poor, and regard themselves as such, if excluded from normal lifestyles because of an insufficiency of resources.

This new approach brought with it new ways to measure poverty. According to the concept of relative poverty, individuals and groups at the bottom of the scale will still be regarded as poor in as much as they are unable to participate in accepted living standards. In such terms, the shape of the country's income distribution is crucial for establishing who are the poor. An income distribution with a wide range and a long tail at the bottom represents a pattern of poverty even where those at the bottom have sufficient resources to meet their basic needs. This has to be qualified by the recognition that transfers in kind or subsidised services may alleviate the condition of those on low incomes; in such cases, the shape of the income distribution would not be sufficient in itself to indicate poverty. For the concept of absolute poverty, the location of the income distribution is more important — how many individuals are above the independently derived poverty line?

Operationalising the concept of relative poverty has taken three distinct forms. In their early work, Abel-Smith and Townsend took the national assistance scales as the benchmark and, using Family Expenditure Survey data, estimated the numbers of households with incomes above and below the scales. Their justification for using national assistance scales was:

> "Whatever may be said about the adequacy of the National Assistance Board level of living as a just or publicly approved measure of poverty, it has at least the advantage of being in a sense the official operational definition of the minimum level of income at any particular time."[9]

But, since national assistance scales had been directly derived from Rowntree's methodology,[10] their use implied a return to measures of absolute poverty. Partly in recognition of this dilemma and partly because of the very low standards of living permitted by such scales, it became customary to regard 140% of the scale as the poverty line.

A more sophisticated approach adopted by Townsend[11] was to create an index of items which defined a 'normal' lifestyle. Some of these referred to household amenities and possessions like a refrigerator, some to activities like taking evenings out, and others to consumption such as regularly having a cooked breakfast. The index of deprivation could be measured by the degree to which a particular household failed to possess such amenities and was unable to participate in these activities. This appeared to provide a true measure of relative poverty by focusing on social exclusion.

A third approach has been to explore the level of agreement among the population at large as to what constitutes poverty. In a survey carried out by MORI in 1984 for London Weekend Television, individuals were asked to declare what they regarded as necessities, the absence of which would constitute poverty.[12] There appeared to be a general consensus around a range of items which paralleled Townsend's index. Poverty could thus be defined relative to the views of a cross-section of the general population. The results of applying all three approaches suggested that during the entire period of the development of the British welfare state, significant numbers of the population remained in poverty with some estimates putting the figure at over 7 million people.

While poverty research presented findings that were a powerful critique of the capacity of a relatively rich society to eliminate deprivation, there remained constant dispute about the methods employed and the nature of the findings. For example, Piachaud[13] suggested that the attempt to find an objective index of deprivation through measuring possessions and consumption patterns was flawed. Life styles may diverge greatly because of different tastes — health-conscious vegetarians, for example, may permanently avoid cooked breakfasts. A failure to participate might therefore reflect a reluctance to conform rather than an insufficiency of resources. Moreover, Sen was concerned that the preoccupation with relative poverty would divert attention from those still living on or below subsistence levels, i.e., in absolute poverty: "....the approach of relative deprivation supplements rather than supplants the analysis of poverty in terms of absolute dispossession."[14] Also, attempts to estimate the numbers living in poverty were still fraught with methodological complexities. Sawhill[15] has suggested that the process involves at least four stages:

1)  defining needs, either in absolute or relative terms, and with due allowance for family size and circumstances;
2)  deciding what constitutes the resources required to meet such needs — particularly with respect to in-kind rather than monetary transfers and wealth;
3)  defining the appropriate income-sharing unit: the household, the family or the extended family;
4)  and finally establishing an appropriate accounting period for measuring flows of income and expenditure.

At every stage difficult decisions need to be made and so, it is not surprising that little consensus existed about the nature and extent of poverty. While relative poverty was said to reflect better the relationship between the poor and their social environment, it did contain conceptual weaknesses. In periods when there is a general decline in GDP and living standards, those at the bottom of the income distribution might fall below subsistence levels without seeing any deterioration in their relative position. According to the notion of relative poverty, they would be no poorer. Moreover, the tendency to engage in head counts of those below a poverty line tended to ignore the varying degrees to which the incomes of different sections of the poor fall below that measure.

This idea of an income gap may be just as significant as the actual numbers below the poverty line. With large numbers of people on or immediately below the poverty line, small changes in its definition could apparently bring very large numbers out of poverty, without having any effect on those whose incomes fall far below it.

Despite these problems, the proponents of relative poverty have, in the main, continued to employ the device of a poverty line, albeit set at different percentages of national assistance/supplementary benefits, and have used them to produce head counts of the poor. In the early 1980s the academic debate about the measurement of poverty had failed to achieve a consensus.[16] At the same time, there had developed widespread pessimism about the redistributive impact of state services.[17] Some[18] have argued that this pessimism was fundamentally misplaced, being derived either from illusory expectations or incorrect interpretations of the data. However, the idea that the welfare state had failed, remained powerful.

Equally, organisations, like the Child Poverty Action Group (CPAG), were complaining about the complexity, the low take-up rates and the low scales of the benefit system. A climate was created which suggested that a radical transformation of the system was required. Yet, the only body with the power and capacity to effect radical change was the Thatcher government. It had its own ideas about what was wrong and what changes were required.

## The Conservative Assault on Poverty

"The rich admire the poor less and less, partly because the poor are not as poor as they used to be, but also because the poor fritter their money on such trash — video cassettes and cars with fluffy mice that joggle in the back window."

Ferdinand Mount, former adviser to No. 10 Downing Street, 1982.

Although Conservative governments participated in the welfare consensus established after the Second World War, there remained influential figures in the party, and indeed in the Cabinet, who saw the development of welfarism as both economically and politically dangerous. Enoch Powell, for example, consistently maintained that an institutional welfare state, i.e., one which pursued substantially redistributive goals, would create a permanent dependency syndrome among claimants, undermine the incentive for profit and, through the encroachment of bureaucratic power on individual freedom, create the conditions for totalitarianism. In his view: "The translation of a want or a need into a right is the most widespread and dangerous of modern heresies."[19] Thus, the very concept of welfare rights is based on a fallacy. The state has no obligation to attempt to eradicate poverty. Rather, it has a responsibility to act to alleviate destitution, which is recognised as a possible consequence of a free society based on a competitive market place and private property. In the final analysis, the problem of poverty will only be solved when the poor are encouraged to participate fully in the opportunities created by the market place.

Rhodes Boyson[20] also pointed to the dangers of overemphasising the need to deal with poverty. Support for the poor is only achieved through a fiscal transfer from those who are working. The rights of the latter are trampled on when the state compulsorily confiscates part of their earned income and transfers it to the poor. This idea that welfare transfers are essentially immoral comes from Nozick[21] who argued that each person had the right to distribute as they saw fit the rewards of their own labour. Taxation as a means of financing state activities should therefore be kept to a minimum. Social intervention by the state should not be countenanced.

Although one strand of Conservatism remained highly suspicious of state interference, Conservative governments continued to react to increases in unemployment by injecting demand into the economy and sustaining the growth of welfare spending.[22] Even the Heath government (1970-74), although committed to the disciplining of British industry by means of the market, reversed course when faced with the possible closure of Rolls Royce. By the mid 1970s, however, it was no longer clear that state intervention was capable of maintaining full employment and, as indicated earlier, there was widespread dissatisfaction with the functioning of the welfare state. In 1976 one influential book[23] argued that the primary cause of Britain's economic ills was 'structural imbalance': an overdeveloped public (or non-market) sector, sustained by excessive taxation. The burden of taxation fell inevitably on the market or private sector where wealth was generated. In response to this burden, the private sector used productivity gains to shed labour rather than increase production. In this way, public spending was directly responsible for unemployment. Moreover, the jobs created by public spending to compensate for labour shedding elsewhere in the economy, could only be maintained by permanent subsidy, hence exacerbating the problem.[24]

While the Labour government of 1974-79 faced the problems of economic management with diminishing confidence and came to rely on a combination of efforts to restructure large-scale industries, like shipbuilding and aircraft manufacture, and the Social Contract, there was a virtual absence of ideas about how it might make progress towards equality and other social aims in a period when the economy was stagnating. Crosland[25] suggested that it was still possible to create a sense that Labour had a vision of social change through choosing a limited number of priorities and acting on those. Others, like Benn, argued for even greater state intervention and more efforts at fundamental redistribution. Neither of these approaches was considered practical. Instead, public expenditure restraint was adopted, partly legitimating the programme emerging from the new Conservative leadership.

The two bulwarks of Conservative economic policy under Margaret Thatcher have been monetarism and supply side economics. Earlier chapters have described the ways in which monetarism attempted to restrain social expenditure. To legitimise that restraint, the means had to be found to argue that the existing forms and scale of social expenditure were wasteful. This was particularly relevant with regard to measures of income support — the transfers which went to the poor. These can be evaluated in terms of their effectiveness (the degree to which poverty is eliminated) or their efficiency (the percentage of total expenditure which is received by the actual poor).[26] By emphasising the latter, the Conservatives were able to argue that major benefit programmes were insufficiently targeted at the most needy groups. For example, on this criterion, supplementary benefit was regarded as 100% efficient, compared to only 21% for child benefit which, it was argued, involved too much seepage because it entailed payments to all families, some of whom did not really need them. Little attention was paid to the effectiveness of child benefit resulting precisely from the fact of its universal coverage. Instead, means testing was to become the major allocative mechanism in other benefits since this did achieve the required targeting. The tendency for means tested benefits to have low take-up rates was not considered important. The Conservative emphasis on efficiency further enabled criticism of the 'welfare bureaucracies', said to be overstaffed and insensitive to consumer needs.

At the same time, the media attention paid to benefit fraud dramatically increased.[27] The popular press, in particular, generated sensational headlines about relatively minor cases of abuse. This helped to create the idea that benefit abuse was widespread and confirmed the view that much of the resources were being squandered. Consequently, the government announced a crackdown on social security fraud and increased the number of social security investigators.

Supply side economics also played a role in the poverty debate. This approach suggested that economic growth could best be achieved by removing all restraints on the operation of the market. Industry had to be deregulated and managers liberated. The two major bottlenecks to the free market were, on the one hand, trade unions bolstered by legislative concessions prised out of

Labour governments and, on the other, the benefit system. The latter was supposed to restrict the supply of labour. Individuals would 'obviously' refuse to work if benefit levels approximated to the net wage levels they could command in the market place. Yet neo-classical economic theory suggested that only by lowering the price of labour could surplus labour be absorbed into jobs. Benefits therefore acted to reproduce unemployment.[28]

Supply side economics demanded that new incentives to work should be created. Since increasing wages would merely add to labour costs, however, and make industry less profitable, the real value of benefits, particularly to the unemployed, had to be cut. As Margaret Thatcher said in 1980: "I believe it was right to cut the increase in unemployment benefit, because I believe it is right to have a larger difference between those in work and those out of work."[29]

A further implication of this new approach was to differentiate between the various groups suffering poverty. Since the essential rationale was to ensure an appropriate supply of low cost workers for the labour market, those capable of entering the labour market were subject to special attention. Of course, this has always been a feature of the British system of social security. It was exemplified in the wage stop (a device by which benefits could not exceed the level of wages when working) in the 1970s and the refusal to give long-term rates of supplementary benefit to the unemployed. This was to become the dominant feature of the system under the Conservatives. In 1980 the link between uprating benefit levels and increases in earnings was abolished. The earnings-related supplement to unemployment benefit was also ended. In the same year, the Supplementary Benefits Commission was abolished and replaced by the Social Security Advisory Committee. School-leavers were denied entitlement to claim supplementary benefit until the end of the school holidays. In November 1981 the benefits were uprated by 2% less than inflation. In 1984 a new benefit anti-fraud campaign was announced and in 1985 a green paper was published proposing a major transformation of the benefits system. By 1988 the new benefits system was in place and the majority of agencies working with the poor expressed considerable concern about the level of support provided. The purpose of these changes was not merely to save money, though that was very important, but to restructure benefits so that they did not undermine the incentive to work.

Certainly, the Conservative government believes that it has achieved a wholesale transformation of the supply side of the economy. As the then Chancellor told the Institute of Economic Affairs in 1988:

"There can be no doubt that the transformation of Britain's economic performance during the Eighties, a transformation acknowledged throughout the world, is above all due to the supply side reforms we have introduced to allow markets of all kinds to work better."[30]

Nevertheless, the government found that it was difficult to reduce state support for the poor without being subject to considerable criticism about the growth of poverty. Not only the Opposition, but the poverty lobby and the majority of academics concerned with these issues consistently condemned the government's approach to the most needy. The government could not simply reply that these hardships had to be borne in the interests of turning the whole economy around, since they were being suffered disproportionately by only certain sections, and those the most vulnerable, of the community. Rather, it tried to claim that such criticism was fundamentally misplaced. There was no growth of poverty, merely a growth of the poverty industry, i.e., organisations campaigning for the poor whose self-interest was served by asserting the widespread nature of the problem.

The government and its supporters felt obliged to launch an assault on the concept of poverty itself. In particular, they attacked the notion of relative poverty since this required more than residual social intervention and so was especially dangerous for a government determined to reduce such intervention.

What was regarded as the central weakness of the concept of relative poverty was fully exploited. Those concerned were accused of confusing poverty with inequality. In the Conservative view, social inequality is inevitable given the unequal distribution of talent, initiative and hard work within the population. Some people will always be better off than others, and this is entirely acceptable since it is a reward for their or their ancestors' labour. Inevitably, others will be denied access to the predominant lifestyle in the country without necessarily being very badly off. Indeed, in advanced industrial societies, particularly in periods of economic growth, this is more likely to be the case. The poverty lobby had, therefore, replaced a legitimate concern with destitution with the political object of creating an egalitarian society which, of necessity, restricted the freedoms of the market. In 1975, even before coming into office, Margaret Thatcher had asked:

"What is it that impels the powerful and vocal lobby in Britain to press for greater equality.... Often the reasons boil down to an undistinguished combination of envy and what might be termed 'bourgeois guilt'."[31]

The most celebrated example of the government's challenge to the poverty lobby was the speech made by John Moore, then Secretary of State for Social Security, in May 1989. He claimed:

"Not only are those with lower incomes not getting poorer, they are substantially better off than they have ever been before.... It is hard to believe that poverty stalks the land when even the poorest fifth of families spend nearly a tenth of their income on alcohol and tobacco."[32]

John Moore argued that since even those in the bottom fifth of the income distribution had access to cars (50%), colour televisions (70%), washing machines (85%), central heating (50%) and refrigerators (nearly 100%), it was no longer possible to regard them as being in poverty.[33] Such people were only labelled poor because of the application of a poverty line based on 140% of benefit levels which was wholly inappropriate. The use of this poverty line implied that one in three people in Britain were in dire need, which he said was both 'false and dangerous'. The concept of relative poverty was strongly attacked: "Does it mean that in a rich community where most people have three cars, the people with one car are poverty-stricken?"[34] Definitions of relative poverty were, in his view, essentially politically motivated: "since by its use the fires of resentment and envy are kept forever stoked, and no matter how much we succeed they can always claim that we have failed."[35]

In more neutral language, the DHSS had developed a similar argument in a document produced the previous year.[36] Supplementary benefit was not an appropriate measure of poverty, not only because families obtained additions to the basic scales and had housing costs paid through housing benefit, but also because the more generous the scales, the greater the numbers registered as poor. Thus, the attempt to measure poverty by the principal instrument used to alleviate it was circular. The use of the line, 140% of supplementary benefit, was "particularly open to question". For example, in 1987 the equivalent for a two-child family would be 77% of average gross earnings. But for a four-child family, the figure would actually be above average earnings. Of course, this line of argument overlooks the problem of comparing wages, which are paid to a single person, to a benefit level on which an entire family subsists. Families may depend on one set of wages, but, even where they do, child benefit would provide a further proportion of family income. This is not the case with income support where child benefit received is deducted from the amounts paid.

The Conservatives have attempted to effect a new rediscovery of poverty which overturns efforts to relate the phenomenon to its social context. This attempt is not merely scientifically invalid but politically malicious. It was their overall strategy of freeing up the labour market and creating a more 'flexible' labour force, rather than any concern about poverty that propelled them to intervene in the poverty debate. In particular, they wanted to establish that there was no necessary relationship between being unemployed and being poor. Real reductions in benefit levels, as a means of compelling those allegedly unwilling to re-enter the labour market, could then proceed. The use of instruments like Restart, targeted initially at the long-term unemployed and designed to facilitate re-entry to the labour market, involved a coercive dimension — the threat to withdraw benefit.

This approach could only be sustained by the selective use of evidence. In 1979, there were 100,000 families with a head of household who had been unemployed for more than three months, who were living below supplementary benefit levels. By 1983, the figure had increased to 370,000 families.[37] In 1979 such families were 7% of all families living below supplementary benefits levels. In 1983, they were 17.7%. The growth of unemployment has been therefore clearly associated with a substantial increase in the number of families, not living below 140%, but below the scale rates. It is difficult to see how this can be interpreted except as a large scale growth in poverty.

Yet simultaneously, another rather different dimension to Conservative strategy on poverty was emerging. The inner city riots of the early 1980s had generated a fear that the combination of urban decay and personal deprivation would catapult young people into periodic, but serious, confrontations with the police. A number of ad hoc measures were introduced, particularly under Michael Heseltine, to upgrade some of the more depressing environments. Moreover, although the 1987 election ended with a Conservative majority of over 100 seats, there had been some unease during the campaign that the opinion polls might suddenly swing towards Labour. In the event, the swing was insufficient to damage the Conservative hold on the Commons.

Nevertheless, immediately after the declaration of the result, the Prime Minister announced that some initiative was required in the inner city areas, which, if they continued to decline in the midst of general economic growth, might, like Scotland, almost wholly reject Conservatism. An inner urban programme was needed and this had to have the character of an anti-poverty programme. Thus, a government which, in the words of the Low Pay Unit "was trying to define the poor out of existence",[38] ended up trying to develop a strategy to combat urban poverty.

The details and results of that strategy are provided in Chapter 6. Its essential features were in line with the government's overall policies for the economy. Rather than provide welfare support for the poor, it sought to generate a private sector-led economic revival to create jobs in new, predominantly service sectors. The main instruments were to be private corporations with specific responsibility for urban regeneration. The advantage of this approach was that it firmly located the resolution of inner city problems in the economic realm rather than welfare activity. The disadvantage was that the wholly privatised agencies have frequently bypassed the very communities they were supposed to be serving while the benefits of post-industrialist growth have been selectively enjoyed.

To sum up, the Thatcher government's strategies on poverty have operated on the assumption that the poverty lobby exaggerated the scale of the problem, and, in consequence, the government has been prepared to allow the real value of welfare support for the poor to decline, particularly with respect to social security. On the other hand, it has been willing to provide resources for inner city regeneration, but with an almost exclusive emphasis on private development. This has dramatically shifted the direction of anti-poverty programmes, in line with the government's overall approach. We need now to turn to the question: how have these policies been put into practice in Northern Ireland?

## Poverty in Northern Ireland

As indicated earlier, the bulk of poverty research has tended to find greater concentrations of poverty in Northern Ireland than in other regions. In Townsend's major study of poverty in the UK,[39] he ranked the degree of poverty in regions according to eight different criteria. On six of these, Northern Ireland came first, and it was respectively second and third on the other two. Indeed, he contended that the only advantage enjoyed by the poor in Northern Ireland was less pollution. Another researcher, Evason produced a series of pamphlets from the mid 1970s[40] documenting various dimensions of poverty in Northern Ireland; throughout the period, she accepts the contention of its uniquely disadvantaged status. For example, she produced figures to show that 38% of households were in poverty in Northern Ireland compared to 30% in the next highest region, Wales. She has demonstrated that in the mid 1980s, 23.5% of the total child population in Northern Ireland were dependent on supplementary benefits compared to only 13.4% in Britain. She argues that: "The degree of dependence on certain benefits gives a guide to the volume of poverty in Northern Ireland"[41] and dismisses the government's view that benefit dependency is not necessarily associated with poverty.

Contrary views have been expressed. For instance, Fieghen, Lansley and Smith[42] ranked regions according to the 'risk of poverty' (the proportion of the sample who were actually poor). Northern Ireland had the lowest risk of any UK region at 4.9% compared to Wales 10.3%. The validity of this result has to be qualified by the very small size of the Northern Ireland sample. Also, the poverty line employed was the standard supplementary benefit scales, and since the income distribution may be particularly dense at this point, the reduction from the more normally employed 140% to 100% might well have excluded large numbers of Northern Ireland households from poverty. A more recent account, the Northern Ireland Continuous Household Survey 1987[43] found that, in a sample of 2,772 households, 42% had a gross annual income of less than £5,000. This finding runs counter to data produced in Regional Trends and indicates a substantial proportion of households on very low incomes. Further, the Survey found:

"....a marked contrast in the level of income between households where the head is working and households where the head is out of work, either unemployed or economically inactive [ out of work and not looking for work]. Almost three-fifths of households with the head working had a total income of £10,000 or more. Three-quarters of households headed by an unemployed person, and 71% of those headed by an economically inactive person, had a total income of less than £5,000 per annum."

Households with an unemployed or economically inactive head constituted more than half the sample.

Whatever the debate about the level of poverty in Northern Ireland, there can be little doubt that, with the exception of old age pensions where the region has a lower percentage of its population in the relevant age group, there is a much higher degree of benefits dependency. A greater proportion of average household income is benefit derived and the proportions in receipt of unemployment and supplementary benefits have been higher than in other regions (see Chapter 2). Consequently, the relative numbers affected by the transformation of the social security system have been greater. Thus, the changes which the Conservatives have been attempting to achieve through the reform of social security may well be more evident in the region.

## The Reform of Social Security

The 1986 Social Security Act came into force in April 1988. The Green Paper on Social Security, published previously, argued that the existing system had lost its way and was becoming incomprehensible both for claimants and those who operated it. The new benefits were expected to apply common criteria on such issues as income and capital. They were intended to be simpler to operate and easier to understand. Finally, they were supposed to be fairer, with better targeting of those most in need and establishing a clearer difference in income between those in and out of work. This new approach was opposed by groups like the Child Poverty Action Group, the Low Pay Unit and the National Association of Citizens' Advice Bureaux.[44] Under the new regulations, supplementary benefits, based on the calculation of individual needs, was replaced by income support, paid according to the client group to which the individual belonged. A standard feature of supplementary benefits, the so called additional requirements, given on the basis of special dietary or other needs, was also abolished and replaced with premiums paid to particular groups. Single payment grants also vanished and the social fund, concerned mainly with offering loans rather than grants, was substituted. Family income supplement was replaced with family credit and significant changes were made to housing benefit.

The Minister responsible for the introduction of the new system in Northern Ireland, Richard Needham, was optimistic about its impact:

"Apart from targeting help to those who most require it, the reforms should ensure greater equity between those in low paid work and those relying on income support. In particular, the effect for those on low earnings should be of considerable importance in Northern Ireland where some £32 million more cash is being provided for Family Credit than was spent last year on the former Family Income Supplement. Indeed the Northern Ireland economy would benefit from an increase of some £43 million for all weekly income-related benefits and family benefits this year."[45]

However, other estimates of the effects of the reforms have been less sanguine. When the Act was first introduced, the Labour frontbencher, Michael Meacher, used a computerised social security model to calculate probable effects in Northern Ireland.[46] On that basis, it was anticipated that 138,183 claimants would lose out. The bulk of these would be pensioners aged between 60 and 79, where the loss of additional payments under supplementary benefits would not be compensated by the new premiums. Over 10,000 low paid families and nearly 10,000 unemployed families were also expected to see benefits reduced by £3.00 to £5.00 per week. Further, it was anticipated that the abolition of single payments would have a grave effect. In 1985, pensioners received on average £170.31, while the unemployed received £167.42 in single payments. Since the bulk of the social fund was to be distributed in the form of loans, these figures represent a permanent loss of income.

In the first two months of the new system, the Northern Ireland Citizens' Advice Bureaux monitored the impact on claimants by conducting a survey of those seeking advice. While the sample is clearly biased towards those who had problems with their revised entitlement, it does provide information on where the reforms have failed.[47] They found that 15% of claimants were better off, 26% experienced no change of circumstances and 59% felt they were worse off. These figures are even worse than the Meacher calculations, which foresaw about one in three claimants being worse off. In answer to a parliamentary question,[48] Richard Needham admitted that the social fund budget for 1988-89 was only just over half the value of the single payments made in 1986, when Northern Ireland claimants obtained 10% of all expenditure on single payments even though they constituted only 5% of all UK claimants. Moreover, in 1988-89, every single social security office in Northern Ireland underspent their social fund allocation,[49] so the difference between single payments and social fund allocations actually made was even greater. The major beneficiaries of the reformed social security system were intended to be the low paid, in keeping with the central objective of upgrading work incentives. Yet, in November 1988, John Moore admitted to the Commons that the take-up rate of family credit in the UK was only about 40%. In Northern Ireland, spending on family credit in its first year was around 50% of the allocation.[50]

There are strong grounds for believing that the overall impact of social security reform has reduced the resources of a substantial proportion of claimants. For the unemployed, the new 1989 Social Security Act introduces even more rigid tests of availability for employment, again with the threat of the removal of benefits. The new legislation was prompted by persistent Conservative concern that the unemployed were refusing to work for 'realistic' pay levels.

At the same time, specific programmes to combat poverty in the inner city also emerged in Northern Ireland. A detailed analysis of these initiatives is provided in a later chapter. Nevertheless, the assumptions on which they have been developed are very similar to those in Britain. They are designed essentially to encourage a grassroots entrepreneurialism and to create a community base for the enterprise culture. The public spending plans, unveiled in November 1989, indicated that nearly £100 million would be devoted to these programmes over a five-year period. This is clearly an important increase in resources which hopefully will make a difference in the most disadvantaged areas of Belfast and Derry. However, the scale of the additional resources has to be evaluated with respect to both the enormity of the problem of long-term unemployment and the other, more negative changes taking place in public expenditure. For example, the official register demonstrates a fall in unemployment of nearly 25,000 between the end of 1986 and 1989. If the average level of benefit paid to each unemployed person is just £30 per week, then there has been an annual saving of around £39 million. Over five years this would considerably exceed the resources being made available for inner city poverty programmes. Similarly, if the average cost of creating a single job is around £4,000 (LEDU figures), eliminating unemployment in West Belfast alone, the most concentrated area of unemployment in Northern Ireland, would require £44 million. This is indeed the figure arrived at by consultants working for an independent group Obair.[51] In general, the savings by government as a result of its changes to the benefit system have more than matched the additional resources it is allocating inner city programmes.

## The New Poverty: The Underclass

The combination of benefit changes, inflation in house prices and the continuing high level of unemployment have driven gaping holes through the safety net formerly provided by the welfare state. This new form of poverty, the growth of an underclass, has received a great deal of attention recently. At one level the term has been used to describe not just the poor but those embedded in cultures which inhibit active efforts to escape poverty. This approach looks at correlations, for example, between illegitimate births and unemployment and seeks to explain both by a third factor, usually culture. It thereby reproduces the old distinction between the deserving and undeserving poor. A different version refers not merely to the growth of homelessness — the 'cardboard cities' that have sprung up especially in London — and also includes many of those almost wholly dependent on state services and who suffer greatly when these are reduced. In December 1989 all the major churches in Britain launched a common declaration, '**Hearing the Cry of the Poor**' which accused the government of "hurting, damaging and discounting the poor" and declared that it was not right for some people to have to subsist on £60 per week while some of the very well off regularly obtained £3,000.[52] This critique was followed in January 1990 by the Church of England report,

**Living Faith in the City**, which claimed that changes in taxation and social security had significantly accentuated the gap between rich and poor.

It may be that the relatively greater availability of public sector housing in Northern Ireland, coupled with the smaller decline in other forms of public expenditure, has inhibited a similar growth of an underclass. For example, in Catholic West Belfast, which is generally regarded as containing the most concentrated deprivation in the city, there is a massive unemployment problem, but over 50% of households live in public sector housing, the majority of which has been built since 1960. Moreover, the grades obtained by school-leavers in this part of the city compare favourably with the Northern Ireland average.[53] It therefore lacks the combination of conditions which generate a true underclass.

Nevertheless, reports from organisations like the Saint Vincent De Paul charity indicate a phenomenal growth in requests for help. Its regional director, in a statement released in December 1989, declared that: "Since the government's single payments for the needy were changed into loans, demand for our services has increased dramatically.... people who managed to cope in the past are now turning to us in desperation."[54] She reported a twenty-fold increase in requests for help in certain branches since September 1988. Thus, there can be little complacency that a relatively better social welfare infrastructure in Northern Ireland will hold a safety net in place.

Although Northern Ireland has benefited from specific programmes to combat inner city poverty and while these legitimately emphasise job creation, it has suffered from the dual nature of the Conservative approach. Operating under the concept of absolute rather than relative poverty, the Conservatives have simultaneously reduced the measure of benefits support for the most dependent groups while emphasising job creation programmes. Within the region, this has resulted in proportionately greater hardship because of the higher benefits dependency ratio. On the issue of poverty, the judgement on Conservative policies must be negative.

# 5. The Tory City: Urban Blues

The economic restructuring experienced in the Thatcher period has had specific spatial consequences in the country's major conurbations. In this sense:

> "Uneven development across cities, regions and nations is not a mechanical process of economic relations in isolation from other important factors. Cities change not only as a result of the requirements of global or local capital but also as a result of state policy at the local and national level."[1]

Interestingly, in Britain over the last decade most of urban local government, which is mainly Labour-controlled, has faced sustained hostility from the Tory central government. This tension has been a major factor in shaping urban policy in the 1980s. The question is to what extent the actual outcome has been significantly different from the pre-Thatcher period, and whether this urban policy has been similarly applied to Northern Ireland, where the contest between central and local government is engaged around different issues. It so happens that Belfast currently faces a new strategic plan to guide its development over the next 20 years, and this provides an opportune focus for consideration of this comparison. In the British context, one of the major instruments for this form of redevelopment has been the Urban Development Corporation (UDCs).

## Urban Development Corporations in Britain

Urban Development Corporations were established under the 1980 Local Government, Planning and Land Act, which give them planning control over development in their designated areas.

They can acquire — ultimately through compulsory purchase — maintain or dispose of land and other property. Apart from the creation of a good infrastructure, they can distribute financial aid to attract or lever private investment and development.

It is clear from the experience of the London Docklands Development Corporation (LDDC) that, while such an organisation can facilitate and subsidise commercial activity, its overall contribution, as well as accountability to the local community, fall far short of being adequate. The Thatcher government applauds the near £7 billion worth of private sector activity in London Docklands. But the indirect state investment has been considerable. By 1992 the Isle of Dogs Enterprise Zone, for example, will have given tax holidays likely to total around £1.5 billion. This is not including exemptions from rates, which amount to around £24 million a year. Similar exemptions operate on some of its other key development sites such as Canary Wharf. Moreover, the free-for-all market approach has created a potential glut in the area's property markets, thereby inducing high risk since again much of the development is speculative:

"....there is also much nervousness about whether Docklands can really compete, as it aspires to, for City finance houses, the West End's shoppers and eaters-out, and the residents of posh Fulham and Hampstead."[2]

In any case, to suggest that this level of investment activity can be repeated elsewhere ignores the unique location of this particular Development Corporation with its convenient proximity to the expanding financial services sector in the City of London. Other Development Corporations such as the one on Merseyside have reflected, more than they have changed, the depressed economic state of their hinterland:

"By the end of 1986-87 only about one-third of available commercial and retail floorspace owned by the Merseyside Development Corporation was occupied; only three sites had been sold; and the MDC had attracted less than £20 million of private sector investment....Because industry has not been attracted to the MDC's area, permanent jobs increased only from 1,500 to 2,500 by August 1987."[3]

It is notable that in government spending plans announced in 1990 the LDC is to receive an extra £359 million, whereas an extra sum of £28 million is allocated to be shared by the other nine UDCs. Unquestionably, thousands of jobs have been generated in London's Docklands. But the majority, have been filled by outside commuters or new residents. This 'leakage' in the labour market clearly demonstrates that targeting resources at particular geographical areas is a poor substitute for targeting them at the people who reside in them:

"The escalation of land prices in the LDDC area has forced many local firms to move out or close....Unemployment in the three Docklands boroughs rose by over 10% between 1982 and 1987— over twice as fast as in London as a whole. Projected employment growth is high due to major office developments, but most jobs will go to commuters, not local people — except for ancillary and cleaning work."[4]

This pattern of limited jobs growth, and the skills mismatch which results in even less new employment for local people, is true of many of the run-down areas in Britain's cities. As one comprehensive review concluded: "....perhaps the best estimate is that something like 85% of new jobs in inner cities have gone to people living outside the area."[5] Another feature of this displacement of 'natives' to accommodate the up-market 'newcomers' is what has happened to housing in many of the riverside developments. The London example of exclusive, prestigious apartments fronting the Thames has been well reported. But much the same pattern is becoming evident in other schemes:

"....an entirely new type of resident is moving into the centre of Salford (Quays). Middle managers, executives and yuppies are coming to live in an area which once provoked only fastidious shudders."[6]

A similar prospect is possible in Belfast's Laganside (the flagship project of Belfast's new Urban Plan) where prior consultation with the well established local communities has been negligible:

"To prevent the 'waterfront wonderland' becoming debased and turning into another sector of low grade housing, Needham [the Belfast Minister] is pinning his hopes on private sector funding for new riverside residences".[7]

Yet such claims about the yuppification of the area are vehemently rejected by the Chief Executive of the Laganside Corporation, Mr Mackey who has said: "We would like to build a paradise but it will not be a paradise for the elite. There are plans for some excellent first starter homes".[8] In February 1990 the Laganside Corporation indicated that it may conduct a local skill profile and adopt training schemes which would facilitate local residents taking up job opportunities in the development. It could, of course, be argued that a more socially mixed residential pattern and occupational profile will emerge in the Belfast scheme because lessons have been learned from the experiences of places like London. As noted by the House of Commons Employment Committee:

"It is not good for the health of a community for the original inhabitants of an area to see others benefiting, as they see it, at their expense, while they suffer from increased road traffic congestion, higher house prices and associated ills. Nor is it just".[9]

There is also some evidence that the Development Corporations in Britain have recently invested greater effort in facilitating negotiations between local communities and the developers.[10] However, so far, the amount gained by communities in this process is modest in scale relative to the 'betterment' value of the development. Moreover, the negotiations are often subject to commercial confidentiality, lack contractual status and generate mainly those concessions congruent with the development objectives. It remains the case that the social costs of these UDC projects are underestimated. Orthodox evaluations emphasise total new investment, leverage ratios and acreage developed. Less attention is paid to the net impact. In other words, they do not take into account job and industry displacement, the costs of reclamation and infrastructural improvement borne by the public sector, the longer term costs of increased congestion and the effect on local residents of increasing land values. Before examining recent developments in Belfast, it is useful to consider their historical context.

## Planning in Belfast: A Brief History

Belfast did not experience the systematic urban reconstruction which occurred in many cities in Britain in the post-war period, whereby the inner cores were redeveloped to accommodate large-scale tower block housing, new shopping centres and motorway development. As part of this process, sections of the inner city population were given incentives to move out to suburbs and new towns, which also offered green-field site development opportunities for new mass production industries. Despite its declining industrial performance, Belfast had to wait another 20 years before similar urban renewal was seriously implemented. Even then, the diversification and regeneration of the city's economic base were not assisted by the tendency of local capital to be increasingly attracted to a more lucrative investment potential in Britain.[11] Belfast, like the rest of Northern Ireland, was also at this stage lagging behind in terms of social provision. For example, in 1944 a report from a planning advisory board estimated that 90,000 new dwellings would be needed to bring Northern Ireland's housing up to standard.[12]

While the conservative Unionist governments were generally ill disposed towards the social management of the economy, they were not immune to some of the imperatives of greater state planning typical of post-1945 social democratic politics.[13] The achievement of parity of provision with Britain required the development of a local welfare state. Moreover, in a new world of internationally mobile capital, Unionists had to begin systematically to erect an infrastructure suitably impressive to British and later other sources of inward investment. A related concern was the way in which Belfast's market pull had engendered a skewed geographical distribution of industry which neglected the rest of Northern Ireland.[14] Despite this, during the 1940s and 1950s there was no local parallel to Britain's post-war legislation such as the Town and Country Planning Act or the Distribution of Industry Act.

By the early 1960s, government reports[15] implicitly acknowledged the inadequacy of state intervention to date in achieving economic modernisation. The Matthew Report[16] specifically recommended the dispersal of industry from the Belfast Urban Area to Greater Belfast and to new 'key' and 'growth' centres. To encourage the requisite labour mobility, a stop line on Belfast's further expansion was proposed, together with new town developments, in particular, Craigavon. Matthew also emphasised the urgency of a concerted attack on the derelict built environment to enhance Belfast's image in the eyes of outside investors.

These reports culminated in the 1969 Belfast Urban Plan. The consequence of having delayed new housing programmes was the need for considerable demolition and comprehensive redevelopment for many traditional Belfast working-class communities. Apart from new build housing, land in the inner city was designated for major elevated motorways and new commercial/industrial development. Sections of the population were encouraged to 'decant' to the suburbs and new towns, the locations for much of the anticipated multinational investment.

There was little evidence that the consultants were enthusiastic about the kind of public participation and planning which the 1968 Skeffington Report had advocated in Britain. They did, though, suggest that the Stormont government adopt overall responsibility for strategic planning, land development control and conservation.

The implementation of Belfast's redevelopment coincided with the onset of the 'Troubles', which complicated the process by contributing to population shifts and urban dereliction. By the early 1970s, the oil crisis and related industrial recession upset predictions about investment and consumption patterns, car ownership, and economic growth. For example, the consultants were over-optimistic in anticipating the demise of small corner shops as a result of a richer and more mobile population with more leisure time taking more frequent trips to larger shopping complexes. The public spending implications of this ambitious Plan were also subjected later to revision as government adopted greater fiscal restraint.

At the same time, political and administrative structures in Northern Ireland were changing. In 1972 Direct Rule from Westminster replaced the regional government at Stormont. A year later, following a review by the McCrory Commission,[17] local authorities in Northern Ireland were stripped of many of their traditional powers. They were judged to have been guilty of discriminatory practice.[18] Most planning responsibilities were concentrated in a newly created Ministry of Development. But while this shift appeared to have been motivated by a desire to erode Unionist patronage, the process coincided with tendencies in Britain to centralise local authority functions in new structures of corporate management in a drive for greater efficiency and budget control.[19]

A combination of community protest and the harsher economic environment of the 1970s induced a reconsideration of the main proposals of the 1969 Plan. Most obviously, this resulted in a scaled-down version of the grandiose elevated motorway proposals.

As noted earlier, Northern Ireland's economic strategy for the 1960s was successful for a time. New companies, many in new industrial sectors, did invest. By the early 1970s, 45% of all manufacturing firms employing 500 or more workers were controlled from Britain, double the share of those originating in Northern Ireland.[20] The new jobs created by these companies helped compensate for the job drain in declining traditional industries. But significantly, manufacturing was still seen as the basis of future prosperity.

But the decade of the 1980s turned out very differently, with considerable shifts in the international division of labour and the location of production. Attracting mobile capital to depressed regions like Northern Ireland became much more problematic. As we have seen, the local economic development agencies have currently less faith in the prospect of consistent new inward investment which could restore the region's manufacturing base to its former status. Consequently, the 1989 Belfast Urban Plan is of a different character to its 1969 predecessor. For example, it does not include major new housing and road proposals with their concomitant disturbance of population. Instead, the Plan is intended to identify and satisfy the land development needs of the current most active sectors of a frail local economy, in particular, retailing, leisure and tourism. The city's economy. which has been based for over a century on production, is to be converted into one largely dependent on services. An analysis of the principles and policies of the new Urban Plan needs consequently to address this fundamental question of whether its vision of a transformation to post-industrialism is viable, and secondly to assess how far the Plan is congruent with the tenets of Thatcherism.

## The Belfast Urban Plan 1989

One of the major proposals is to accord retailing a special importance and to further concentrate it in the city centre. Particular support is to be given to speciality shopping and the growing trend of warehouse retailing. At present, the city centre accounts for some 30% of total shopping floorspace, and 50% of all the Belfast urban area's retail sales. While the urban core has a higher share of quality up-market shops than comparable cities in Britain, it also contains a higher proportion of poor shops,[21] a reflection of the big gap between affluence and poverty in Northern Ireland.

The decision to endorse a pattern of centralised retail activity has different implications for consumers, depending on their age and social class. Currently, it is the higher socio-economic groups who shop most regularly in the city centre, whereas the less mobile — the poor and the elderly — depend more on shopping facilities closer to home. Yet, local shopping facilities have suffered consistent decline, which has adversely affected the most deprived sections of the city, producing a negative impact on much needed local job opportunities. For example, North Belfast accounts for only 6% of net retail space in the whole urban area, and West Belfast only 9%. On almost every social indicator, these areas suffer systematic disadvantage relative to other parts of Belfast.[22] The Urban Plan has no proposals to compensate for this spatial bias generated by differential spending power.

117

But the Plan has acknowledged that growth in retail space in Belfast: "....will be more closely related than before to the future rate of growth of household income and expenditure in Northern Ireland...." This is largely because much of the new design and 'niche' marketing effort in retailing is targeted at those with high and expanding disposable incomes, for whom issues of quality, diversity and fashion can take precedence over price. This more acute social division in shopping throughout the UK has also to be seen in the context of shopping in Belfast being more expensive. It is ranked by Reward Regional Surveys as the UK city with the third highest High Street prices.

Other important contrasts, as well as similarities, can be drawn between Belfast and cities in Britain. In respect of the structure of their retail trade, the similarity is marked. On the other hand, while out-of-town shopping developments have been, up until recent years, resisted in Britain, they have comprised most of the new schemes in Belfast over the last decade:

"The city, in fact, was characterised by laissez-faire retail planning throughout the 1970s and early 1980s.... In late 1983, the Environment Minister announced that future applications for suburban or out-of-town shopping centres would be resisted by his department. At the same time, a £35 million package of measures to revitalise the centre of the city was announced."[23]

In other words, perhaps in response to the bomb blitz years of 1970-75, a deregulated approach was largely adopted — even by the last Labour administration. Surprisingly, it has been the Thatcher administration in Northern Ireland which has adopted a more interventionist position. The result is that the reverse of the previous pattern now applies. Whereas Belfast is seeing a concentrated effort in its urban core, one half of retailing floorspace being built now in Britain is located out-of-town. The motivation for such suburban investment is that land is cheaper, parking more plentiful and site assembly easier, and the government seems to be becoming more sympathetic to these considerations. A recent government policy guidance paper on the issue, while recognising that new retailing schemes can help reshape and update flagging town centres, does not show any urge to steer development in that direction as opposed to out-of-town sites. The general drift of policy in Britain, in fact, is that the planning system needs to operate with suitable flexibility and agnosticism to ensure that developers and retailers are permitted to invest on the basis of competitive market principles.[24] The policy in Northern Ireland appears different. It seems to be influenced by the arguments which suggest that: "investment in the centre is crucial to urban regeneration in the widest sense, not least to adjoining inner city areas."[25]

Returning to the similarities between Northern Ireland and Britain, the UK retail sector as a whole has seen an increasing concentration in ownership, evident in the dominance of the large retail multiples in every High Street. For example, in Belfast's Central Shopping Area, around 40% of the 49 shopping units owned by UK multiples are controlled by just three companies. This pattern of takeovers and mergers, concentrating as it does commercial power within a relatively small number of large firms, has important significance for planning. Regarded by government as pre-eminent investors and employers in a modern urban economy, they are in an influential negotiating position to determine land use decisions favourable to them.

Indeed, the formative period in the development of a strategic plan permits what have been called 'hidden negotiations',[26] particularly with major economic interests. In this respect, the fact that Northern Ireland's political administration is not locally accountable has facilitated this practice. The land use needs of the large developers, volume house builders and multiple retailers can be communicated either directly in negotiation or indirectly through the consultative studies which shaped the current Urban Plan.

Major UK multiples have been extending their presence in Belfast in recent years, attracted by the reduced security risk, the relatively low occupancy costs, and sound trading figures. This expansion has in turn resulted in a significant rise in rentals, which itself has encouraged the property developers to boost investment and construction. Recent prestigious developments such as the mega retail centre, Castle Court, located prominently in Belfast's city centre, suggest that there is a speculative element to this boom. Building began in Castle Court before an anchor tenant was committed. The problem with such speculative schemes is that they can increase competition for land, and thus inflate land costs for other much needed social consumption such as housing, schools or hospitals. But, from the viewpoint of the Northern Ireland administration, such developments, with their hi-tech architecture, signal not just an economic revival but also a political recovery for a city subjected to years of bombing and destruction. As one Northern Ireland Minister expressed it:

"You cannot be anything but impressed by the new skyline of Belfast city centre as shops and offices rise to herald a new era of prosperity. On the cultural and entertainment side, too, there is an encouraging spirit of enterprise."[27]

This effusive ministerial pride demonstrates the symbolic importance attached to development — almost any kind of property development — in Belfast's centre. There, in a visible form and in a concentrated space, is evidence of the ultimate triumph of government over a sustained paramilitary campaign designed to deny the normality and stability of existing political arrangements.

## Prospects for the Retail Sector

The factors behind the consumption-led reflation of the late 1980s have been alluded to earlier in Chapter 3: the abandonment of monetarism; the deregulation of the financial sector which facilitated a credit expansion; a significant decline in the savings ratio; fiscal relaxation; a rise in real earnings; and a fall in interest and exchange rates. This somewhat unique combination of events stimulated a rapid retail boom which appeared to augur well for further growth. In Northern Ireland in the 1980s employment in the retail sector increased by nearly 10%, much of it female and part time.

| Table 23 | Employment in the Retail Sector in Northern Ireland, 1979-89. | | |
|---|---|---|---|
| | 1979 | 1989 | % Change |
| Male | 20,700 | 19,930 | -3.7 |
| Female | 25,000 | 30,220 | +20.9 |
| Total | 45,700 | 50,150 | +9.7 |
| *Source: Coopers & Lybrand Deloitte, January 1990* | | | |

However, optimistic predictions about future patterns of retail growth, made at the height of the consumer boom in 1987, have proved rash. The big retail corporations expected high consumer spending to help offset their investment and borrowing, which produced a spiralling of property values, rents and rates.[28] But this credit-based boom sucked in imports and stoked inflation to such an extent that the then Chancellor was compelled to cool the overheating and its attendant trading imbalance. The use of penally high interest rates has made the prospects for retailing in the early 1990s more bleak.

## On the Waterfront

The showpiece of the Belfast Urban Plan is a visionary regeneration proposal for that part of the River Lagan adjoining the centre of the city. Laganside, the name given to the scheme, was originally costed by consultants at £240 million. More recent estimates suggest that the total costs may be in the region of £700 million. It aims to transform the neglected waterfront into a leisure and tourist complex which will contain sites for a harbour village including residential accommodation; marinas and a maritime museum; a leisure island; and a business village for light industry and offices. In addition, the Belfast City Council has proposals for a conference/concert hall/ice rink/hotel complex at an adjacent site to be called Laganbank. Laganside itself accounts for some 40% of all land in the city centre, some 300 acres, of which 115 are already in public ownership.

The Northern Ireland Department of the Environment (DoE) argues that the city needs such a project. The rationale is that there is little point in continuing to subsidise the declining traditional industry in the vicinity. Moreover, the riverside represents a major urban asset which, if converted from dockland, would provide new market opportunities for modern development. The Department points to the way in which similarly located cities in Britain have already adopted this approach and warns of the dangers of being left behind. The realisation of this innovative concept would provide an up-beat image for the inner city, thus encouraging an increase, not merely in tourism, but in external investment.

As with similar projects elsewhere in the UK, the scheme involves a movement away from the traditional development plan approach to planning and implementation. The local Environment Minister has announced the formation of a Laganside Corporation charged with the responsibility to implement the proposals. Even before the Public Enquiry into the Urban Plan had recorded its verdict, the Corporation had been busy promoting and marketing investment opportunities.

Though this body is similar to the Urban Development Corporations operating in Britain, it does not have the same extensive planning powers. Rather, the Laganside proposal has the status of a 'concept' plan, which merely invites developers to comply broadly with its vision. Particular major development proposals may still be subject to the need for planning approval. However, this is not likely to prove an obstacle to a developer since the DOE, which is ultimately responsible, has blessed the general idea and is keen to see rapid progress.

The argument for such a Corporation in Belfast, as in Britain, is that a single-purpose body, freed from political constraints and staffed with individuals expert in property development, is able quickly to overcome problems of fragmented land ownership, assemble appropriate packages of development land and thereby reverse dereliction.

## Planning for Post-Industrialism?

The almost exclusive emphasis on the development of the service sector as the mode of economic regeneration raises the issue of opportunity costs. While the arguments for allowing declining industries to disappear may be valid in terms of strict business efficiency, this approach does not consider the idea of the 'democratic modernisation' of the industrial base. This alternative would involve developing a new regional sectoral specialisation, concentrating on new growth industries, but through negotiation with, and retraining of, those employed in older industries. It would embrace formal discussions with local communities about the ways in which they would benefit from new investment, and would be located within the framework of a popular planning model for the regional economy.

The new Urban Plan adopts a different course. Over the past two decades, deindustrialisation has resulted in a significant loss of manufacturing jobs, and meant that service sector employment has assumed greater importance. Of course, service sector growth is partly due to the tendency for the composition of demand to change with advances in economic growth. As national wealth increases, a greater share of resources tends to be devoted to the service sector. In addition, greater productivity gains are easier to achieve in manufacturing so that, in a situation of little or no growth in demand, jobs are likely to be shed faster in that sector than in services.[29]

Accordingly, some see this stress on the service sector as auguring a more optimistic future for urban development. While manufacturing industry has contracted or been able to relocate to suburban or new town sites in order to escape the high costs of unionised labour, congestion and transport, it is argued that the service sector cannot similarly choose to locate outside the city. By its nature and function, it has to be conveniently located to large population settlements. Thus, some see the expansion in activities such as retailing, business and financial services as offering a good prospect for arresting, and maybe even reversing, the fall of urban employment.[30] However, the force of this argument is weakened by the fact that the new information technologies themselves allow a decentralisation of some of the activities associated with these services.

The question, also, should not just be about the number of jobs It should include considerations about their quality, in terms of skill, remuneration and security. Recent studies[31] indicate the growing pattern of feminisation, casualisation and non-unionisation, for example, in the retail sector. Employers are increasingly demanding young female labour, removed from Wages Council protection, and prepared to work flexibly to respond to peak demand periods.

Besides such reservations, it can also be argued that faith in an expanding service sector should not distract urban development efforts from renewing the manufacturing base. Many services, after all, still largely depend on a wealth-creating industrial sector in the first instance:

"There is [a] contradiction in government's emphasis on service sector solutions. Only if real wages in production were to expand so that the total production wage bill was at least as large with much reduced employment as it had been previously, would there be the resources available locally to purchase the services and thereby create employment."[32]

The Belfast Urban Plan devotes inadequate attention to this requirement for the consumption of goods and services to be related to their domestic production. It must be said, however, that the contention that manufacturing is being relegated to a subordinate role is strongly contested by the Northern Ireland Office. Its Information Service frequently extols the job creation achievements of the Industrial Development Board and the Local Enterprise Development Unit. Recently, it has cited a significant example of new manufacturing investment in Belfast — the French company Montupet.

But while such developments are welcome, they do not compensate for the scale of labour shed by other industries. Certainly, manufacturing as a process is undergoing change. The argument here is not to support, with endless subsidy, sectors which need to be restructured. Rather, the contention is that a reliance on services is no substitute for systematic industrial modernisation. Nor do we propose a false dichotomy between the productive and service sectors. What is required is a strategic integration of the two, without which job creation targets in Belfast over the next decade face formidable odds.

## The Urban Plan and Job Creation

The Plan's technical supplement on Industry and Commerce opens with a bald statement about the decline of jobs in Belfast:

"This decline in employment opportunities in inner city Belfast is characteristic of other cities undergoing physical and economic change. Opportunities need to be identified in the inner areas to arrest the employment decline and achieve a more balanced structure of jobs within the city."[33]

There have been a variety of analyses of the decline of jobs in cities. Massey[34] identifies industrial recomposition as the principal cause where "regional sectoral specialisation" — the location of entire sectors usually within cities in particular regions — gave way to a more hierarchically organised process of production involving the centralisation of key managerial functions in the metropolis accompanied by the dispersal of production to greenfield sites. Others like Fothergill and Gudgin or Moore and Rhodes[35] have focused on the increasing marginal costs of establishing production capacity within cities and the consequent incentives to move elsewhere.

Belfast has not been insulated from these processes, but its specific politics have also had their effects. The North and West of the city saw the collapse of its traditional linen industry and its replacement by artificial fibre manufacture in the satellite towns of Carrickfergus and Antrim. The traditional shipbuilding and engineering industries of East Belfast with their predominantly Protestant workforce, also suffered decline, but they obtained a high measure of public support that prevented closure. As late as 1987 the annual subvention to Short Bros & Harland and Harland & Wolff accounted for 33% of all industrial subsidy. Job losses in Belfast have to be understood in terms of both general economic change and specific political interventions.

In fact, processes of change in the UK as a whole have been even more complicated. For example, over the past 15 years, the working population of the inner cities has declined, though not as fast as job opportunities. The relocation of employment to suburbs and rural areas has been partly responsible for outward migration from the city. However, the working population living in the suburbs expanded faster than the number of jobs available there. As a result, suburban residents have increasingly commuted to city centres.[36]

Intersectoral developments have complicated this trend. The decline of certain manufacturing industries, formally located in the inner city, made redundant many of the traditional skills of inner city residents. Coinciding with that decline there has been an increase in inner city employment in banking and insurance, finance and administration. However, most of these jobs are filled by suburban commuters. The operation of these two processes has combined to produce a growing gentrification in certain pockets of the urban core.

All of this demonstrates the complex and changing relationship between labour market and space, none of which was adequately represented in the Belfast Urban Plan. Further, it does not attempt to relate strategies for urban regeneration to the causes of decline. Instead it projects an optimistic assessment for the future growth of the regional economy and asserts that Belfast will obtain a significant share so long as the right conditions are created to take advantage of future investment opportunities.

But, as explained earlier, there has been no complete, let alone simultaneous, correlation between the development of the economy in Northern Ireland and whatever economic improvement has been seen in Britain. One indication of this, relevant for any projections of growth in services like retailing, is the trend in consumer demand. Between 1983 and 1986, in the UK as a whole, total personal disposable income grew by 26%, whereas in Northern Ireland, it grew only 13%, or half the UK level.[37]

Several recent trends and potential policy shifts suggest that local spending capacity will be depressed further in the foreseeable future. These factors include:

☆ Future employment prospects, which include the growth of female and part-time jobs at the expense of full-time male jobs; the continued drop in manufacturing employment; the increasing use of flexi-time; and the reduction in the number of middle managers;[38]

☆ Further restrictions on the growth of public expenditure in the light of gloomy predictions about a slow-down in the economy over the next two years;[39]

☆ Changes in social security to reduce dependency which, in effect, will erode the relative living standards of the poor, particularly in a region with such high levels of dependency on social security;

☆ The possible delinking of depressed regions like Northern Ireland from national wage negotiations on the pretext that reduced real wages will increase the demand for labour;

☆ Higher charges for services about to be privatised, such as electricity;

☆ The extension of indirect taxation necessary to comply with the internal market of the European Community by 1992. A recent analysis[40] estimates that the European Commission's plans for tax harmonisation across the community would place an extra 15.5% burden on the poorest 10% of households; the extra spending pressure on the top 10% of households would amount to only 5.5%.

Should this prognosis for sluggish future demand in the Northern Ireland economy prove correct, the only way a sector, such as retailing, could expand would be if it diverted demand from elsewhere.

## Thatcherism and the Belfast Urban Plan

The key principles which inform the 1989 Belfast Urban Plan echo many familiar themes of Thatcherism. Post-war planning in Britain was, at least nominally, committed to the compensatory and redistributive values of welfarism. This is notwithstanding the valid criticism that it lacked real democratic accountability and that it was misrepresented as a neutral technical exercise engaged in by disinterested professionals beholden to some vague public good. Behind the jargon of planning rationale lurked considerations of class, particular interests, social costs, power, ideology and the market, all of which the 'gatekeepers' were eager to underplay.

Nevertheless, the concept of planning as a potential instrument to contain the spatial and social inequalities which would otherwise be generated by the free play of capitalism, could still command a certain credibility. But that conception was challenged by Mrs Thatcher. For her, ideally the most effective processes were not planning, but deregulation and privatisation. Unsurprisingly, current urban policy to stimulate the desired renaissance in Britain is heavily influenced by this approach.

The Belfast Urban Plan adopts an almost identical development model to that being applied to many former dockland and shipyard cities like Liverpool, Cardiff and Southampton. It is based on the same 'trickle down' theory of development, which assumes that gains to private capital will in time percolate downwards, via the multiplier effect, to the general community. In other contexts where this approach has operated without social accountability, the gains have bypassed lower income groups.

The process has also involved considerable social costs, including community dislocation and effective disenfranchisement. The scale of public subsidy to the private sector, including the transfer of public land to private use, has also had high opportunity costs. It is a strategy which mistakes spectacular property development for less glamorous, long-term, economic development. Moreover, the greater the number of areas which adopt this development package—emphasising private capital and investment in leisure and tourist industries — the greater will be the diminishing returns. One development centre with conference venues, marina, and trendy wine bars may well take off. But, if this is replicated in every development area of the UK, it will amount to little more than self-defeating duplication.

Whatever the relevance of the Thatcherite approach for declining areas of Britain, there must be grave reservations about its viability in a city like Belfast with such particularly acute economic, social and political problems.

## Belfast: A Different Politics

We have seen that Belfast like other industrial, particularly dockland, cities in Britain has participated in the general manufacturing decline and been subject to similar government solutions, although often with a time lag. But the city's particular political and administrative context has influenced the manner in which such changes have taken place. This contention is supported by Byrne.[41] Having reviewed the way in which the recent construction boom has, under the government's free-market policy, transformed irreplaceable industrial land into unplanned and speculative services-oriented development, he explores the capacity of the labourist traditions of Northern industrial cities in England to resist and reverse this pattern. But he is more hesitant that a similar political response is possible in Belfast:

"The only other place I know well enough to make specific comments about is Belfast. Again this is a great estuarine shipbuilding city and I know that much of the analysis already holds for its industrial base, and will hold entirely with the privatisation of Shorts and the shipyard. However, sectarianism is so central as a base for politics that it is difficult to see how an industrial-welfare labourist politics can ever take hold. If it does not, the outlook for Belfast's working class is appalling."

The sectarian character of Belfast politics, rooted partly in the different material position of the two religious communities, does unquestionably impede the prospects of unified opposition. West Belfast Catholics are not going to be unduly alarmed at the potential loss of jobs at the newly-privatised East Belfast shipbuilding and aircraft plants, from which they have long felt themselves excluded. Nor are East Belfast Protestants likely to applaud demands for substantial extra resources for the West of the city, where they consider Republican paramilitarism to be the primary author of its misfortune. This is not to underestimate the impact of sectarian or racial discord in cities such as Glasgow, Liverpool or Birmingham. But one has to acknowledge the particular ferocity and impenetrability of an antagonism not only historically entrenched but also severely exacerbated in the polarisation of the last two decades.

Uniquely, in Belfast, there is a physical wall euphemistically referred to as the Peace Line, built to keep the sectarian camps apart in the most troubled spots. Uniquely, in Belfast, a substantial part of the funds from a new urban programme, **Making Belfast Work**, designed to resuscitate the worst-off areas, has had to be spent on demolishing newly constructed public housing because it was located at a sectarian interface. Uniquely, in Belfast, there has been a sustained guerrilla campaign by the IRA, which has exacerbated the dereliction of the built environment. In these, and other respects, it remains inaccurate to characterise urban change and politics in Belfast in the exact same model applicable to cities in Britain.

## Thatcherism and Urban Change: An Overview

A glib judgement on Thatcherism and the city would refer to its deregulative and privatising impulses and would point-out the contradiction between its rhetoric of free-market individualism and its practice of greater state centralisation. In this view, the legitimacy of planning itself has been eroded under Thatcherism. In his book, **Whatever Happened to Planning?** Peter Ambrose notes in relation to London:

"....the post 1947 planning system has been effectively bypassed in docklands since 1981. The area has been 'taken into care' by central government because its natural parents, the local boroughs, were too leftish, too committed to local needs and too sensitive to local feelings to carry out the kind of private sector led redevelopment strategy the Thatcher government had in mind."[42]

But Thatcherite urban policy is not exclusively about an anti-planning free-for-all. Indeed, it may be more helpful to conceive the current situation in terms of several planning systems rather than a single system operating uniformly and universally. A recent attempt to construct a typology of planning styles under this government distinguishes between booming areas where planning operates with the grain of a buoyant market; marginal localities where, despite some decline, there is potential market interest which could be stimulated by leverage planning whereby the public sector can 'pump prime' private investment; and, lastly, severely run-down areas with comprehensive problems where the market is so depressed that subsidies are needed to promote initiatives such as private management.[43] This distinction is partly reflected in public policy in Belfast. The planning approach to the retail core of the city is largely responding to the development needs of that relatively buoyant sector, while the Laganside proposals can be understood in terms of public sector leverage to cushion risks for private sector activity. But what is also apparent in Belfast is a differentiated response in the third category, i.e., depressed areas with restricted market pull. For example, West Belfast has a high profile, containing areas of symbolic importance of both Loyalism and

Republicanism. As such, it is the recipient of much of what is going in the form of government urban programmes. North Belfast, on the other hand, despite its acute deprivation, receives less attention from both media and government. Clearly, there is a fourth category of informal planning zones — those which are bypassed by the market, yet command too little political significance to compel compensatory action by the public sector.

This greater differentiation of urban areas and planning responses mirrors the greater spatial and social distinctions arising from the increased inequalities in the Thatcher era. We have not yet reached the position advocated by the Adam Smith Institute that different parts of the UK should be subject to different zoning representing varying degrees of planning constraint.[44] But it does begin to conform to the position advocated by neo-liberals like Sorensen,[45] who contend that planning ultimately has to be an instrument which facilitates the market working at its most efficient. To do this, he argues that planners must be appreciative of enterpreneurship, the role of profit and the necessity of speculation.[46] Of course, it might be argued by the sceptics that this is little different from times past. From the neo-Marxist perspective it has always been the case that planning problems and limits to planning arise out of the existence of a private market in land and capital.[47] Even from a more Fabian perspective, recognition of the modest and incremental potential of planning has been widely canvassed.[48]

One Thatcherite theme in the last decade has been its constant harping on the allegedly interfering nature of local government, its unresponsiveness to entrepreneurial possibilities and the imposition of financial and planning constraints on business. This is not particularly relevant to the circumstances of Northern Ireland. In overall urban policy the increased emphasis attached to the market is not unproblematic for its advocates:

"When the inevitable risks, which are taken even by security-conscious investment agencies, result in losses rather than profits, the private-sector solution will be to withdraw. The 'mistakes' of the property market then show up as under-occupied or empty buildings and stand as a long-term reminder of the short-term commitment, footloose character and inherent instability of much private-sector investment".[49]

Moreover, a market-oriented approach, which effectively disenfranchises whole sections of the urban population considered surplus to the needs of modern production and politically peripheral, threatens a social fragmentation which itself can become a source of insecurity to property and profit. For communities in great need, the contradictions of the strategy promise little alleviation. Rash assumptions are made about the availability of mobile investment for an urban environment beset by disadvantages vis-a-vis suburban and greenfield sites. Unemployment blackspots are invited to compete in a zero sum game considering the chilly climate for sizeable new industrial projects. Plaudits are bestowed on the regenerative role of small business, with little apparent appreciation of its limited capacity for new job creation. Perhaps many of the tensions of the policy are exemplified in the crucial area of training:

"[In the] question of the need for massive and retraining targeted at individuals within the labour market....two points of importance arise. First, the problem of persuading a government committed to market forces that special measures are justified for the most disadvantaged people within the labour force....The second point is the suggestion that if the unemployed are given special training then it is at least likely that they will simply move out of the community to where the jobs are. Training would act as a filter providing a one-way ticket to those who can benefit, leaving an even more fragmented, deprived and unskilled community in the peripherals."[50]

But it is not just these kinds of contradiction that undermine government targets for urban revival. It is also the self-defeating ideological pursuit of goals, such as the curtailment of local authority power, even where this prevents local government co-operating with the Thatcher agenda. In this regard, the controller of the Audit Commission, Mr Davies, who is personally sympathetic to much of this agenda, commented:

"Local authorities have now, by and large, come to accept the government's view that private sector-led growth is the main long-term answer to urban deprivation. But the government do not seem to realise that they have won the argument."[51]

There is something here of a tendency for the government to snatch defeat out of the jaws of victory in the frenetic drive of its 'permanent revolution'. It remains a central obstacle to government urban policy in Britain in a way that it need not be in Northern Ireland, as the next chapter will seek to show.

# 6. Inner City Strategies: Reclaiming the Core

The previous two chapters have focussed on Tory policies relating to poverty and planning. The arena of the inner city represents the conjunction of both. Inner city programmes have combined elements of planning and anti-poverty initiatives. This chapter examines such developments in Britain and assesses their application to Northern Ireland.

## The Experience of Inner City Programmes: Britain and Northern Ireland

The urban programmes which began in Britain in the late 1960s were billed as innovative experiments to redress what government projected as a problem of residual poverty located in scattered pockets of Britain's inner cities. Optimistic assumptions about the capacity of the welfare state to reduce class inequality and of regional policy to minimise spatial disparities were, at this stage, regarded with some scepticism. Studies of the effects of the massive post-war urban redevelopment programme[1] suggested that the process had often involved 'throwing out the baby with the bathwater', insofar as positive aspects of working-class communities, such as the informal networks of mutual support, had been sacrificed in the social and physical dislocations the dispersal policies involved.

One of the largest and most influential of the new urban programmes was the Community Development Project (CDP) launched in 1969. It saw the answer in imaginative forms of community work, which would improve communication channels between local communities and their city councils; achieve better service delivery; develop greater policy coherence and administrative co-ordination within local government; facilitate public participation in local decision-making; and adopt positive discrimination in favour of the most disadvantaged communities. The CDP teams were also to mobilise self-help activity within the worst-off localities so that a balance between self-reliance and state support could be attained.

However, in the course of the project, analysis by the staff markedly changed these perspectives. Instead of the deodorising and confusing concept of community, they tended to emphasise that of class. Instead of the issue of poverty, they stressed the impact of inequality. In other words, they argued that urban deprivation could not be seen in terms of simple geographical demarcations. The determinants of deprivation were not in the main locally generated, and thus solutions could not emanate from within resource-starved neighbourhoods. Rather, urban poverty was an inevitable, indeed functional, consequence of a wider social inequality, rooted in a global market system. The focus should be on the unaccountable power of the "commanding heights of the economy" and local and central state structures, which prioritised facilitating the capital accumulation process.

Unsurprisingly, these somewhat economistic and reductionist conclusions did not find favour with governments of either political complexion in the 1970s.[2] The Labour administration developed a new initiative in 1977 — the Inner City Partnership Programme (ICP). This travelled a lot of the-by now-familiar territory about the need for more co-ordinated partnership between central and local government, with some opportunity for consultation with community organisations from deprived areas in decisions about how to allocate the modest extra resources involved. There were some distinct departures from previous interventions. For one thing, the new policy endorsed one element of the earlier CDP prescription that the problem should not be tackled in purely welfarist terms but rather understood in terms of the way such areas were enduring the costs of industrial restructuring. But the economic dimension to the policy was hardly radical. It merely spoke of the need for local authorities to be entrepreneurial in their efforts to attract commerce and industry. In particular, they were advised to value and foster the energies of small and medium size enterprise, which, it was believed, could restore vitality to derelict inner cities. The role of the public sector was mainly to create the right conditions which would inspire private investor confidence.

Northern Ireland, by this stage under Direct Rule, received its version of the programme. Known as the Belfast Areas of Need Project (BAN), it was based on a study called **Belfast Areas of Special Need**,[3] which used data from the 1971 census and other government sources to construct a league table of relative deprivation by ward. The study itself, and the subsequent series of consultations with community representatives in the most deprived wards, confirmed that the two most pressing issues were jobs and housing. Nevertheless, the BAN project became a largely traditional welfarist programme. Its most obvious impact on the ground lay in the development of a number of youth and leisure facilities. One important difference between the Belfast programme and its counterparts in Britain involved the role of the local authority. Since there had been a substantial erosion of local government powers in Northern Ireland from 1973, the local version of this anti-deprivation strategy involved the Central Stormont administration working directly with the mainly nominated agencies responsible in Belfast for services such as health and education.

An updated analysis of deprivation, **Belfast: Areas of Relative Social Need 1981 — Update,**[4] indicated little significant change in the spatial distribution of disadvantage in Belfast. This has to prompt serious scepticism about whether marginal social intervention of this type can be at all commensurate with the scale and pace of the urban decline it addresses.

In short, from the late 1960s to the late 1970s UK government policy on the inner city acknowledged the efficacy of some degree of positive discrimination to compensate for spatial and social inequality. But the extra allocations made were never significant. Instead, much emphasis was placed on such matters as improving awareness and take-up of existing welfare provision. True, by 1977 official analyses of the 'urban problem' did include a more specific economic dimension because orthodox theories of urban poverty were no longer credible. These depicted the problem as largely one of cultural underdevelopment or social pathology suffered by minority groups which were regarded as being on the periphery of society and trapped in 'zones of transition' typical of the inner city.

Instead, it was now more widely acknowledged that urban decay was mostly a function of structural economic change—involving processes such as de-industrialisation, relocation of capital and rationalisation of production. In the 1970s priority was given to environmental improvement to enhance the living conditions of inner city residents and to create a suitable physical infrastructure for industrial redevelopment. The question is how far have these strategies been continued or reformed under Thatcherism?

## Thatcherism and the Inner City

In general terms it would appear that even these mild forms of indicative planning and compensatory programmes have been substituted under Thatcherism by a more rigorous market-led strategy, less accountable to local democratic institutions. However, to say that would be a gross over simplification. In Britain, elements of previous interventionist approaches remain. There are still Inner City Task Forces and Action Teams charged with the well-worn brief of co-ordinating government action and promoting public participation. They operate on budgets that allow only modest exercises in positive discrimination: "It is true that the government early on changed the emphasis of some of these programmes, demanding that submissions under Urban Aid be ones 'which would assist in wealth creation rather than consumption, (and) engage the private sector'...."[5] And the greater importance attached to the economic is evident in the expenditure: "Economic projects have grown to account for nearly 40% of the programme, and social projects have declined from over 50% in 1979-80 to 42% in 1984-85."[6]

Alongside these familiar instruments, more distinctively Thatcherite programmes, such as Urban Development Corporations and Enterprise zones, also operate. Indeed, the most blighted parts of the major cities in both Britain and Northern Ireland are currently besieged by a plethora of such statutory interventions. What incoherence is manifest in Britain can be partly attributed to the confusion and indeed rivalry amongst the various government departments, each charged with partial responsibility. The Audit Commission has described the programmes as "a patchwork of complexity and idiosyncrasy". It notes:

> "The rules of the game seem over-complex and sometimes capricious. They baffle local authorities and business alike. They encourage compartmentalised policy approaches rather than coherent strategy."[7]

In Northern Ireland the situation is less muddled, since a highly centralised administration has greater freedom to clarify objectives and secure co-ordinated implementation. However, the administrative context is different, as are the political imperatives which shape policy. After the 1987 election, Mrs Thatcher proclaimed her desire to extend her hegemony — "next time also the inner cities". However, such an ambitious goal confronts the reality that, in most of Britain's major cities, Tory parliamentary presence has vanished. Should the government seriously intend to capture some of this hostile political ground, it would probably be compelled to gentrify it. A case in point is London's Battersea, the sole inner city seat taken by the Tories in 1987. The party's success there can partly be explained by the process of 'yuppification' in the area. House prices soared with the initial influx of the middle class, which in turn pressured sections of the traditional population into leaving. At the same time, some of the Council's tower blocks were sold to developers, renovated, cleared of their tenants and converted into luxury apartments. These kinds of processes have contributed to a change in the constituency's electoral complexion to the advantage of the Tories.[8]

But, even if such patterns were replicable elsewhere in Britain, no such political gain can be made in Northern Ireland, where only very recently have the Tories recognised their first constituency associations. Nevertheless, there is another potential purpose to be served by such population shifts which has more relevance to the region's problems. It could be argued that the image of a tribal city would be ameliorated if the residential part of Inner Belfast became less visibly divided into two sectarian blocs by the inclusion of 'Yuppie' settlements, which act to 'neutralise' more sections of the urban core.

## The Role of Local Government

> "We no longer think primarily of giving grants to the public sector
> bodies to act as our agents. We intend to get involved in partnership
> with the private sector to get inner cities moving. Where local
> authorities will work with us, we will work with them.... But where
> — perhaps for ideological reasons — they obstruct us, they will not
> be allowed to get in the way."[9]

Another distinction between current government urban policy in Belfast and
cities in Britain derives from the different roles played by local government.
In Britain the government often bypasses many Labour-controlled local authorities deemed to be high spending and obstructive to private enterprise:
"Government rhetoric, allied to some specific changes designed to cut down
the local authority role, has contributed to a climate which is less favourable
for co-operation than it might be.... there is inadequate co-ordination of local
strategies, and the totality of government effort is less than the sum of its
parts."[10]

The government is keener to deal over the heads of Councils with local
leaders of industry and commerce, who in Mrs Thatcher's vision are motivated
by civic pride and philanthropy as well as profit. However, herein lies one of
the tensions within the government. For example, in 1987, the then Minister
with responsibility for the inner city, Kenneth Clarke, declared: "To the leaders
of British industry in our cities, I can say this: We need offers of resources,
management and money. You choose exactly which policy you wish to
support. We will identify the department of government who will work with
you."[11] But the optimism behind this open door policy was not shared by his
colleague, Lord Young, also at that time charged with responsibility for inner
city renewal: "There is no way in which any new employers would go into
inner cities. Vandalism is too high and the problems are too great... and that I
fear means self-employment, co-operatives and starting up new business."[12]

This confusion is also evident in Northern Ireland. Behind some of the
government's announcements is the inference that areas like West Belfast,
beset by severe industrial decline and violence, are not attractive candidates
for substantial private investment. The corollary is that a good part of the
solution must be internally generated in the form of self-employment and
community enterprise. Whether communities in Britain's inner cities are better
advised to place their faith in entrepreneurs rather than local state support is a
matter of dispute. But in Northern Ireland the same choice does not operate
since, as previously explained, local authorities in cities like Belfast exercise
minimal powers in planning and industrial promotion. In simple terms, there
is less obvious reason for the Northern Ireland Office to bypass local government. Little of it is socialist-inclined and its current restricted range of
responsibility already sets a benchmark which the Thatcher government would

dearly wish to reach in Britain. Yet, despite this, certain measures adopted in Britain to curtail the role of local authorities are now, somewhat later, being implemented in Northern Ireland.

One example is the move to compel local authorities to open up their in-house provision of Council services to competitive tender by the private sector. In Britain such privatisation forms part of a wider strategy to convert local government into an 'enabler' rather than a direct service provider. As such, it is opposed by Labour Councils as a doctrinaire attack on their autonomy. In Northern Ireland the politics of the issue are very different. A Unionist Lord Mayor of Belfast, Mr Empey, sponsored a meeting open to all 26 local councils — including those under Nationalist control — to discuss a common opposition strategy to privatisation. But concern over the further diminution of local authority influence was only one of his reasons. Other local factors played a significant part. He claimed: "It could lead to the paramilitaries running the refuse collections in some areas, and that is a multi-million pound business."[13] By early 1990 the Councils had reached agreement about a strategy to limit the impact of the privatisation proposals.

Interestingly, this kind of attempt to mobilise a cross-community politics is applauded by government as a welcome sign of normal discourse, and even by media, whose conservative sympathy with the rationale of the policy is superseded by their approval of non-sectarianism. An editorial in the *Belfast Telegraph* commented: "If councillors can demonstrate the ability to work together constructively and in trust on issues *which are not controversial in Ulster political terms* (our emphasis), there could be a beneficial spin-off in grassroots politics."[14]

A standard complaint from many local authorities in Britain has been that the various urban programme funds they receive pale into insignificance when compared with reductions in rate support grant from central government and the use of penal instruments such as rate-capping. For example, in the Inner Area Partnerships between 1981 and 1988, funding under the Urban Programme increased by just over £23 million whereas the Block Grant to these areas fell by over £107 million.[15] It has long been recognised that it is crucial not only to allocate specific extra funds to the inner cities, but also to 'bend' the mainstream programmes towards these areas. Very little of this has happened in Britain, and the same is true for Belfast. While areas like West Belfast benefit from initiatives like **BAT** and **Making Belfast Work**, they simultaneously lose millions of pounds due to other government mainstream policies such as the reforms in social security.

## Enterprise Zones

Another major instrument of inner urban regeneration has been the Enterprise Zone experiment. Such Zones were established in areas of industrial decay on a ten-year trial basis to assess whether a certain deregulation ( via relaxed planning controls) augmented by indirect subsidies in the form of tax and rate reliefs could stimulate business activity. In Britain the cost of the experiment by the late 1980s totalled over half a billion pounds.

| Table 24 | The Costs of Enterprise Zones (from designation to 1987) (£Million) | |
|---|---|---|
| Urban Programme Funding | | 22.0 |
| Urban Development Grant | | 6.0 |
| Derelict Land Grant | | 28.5 |
| European Regional Development Fund | | 13.0 |
| Rate Revenue Foregone | | 124.0 |
| Cost of Capital Allowances | | 230.0 |
| Public Sector | | 150.0 |
| Total | | 573.5 |

*Source: Enterprise Zone Information 1986-87, Department of the Environment, 1988, HMSO.*

Other criticisms of the strategy have been made. While rate relief provides most gain to activities which "are extensive users of property such as warehousing and large scale retail operations,"[16] the real beneficiary may be the property sector:

"....whilst 'rate holdings' were intended to reduce operating costs, the consequential increase in the demand for sites has increased rents by at least the same amount as any savings in rates — benefiting landowners and developers but at public expense."[17]

Another problem is that short distance relocations of firms, involving a shift of resources from other areas, have been common. Over 75% of incoming firms would have been in business in the same region, regardless of the existence of Enterprise Zones.[18] Doubts have also been expressed about what will happen when the status and benefits of a Zone expires after ten years. There is at least a possibility that some of the Zone's firms will relocate again, in search of the latest concessionary policy. In fact, due to the high costs and insecurity of the jobs created, the government indicated without fanfare in

December 1987 that the Enterprise Zone experiment would not be continued after the ten-year span.

Northern Ireland has two Enterprise Zones, in Belfast and Derry. The Belfast Zone is divided into two sites — Inner City and North Foreshore. The Inner City site is typical of a deindustrialised area, made up of disused and decaying industrial space. The North Foreshore, on the other hand, resembles more a green field site appropriate for large firm location and has benefited from considerable infrastructural investment.

| Table 25 | Job Analysis by Industrial Sector: Belfast Inner City | | | | | |
|---|---|---|---|---|---|---|
| | Manufacturing | | Services | | Total | |
| | Companies | Jobs | Companies | Jobs | Companies | Jobs |
| Startups | 15 | 91 | 86 | 776 | 101 | 867 |
| Original Firm | 20 | 1,715 | 53 | 1,351 | 73 | 3,101 |
| Original Firm Moved within the Zone | 1 | 151 | 5 | 52 | 6 | 203 |
| Relocated | 7 | 57 | 17 | 239 | 24 | 296 |
| Storage | 1 | — | 11 | — | 12 | — |
| Non-Industrial | — | — | 3 | 10 | 3 | 3 |
| Totals | 44 | 2,049 | 175 | 2,428 | 219 | 4,477 |
| Manufacturing Companies | 44 (20%) | | Manufacturing Jobs | | 2,049 (46%) | |
| Service Companies | 175 (80%) | | Service Jobs | | 2,428 (54%) | |

*Source: PA Cambridge Economic Consultants, 1987.*

The average firm size in the Belfast Inner City Enterprise Zone is small, with manufacturing firms averaging 46 employees and services only 13. Services also comprise the overwhelming proportion of firms and the majority of jobs.

In the North Foreshore Zone the bias towards the service sector is even more pronounced, accounting for 90% of firms and 83% of jobs. Average company size is also smaller, reflecting possibly the greater proportion of warehousing in this section of the Zone. In terms of net job increases, the achievement of the Belfast Zone is modest. Similar to Britain, jobs already in, or near, the Zone constitute a high proportion of total jobs. Particularly in the North Foreshore, a significant amount of the jobs are relocations. In short, the Belfast Zone contains a large number of small firms, mostly in the service sector, occupying a large acreage of former industrial land. Its achievement has been purchased at high public cost in terms of rate revenue forfeited, land acquisition, infrastructural work and receipt of Urban Development Grant.

| Table 26 | Job Analysis by Industrial Sector: Belfast North Foreshore | | | | | |
|---|---|---|---|---|---|---|
| | Manufacturing | | Services | | Total | |
| | Companies | Jobs | Companies | Jobs | Companies | Jobs |
| Startups | 4 | 32 | 39 | 376 | 43 | 408 |
| Original Firm | 1 | 24 | 2 | 342 | 3 | 366 |
| Original Firm Moved within the Zone | — | — | — | — | — | — |
| Relocated | 4 | 181 | 36 | 459 | 40 | 640 |
| Storage | — | — | 1 | — | 1 | — |
| Non-Industrial | — | — | — | — | — | — |
| Totals | 9 | 237 | 78 | 1,177 | 87 | 1,414 |
| Manufacturing Companies | 9 (10%) | | Manufacturing Jobs | | 237 (17%) | |
| Service Companies | 78 (90%) | | Service Jobs | | 1,177 (83%) | |

*Source: PA Cambridge Economic Consultants, 1987.*

The National Audit Office in its February 1990 report **Regenerating the Inner Cities** suggested that Enterprise Zones were "an expensive means of regenerating run down areas". As an alternative, the government has now proposed Simplified Planning Zones (SPZ), to decrease planning regulations and speed up decisions about development. The Housing and Planning Act 1986 obliged local planning authorities in Britain to assess whether parts of their catchment areas could be improved by being accorded this SPZ status. Belfast is also set to experience an SPZ initiative. This new measure seems to be at odds with the evidence that private investment was attracted into

Enterprise Zones mostly due to the financial incentives rather than planning concessions.[19]

## The Inner City: A Law and Order Problem?

Under Thatcherism the inner cities in Britain have on several occasions imitated the most stereotypical image of Belfast streets. As Stuart Hall commented with some sarcasm in the wake of the 1981 urban riots in Britain:

"After watching rioting in the Falls Road as a nightly spectacle on television — persisting in believing that it is ten thousand light years away and nothing to do with us — here we are with Toxteth and Brixton looking like a war-torn Northern Irish city where, for unaccountable reasons, people have risen up against the state."[20]

Government's initial response to this upheaval was almost exclusively in law and order terms. The Prime Minister told the House of Commons in defiant rejection of the charge that unemployment and poverty were the real culprits: "I do not believe that a shortage of money has been the problem in Liverpool."[21] Yet, within a short period, political discretion got the better of her rhetorical valour and a Minister for Merseyside was nominated and other gestures were made in the direction of social deprivation.

Similarly, in Northern Ireland, government has been reluctant to credit rioting as anything other than a security issue. Nor is this posture peculiar to the Thatcher period. Under Labour's Roy Mason, there were also attempts to criminalise many features of the civil disturbance rather than acknowledge their political import. Indeed, since the mid 1980s there has been a discernible, though modest, shift by the Thatcher administration towards a more sensitive disposition to extremely deprived areas like West Belfast. This is probably less attributable to a new compassionate enlightenment as much as to the global spotlight focussed on an area captured by Sinn Fein and the related attention accorded to the area by the Anglo-Irish Agreement. Nevertheless, this sensitivity does not preclude incidents like that which occurred in January 1990 on the Falls Road where three robbers with imitation weapons were shot dead by undercover soldiers. Previously, young joy riders have been shot attempting to break through road blocks manned by the security forces. These represent a law and order response unparalleled in Britain.

## An Image Problem?

A familiar strain in official explanations for Northern Ireland's development problems concerns the drag of its negative image of sectarian strife. Again, this claim is an echo of government complaint in Britain about the difficulty of 'selling' inner cities beset with violence and crime to potential investors. In other words, the perception factor is credited with great significance. The recent submission from Northern Ireland for financial support under European Community regional funds categorises many of the urban initiatives already referred to here in terms of image. In Belfast the 'image investment' seems to be directed towards a mixture of modernising the architecture and planning the urban core in order to signify the city's capacity to compete in the new international age, reshaping the dockland area to capitalise on the city's past industrialism, and sprucing up the most visible frontages along the main routes which pass through the inner city. This process accords with that feature of Thatcherism — 'regressive modernisation' — to which earlier reference has been made:

> "It is regressive because on the one hand, and in reaction to the current period of crisis, uncertainty and disruptive social change, we are encouraged to seek refuge and security in the values and images of the past. However, on the other hand, we are simultaneously being seduced by the values and images of a 'modern' and 'progressive' world. The critical feature of the overall presentation is that we are given only a partial view; one which romanticises the past, idealises the future, and unproblematically juxtaposes the two."[22]

## Bringing Employment to the Inner City: Making Belfast Work

In July 1988 the latest government initiative for depressed urban areas, **Making Belfast Work** was launched: "....to stimulate greater economic activity, reinforce local enterprise, improve the quality of the environment and equip the people of these areas to compete successfully for available employment". It was to be targeted particularly on West Belfast, operate with a six month budget of £10 million, (later increased to make up a total of £92.5 million over the project's five year period) and adopt an approach which could "harness the goodwill and enthusiasm of all the community."[23]

The focus on West Belfast is understandable. Almost from the beginning of the political crisis in Northern Ireland, West Belfast has been prominent as containing concentrations of both violence and deprivation. The Catholic part of the area is vastly overcrowded because it is regarded as safe from sectarian attack and so thousands flocked there in the 1970s. This has inflated house prices and created long waiting lists for public housing. It is the great urban citadel of Republicanism, with Sinn Fein represented by its only Westminster MP, Gerry Adams, and occupying six out of nine possible seats on the Belfast District Council (after the local government elections in May 1989). The presence of the security forces is manifest in strategically placed barracks, designed like fortresses to withstand grenade or rocket attack, and heavily armed RUC and army patrols. The gable walls are decorated with murals depicting the conflict within a mythology which represents the IRA as linked to the sufferings of both Christ and oppressed peoples everywhere. Claims about the exceptional levels of deprivation in West Belfast can be substantiated by an examination of the Belfast Household Survey 1985.[24] This demonstrates that the area has a younger population than other parts of Belfast, with larger average household size and a greater degree of overcrowding. In general, household incomes are lower and benefit dependency rates higher than the city average. There are also substantial inequalities within West Belfast with the inner city segment and a number of housing estates on the periphery showing most disadvantage.

An index of its levels of deprivation is given in Table 27. For each of the indicators in the table, an index has been calculated expressing the rate in individual areas of Belfast as a percentage of the overall city rate, which is represented as 100. The higher the index, the greater the level of deprivation. A figure of 200 would mean that the area in question had twice the rate for Belfast as a whole. These have then been aggregated to provide a general index of deprivation. It can only be a rough measure.

| Table 27 Deprivation Index for Belfast, 1985 | | | | |
|---|---|---|---|---|
| Indicator | Inner East | Outer East | Inner West | Outer West |
| % of Economically Active Population who are either housewives | 107.3 | 70.8 | 156.2 | 141.5 |
| % of Occupations in semiskilled or unskilled categories | 128.0 | 66.1 | 166.5 | 98.7 |
| % of Heads of Households (HoH) with incomes less than £100 per week | 134.0 | 83.6 | 144.7 | 99.3 |
| % of HoHs on either Unemployment, Supplementary Benefit or Family Income Supplement | 164.7 | 54.2 | 198.6 | 122.9 |
| Total | 534.0 | 274.7 | 666.0 | 472.4 |
| Index of Deprivation | 133.5 | 68.6 | 166.5 | 118.1 |
| *Source: calculated from data in the Belfast Household Survey, 1986* | | | | |

Information is provided on East Belfast for purposes of comparison. Inner West scores highest on every single indicator and has an aggregate index more than twice that of Outer East. Given its low scores on the income and occupational variables, Outer West has a 'better' deprivation index than Inner East. It would appear that the inner city areas suffer greatest deprivation, but that West Belfast as a whole is much worse than East. However, when the specific concern is unemployment, it should be recognised that, while in general the inner city areas suffer higher rates than the outer urban areas, West Belfast as a whole is the exception. In 1985 Inner West recorded the huge unemployment rate of 47%, substantially higher than Inner South (27.7%), Inner East (29.8%), and Inner North (37.6%). And Outer West's unemployment rate of 36.1% is actually worse than Inner South and Inner East and over three times as high as Outer South (10.5%) and Outer East (11.7%).[25] Clearly, the unemployment problem of West Belfast cannot be reduced to orthodox explanations about inner city job decline.

West Belfast is a major concern in the battle for the hearts and minds of the Northern Ireland population. While Sinn Fein attracts around 10% of votes cast in Northern Ireland as a whole, and approximately 33% of Catholic votes, Gerry Adams in 1987 obtained nearly half of all votes cast in the West Belfast constituency. Since it is the main Republican constituency, Sinn Fein is anxious to hold onto the allegiance of as big a proportion of the Catholic population as possible. Thus, it has opened and staffed a large number of advice centres and has been demanding more jobs for the area. Other organisations, like the Catholic Church, compete with Sinn Fein in this field. Church sponsored agencies like Cathedral Community Enterprises are major employers of ACE labour and have become interested in developing enterprises. While the rationale is to intervene in the dreadful concentration of joblessness, the process could also be interpreted as simultaneously providing an alternative to the loyalty enjoyed by Republicanism,[26] a project which coincides with the aims of the main nationalist party, the SDLP. Moreover, the Church has been able to mobilise local business interests to provide experience and expertise for job creation. Unsurprisingly, its organisations have been major recipients of state funds while other projects, closer to Sinn Fein, claim to have been blacklisted.

The central focus of **Making Belfast Work** is thus an area which is both socially and politically significant. It is all the more so, given the ongoing debate about fair employment in Northern Ireland, sustained in part by the persistently higher rates of unemployment for Catholic compared to Protestant males. West Belfast represents a massive concentration of Catholic male unemployment. The Northern Ireland Office has become sensitive to this for two reasons: first, the concern of the government of the Irish Republic, represented through the Anglo-Irish Agreement discussions; and second, the fact that the campaign in the United States around the McBride Principles (relating to fair employment in Northern Ireland) secured support in certain State legislatures.

Turning to the particulars of the Scheme, the first stage of the **Making Belfast Work** strategy consisted of a series of initiatives in the economic and social fields. Under the heading of economic development it proposed:

☆ The creation of Job Clubs and Job Markets; and measures to improve job search skills;

☆ The upgrading of training, including areas such: as Information Technology; literacy and numeracy; and a specific one-year programme for 120 adults in the retail and distribution sector;

☆ The creation of 500 extra ACE jobs, particularly directed towards "self-help community initiatives";

☆ The provision of a "major package of support" for the West Belfast Enterprise Board to assist its establishment of a unit for enterprise development.

In keeping with the government's belief in supply-side economics there was an inference behind these priorities that the major problem preventing economic revitalisation was the lack of appropriate skills and the absence of an enterprise culture. Reference had been made in the past to the dependency patterns in communities such as West Belfast, imputing the blame for the lack of development largely on residents themselves. An alternative perspective would pay greater regard to how such areas have been underdeveloped as a result of the policies of government and capital, particularly in recent decades. The provision of 500 extra ACE jobs does not address the criticisms about the operation of this programme — the lack of appropriate training and the short-term duration of the jobs provided. This is particularly so in an area where it is alleged that a gravely flawed training scheme, unlinked to real labour market prospects, is used as an official instrument to favour some 'respectable' organisations and demote others.[27] Where such political vetting of employment projects occurs, it could dissipate the potential unity of local effort and resources, which is so obviously needed in a community where the inclination to demoralisation is understandable.

In the area of education, the programme set out the following objectives:

☆ Establishment of a new further education college to operate as an out centre of Belfast's main further education centre, Rupert Stanley College, with an initial financial contribution of £300,000;

☆ Provision of £200,000 to assist the amalgamation of four existing Catholic schools;

☆ The allocation of £400,000 to Catholic schools trustees for new technology suites and conversion costs;

☆ The use by the Belfast Education and Library Board of a further £1 million to upgrade the physical environment of all schools and enhance their access to books, materials and new equipment.

Developing facilities for adult and continuing education was long overdue. However, questions about access, control, curriculum content and method remain unresolved. There is substantial local experience of self-organised community education in West Belfast and it remains to be seen whether this resource can be accommodated in any new strategy. The rationalisation of secondary school provision in Catholic West Belfast could have provided an opportunity to transcend the inequity of current distinctions and resource allocations between the Secondary Modern and Grammar sectors to provide a comprehensive education for all local children. Funding for items such as school maintenance raises the issue whether this should be considered an 'extra' rather than a normal statutory obligation.

Under health and the environment the proposals were:

☆ The promotion of better environmental health;

☆ The establishment of an immunisation task force;

☆ The appointment of a second facilitator to assist local GPs in upgrading health standards;

☆ The adoption of additional environmental improvement schemes.

Preventative health care could play a critical role in reducing the area's above average rates of morbidity. However, while such health interventions are necessary, they are insufficient. There is now an authoritative range of health research which suggests that ill health is directly related to social indicators such as unemployment, low income and poor housing.[28] Significant health improvement in West Belfast ultimately depends on their redress as well.

The purpose behind the proposed environmental schemes includes making such areas "more attractive to potential employers". This could well lead to emphasis being given to main arterial routes, which are visible to the outside visitor and investor. In establishing priorities for such schemes, it should be acknowledged that it is more important to improve the living conditions of people within the communities than to impress passing VIPs. In addition to the sums allocated under the previous headings, £250,000 was provided to assist the voluntary sector. Again, whether all elements of the voluntary sector in Belfast are eligible or whether some elements remain politically excluded, remains to be seen.

The initial sum of £10 million included £1 million for the establishment of more **Belfast Action Teams** (another community initiative). The remaining 9 million can be broken down into its component expenditures and these can be calculated as proportions of 'normal' expenditure in Belfast in the 1988-89 financial year (see Table 28).

The extra resources so far associated with **Making Belfast Work** are small relative to total expenditure in Belfast. Moreover, the initial figure of £10 million has to be compared to the same amount of public subsidy spent on the lavish retail project in the city centre, known as Castle Court, where no pressure was exerted to ensure that a proportion of the jobs created there was targeted at areas with high unemployment like West Belfast. A further contrast is with the prestigious riverside development under the Belfast Urban Plan, the Laganside Scheme, with around £25 million of public support and an unestimated amount of Urban Development Grant.

Moreover, the additional amount now being spent on West Belfast has to be assessed in the context of the series of 'public disinvestments' that have withdrawn income from the area. This has been most obvious in the field of social benefits. Some calculations [29] suggest that the decoupling of pension increases from earnings has lost pensioners around £400 per year. Applying this figure to the 7,946 senior citizens in West Belfast[30] gives an aggregate loss of £3,178,400. A similar calculation on the outcome of freezing child benefit adds a further £875,732. Actual Social Fund allocations for 1988-89 were £3,074,903 less than the amount given in single payments by the three West Belfast social security offices in 1986.[31] Taken together, these represent an annual aggregate loss of £7,129,035 to the area, over 70% of the first year's allocation to **Making Belfast Work**.

| Table 28 | Expenditure on Making Belfast Work | | | |
|---|---|---|---|---|
| Programme | Approx Amount Allocated | % of Programme | Total Belfast Spending 1988-89 | % of Belfast Spending |
| Jobs/Training | £3m | 33% | £38m | 7.9% |
| Education | £1.9m | 21% | £143m | 1.3% |
| Health | £2m | 22% | £256m | 0.8% |
| Environment | £2m | 22% | £94m | 2.1% |
| Other | £0.1m | 2% | £49m | 0.2% |
| Total | £9m | 100% | £580m | 1.5% |
| *Source: Making Belfast Work and specific enquiries, 1988.* | | | | |

This calculation of benefit loss makes no allowance for probable reductions in ordinary weekly benefit payments. It is therefore possible that the public disinvestment as a result of changes in the benefits system was about the same sum as was spent by the **Making Belfast Work** programme in its first year. What is more, while Making Belfast Work stressed the importance of the voluntary sector, Belfast City Council in 1988 cut £140,000 from its community service budget, some of which affected West Belfast. Equally, while **Making Belfast Work** stressed the role of preventative health care, the new dental and eye-testing charges imposed a heavy burden on the area's residents. Communities in West Belfast have also suffered from the Thatcher government's macro-economic policies to restructure taxes in order to move people from a 'dependency' to an 'enterprise' culture. While the poorest have lost from the reorganisation of benefits, the richest have gained most from tax changes — the top 1% of earners received 70% of the tax-cutting benefits of the 1988 Budget. Of the £2 billion worth of top tax rate reductions, Northern Ireland received the least amount — only £30 million. The vast bulk of tax reduction (60%) was enjoyed by the South East. Yet, marginal tax rates on earned income, inclusive of national insurance contributions, have actually increased since 1979[32] with a disproportionate burden on lower income earners. Finally, the shift to indirect taxation through increases in the rate of VAT hurts most those with least incomes.

Taking all three factors together — benefit changes, other expenditure reductions and shifts in taxation — it can be reasonably asked whether the poor in West Belfast have lost more through government actions than they have gained, despite the operation of the current Schemes.

To what extent is this Northern Ireland strategy for inner city regeneration and job creation congruent with the orthodoxies of Thatcherism? First, the programme is located within a macro-economic policy environment very similar to that operating in Britain. The same supply-side assumptions inform the same changes in taxes and benefits, employment training, and the deregulation involved in initiatives like Enterprise Zones. The new Belfast Urban Plan further promotes planning deregulation and private sector-led development. Despite these parallels, Thatcherism is not entirely ideologically driven and can respond pragmatically to specific problems. An example, as we have seen, is the thorny problem of West Belfast, symbolising as it does the conjunction of political/military resistance, deprivation and discrimination. Moreover, in the era of the Anglo-Irish Agreement the Thatcher government faces a new set of international pressures. These compel a specific expenditure initiative for West Belfast that is not entirely congruent with the overall policy imperatives of the Conservative government. At the same time, the promotion of voluntary agencies in the renewal process accords with the anti-statist dimension of Thatcherism, while the bulk of the resources going to training is underpinned by supply-side assumptions about West Belfast unemployment. **Making Belfast Work** simultaneously represents the sensitivity of government to this particular area while, nevertheless, drawing on its general principles to develop a specific strategy. Whether it will work or not, is a different matter. The key objective of **Making Belfast Work** is the creation of employment. It should therefore be evaluated in those terms. Using published data, it is possible to estimate how many jobs would need to be created and where they should be located.

While many development programmes frequently cite targets for job creation, they rarely relate these to actual inequalities in the distribution of jobs. West Belfast contains 26% of the population of the Belfast Urban Area. The proportion of its population who are of working age is slightly lower than the Belfast figure (58% compared to 60%). Thus it contains 24.9% of Belfast's population of working age. All things being equal, it should have around 25% of Belfast's unemployment. In fact, in April 1988, 38% of the unemployed and 41% of the long-term unemployed in the four Belfast parliamentary constituencies lived in Belfast West. Indeed, the parliamentary constituency does not cover all of the territory popularly known as West Belfast, which has about 4,000 additional unemployed. However, the Department of Economic Development does not provide unemployment figures for the Belfast Urban

Area, so projections for the number of jobs needed to reduce unemployment relate to Belfast West.

Eliminating unemployment in West Belfast in the context of the numbers out of work in Northern Ireland as a whole would be highly unrealistic. A fairer test of the programme in the short term would be to examine the feasibility of bringing the area's unemployment down to a figure equal to its proportion of the city's population of working age, namely from 38% to 25%. To achieve that reduction, 3,850 unemployed people would have to be taken off the register. Since that would also lower the overall unemployment figure for the city, leaving those still unemployed at more than 25% of the total, an additional 1,000 jobs would have to be found. Thus the jobs target for West Belfast would be 4,850 jobs. If this were attained, then its unemployment share would correspond to that in the rest of the city.[33] Despite the substantial job creation effort being focused on manufacturing, the majority of new jobs remain in services. If the new jobs required for West Belfast reflected the current industrial composition of employment, there would have to be 1,067 production jobs, 242 construction jobs, and 3,541 service jobs, where the total of 4,850 has been divided according to the proportion of total jobs provided by each of the three sectors in Northern Ireland.

This poses a further problem. The majority of new service jobs have been low paid and have been obtained by women, yet the vast bulk of the registered unemployed in West Belfast are men. Moreover, where unemployed men are heads of households with dependent children, even current ungenerous rates of benefit will act as a disincentive to the acceptance of low paid or part-time employment. The under-registration of unemployed women cannot be ignored, nor should efforts be made to inhibit them finding jobs.

However, the object of the **Making Belfast Work** programme is to reduce the unemployment register. This requires that around 3,700 jobs for men be provided. Moreover, these should be net new jobs. If further real reductions in benefit levels drove men into the labour market to compete with women for low paid service jobs, that would simply reduce the numbers on the register at the expense of another disadvantaged group in the community — women. In addition, it would lower aggregate household income for the area. The provision of such jobs would exacerbate rather than reduce poverty. There is a problem in creating immediate jobs suitable to the existing skills of the unemployed. Such skills predominantly correspond to those required by construction and traditional manufacturing sectors, and these offer few prospects of expansion. Alternatively, there is a demand for labour within the service sector, but many of these jobs would involve de-skilling.

Skill and gender mismatches can only be overcome by proper training linked to the job creation process. This suggests a twin strategy is required: in the first instance the effort should be to create a large number of useful jobs, probably in the public sector, to deal with other sorts of need in the area; but alongside this, a comprehensive training programme is needed to upgrade skills appropriate to the development of growth sectors both in manufacturing and traded services.

An additional factor that must be considered in Belfast is the differences in unemployment between the two religious communities. The difference is most marked at the level of the whole of Belfast, but even within deprived West Belfast unemployment is unequally endured. In 1985 unemployment among economically active males was 47% in Catholic West Belfast and 35% in Protestant West Belfast. At the same time Protestant males in West Belfast experienced a significantly higher rate of joblessness than all males in the Belfast Urban Area (23%).[34] This may be understood as the outcome of both traditional economic decline and additional disadvantage factors. The economic decline of West Belfast has generated higher than average unemployment for all its males, but, within that framework, Catholics suffer additional disadvantage. It should be noted that the degree of Catholic disadvantage is as great again as the West Belfast Protestant differential from the Belfast average. Thus, in order to promote religious equality of opportunity, a greater proportion of the jobs that need to be created should go to Catholics. Based on a sample surveyed at Social Security Offices by the Belfast Centre For the Unemployed in 1986,[35] an approximate estimate of the religious distribution of the new jobs to be created would be as follows:

|  | Protestants | Catholics |
|---|---|---|
| Males | 958 | 2,775 |
| Females | 336 | 779 |
| Total | 1,294 | 3,554 |

These figures can only be regarded as guesstimates given the possibility of sampling error. Nevertheless, in the absence of better data, it points clearly to the extra job effort required with respect to Catholics. This attempt to establish an overall jobs target for West Belfast and to disaggregate it in terms of gender, religion and industrial sector, is relatively primitive. However, **Making Belfast Work** does not seem even to appreciate the need to engage in such an exercise. Given the government's better access to data, it could have performed a more sophisticated analysis. The failure to do so perhaps reflects a lack of real concern about prioritising jobs and training in which case, the likelihood remains that the new jobs created under the programme will reproduce existing patterns of inequality. While **Making Belfast Work** is to be welcomed to the extent that any additional resources are urgently required in that part of the city where deprivation is worst, there must be genuine concern about whether this kind of programme is sufficient to combat poverty. Relative to overall spending, the resources are marginal. Further, their impact is undermined by the loss of benefits resulting from social security reform.

And there is little evidence of systematic targeting of the most deprived groups. In the context of broader programmes, it should be said that the Industrial Development Board succeeded in attracting a major new investment to West Belfast in the shape of the Montupet Company. This promises an additional 1,000 jobs. However, since 60% of existing jobs in West Belfast are held by non-residents, there can be no guarantee that unemployment in the area will be reduced in proportion to the jobs created. In any case, there are few indications that the nearly 5,000 jobs required to bring unemployment down to the Belfast average can be attained.

In terms of inner urban policy, there has been a "somewhat surprising degree of continuity in approach between that adopted by the Labour government in the late 1970s and that pursued by ostensibly anti-collectivist Conservative administrations".[36] The whole question of how far Thatcherite inner city policy is ideologically driven is subject to much debate. Some feel it is too unstructured and marginal to be so considered.[37] This is a view confirmed by the National Audit Office which, in its February 1990 report, **Regenerating the Inner Cities,** while acknowledging some piecemeal benefits, argued that there was inadequate information to evaluate the long-term strategic impact. Others see it in terms of a grand design by the centre not only to curtail local heartlands of Labour support, but also to mitigate, and disguise, the severe local impact of industrial restructuring.[38] We have already suggested that in Northern Ireland there is little imperative on the part of government to displace the functions of local authorities which had already been substantially reduced in the 1970s. Nonetheless, the influence of industrial restructuring on inner city policy has been evident in Northern Ireland, though once again the process has been mediated by its specific politics — hence the focus of a particular programme on West Belfast.

The inner city problem has now been around for more than two decades. A variety of government interventions has been attempted and increasingly Northern Ireland has followed similar initiatives to those established in Britain. The general conclusion as to their effectiveness has been that their impact has been relatively marginal compared to the scale of the problems addressed. High rates of poverty and unemployment remain the dominant characteristics of these areas.

However, as the previous chapter argued, the fundamental economic dislocations of the 1980s have had severe spatial consequences for the whole urban environment. Perhaps in the 1990s, it is more relevant to speak of an urban rather than an inner city crisis, with the latter being merely the most extreme manifestation of the former.

# 7. Housing Policy: Accommodating Thatcher

## Hitting Home

When the last Labour government came to power in 1974, it froze rents and set about increasing public sector completions from 107,000 in 1973 to 129,000 in 1975. Faced with IMF pressure to adopt stringent spending cuts in 1976, in return for its financial rescue package amid a sterling crisis, the government caved in. In the housing programme, rents were increased and Council new build housing slumped, so that by 1979 in England and Wales public sector housing completions had dropped to 57% of their 1975 level—74,000 houses.

It is in this context that the new Thatcher administration's 1980 Housing Act must be seen, pushing forward much further in a direction already accepted by Labour in its 1977 Green Paper that home ownership was a "basic and natural" desire. The Act took away the discretion of local authorities to sell, and instead gave Council tenants the right to buy their homes, with the incentive of a discount system depending on length of tenure. It also introduced modest measures to decontrol rents in the private rented sector, and a 'charter' which, for example, gave public housing tenants greater security of tenure and qualified rights to sublet and improve their houses. In addition, a new annual block subsidy was given to local government for Council housing to fill the gap between what Councils needed to balance the books, and the income that government considered should have come from rent. This system of 'deficit finance' effectively gave central government increased influence over rent levels. All told, greater reliance was to be placed on the private sector to boost new build housing and, as one inducement, the obligation to abide by Parker Morris standards was lifted. To encourage more private landlordism, new short-hold tenancies were introduced, whereby letting could now be on the basis of one to five-year fixed terms. The new policy reflected itself quickly in public sector housing where new completions declined by 56% between

1980 and 1983 to a post-war low of 31,500. But there was no evidence over the same period that the private sector was expanding sufficiently fast to make up the shortfall; in fact it only increased its new build completions by 10% for a total of 125,646.

Within a few years, a housing crisis was being forecast. On 20 October 1985 the *Sunday Times* reported the government's suppression of a housing stock condition survey, which had estimated that Britain's Council estates required £20 billion for urgent repairs. Interestingly, the government did not rush to overturn much of their predecessors' housing legislation:

"....the Rent Act 1974 and the Housing (Homeless Persons) Act 1977, both thought to have been ripe for repeal in 1979, have been more at risk from the interpretations of judges than the depredations of Ministers. The government can afford to be tolerant: the former is widely evaded and the burden of the latter falls mainly on Labour local authorities."[1]

As the initial momentum in the number of tenants availing themselves of the 'right to buy' provision slowed, the government sought additional means to sustain the drive to privatisation. In 1985 a law was enacted to permit local authorities to sell whole estates to any DoE-approved private landlord. This has provoked its own controversy. For example, Torbay Borough Council attempted to transfer over 5,000 houses worth some £56 million. Only 15% of tenants voted in approval while 43% were opposed. But the Council decided to count the abstentions among those favourable:

"As far as Conservative-controlled Torbay was concerned, this represented majority approval under the provisions of the 1985 Housing Act . But the ensuing row obliged Nicholas Ridley to call for a second ballot, and the Council eventually withdrew altogether."[2]

Eight years after the 1980 'right to buy', and despite the 1985 legislation, the government was still left with around 5 million Council tenants. A new Housing Bill was introduced in 1988 to address this situation. Proposals included the establishment of Housing Action Trusts (HATs), with £192 million of government funds, to renovate particularly run-down estates. Some 18 estates, comprising 25,000 tenants, were earmarked for this experiment. A House of Lords amendment to the Bill stipulated that such estates should only be transferred to HATs if the majority of tenants eligible to vote supported this option. This was in recognition of the reservations emerging in the estates under consideration that the introduction of these Trusts was a prelude to significant rent increases and a subsequent takeover by private landlords. The government eventually conceded a qualified variation of the Lords amendment, namely that "it will be a majority of those voting".[3] But in one of the designated areas, Sunderland, a test vote recorded 86% of the tenants opposed to the HAT option. Besides the apparent unpopularity of the scheme amongst the consumers, the government was compelled in March 1989 to scale down its HAT target by 50%, following a consultant's report which contended that proper renovation to just nine estates would itself cost £352 million over the following 5-10 years. The problems faced by government in implementing the HAT programme is reflected in the 50% decrease in anticipated spending on the project from £90 million to £45 million in 1990.

The other part of the 1988 legislation offers opportunities for private landlords to bid for Council estates or self-contained parts of them. This marked a significant change from the White Paper's proposal to allow tenants to opt out of Council control and come under another landlord. It was now the case that, faced with the prospect of a private landlord bid, tenants could vote on their preference. Moreover, the voting system itself was strange. It was not to be in terms of a simple majority of those voting because abstainers were to be counted with those favouring the change, as were all empty flats and houses. In its initial Bill, the government rejected a minimum turn-out rule and an Opposition suggestion that transfer should require at least 50% tenant support. But, following a House of Lords amendment, the government relented on the turn-out issue and included a proviso that at least 50% of estate tenants now have to vote. Nevertheless, the democratic credentials of the voting procedure in this so-called 'tenants choice' remain suspect. As a *Guardian* editorial concluded:

> "....on an estate of 100 houses, if only one tenant votes in favour, 49 are opposed and 50 do not vote, the transfer goes ahead."[4]

As the editorial goes on to point out, the electoral rules, together with those applicable to the 'opting out' scheme in the 1988 Education Act (see next Chapter), are at notable variance with the government's draft code relating to industrial action in which it suggests at least a 70% poll. There in paragraph 98 it affirms:

> "A simple (or even a substantial) majority indicating willingness to take (or continue) industrial action might not actually be representative if many of those given entitlement to vote in the ballot did not actually do so."

An early example of the Tenant's Choice Scheme did not bode well for government plans. Council tenants in Hertfordshire largely voted against a hand-over to a Housing Association. The government assumption that tenants were eagerly waiting to be freed of the bureaucratic bondage of a faceless Town Hall Housing Department seems to have been a miscalculation. Indeed, a recent report from Glasgow University's Centre for Housing Research, based on a two-year study commissioned by the DoE.[5] discovered high rates of satisfaction amongst council tenants in both their homes and neighbourhoods. By contrast, Housing Associations, in which the government is investing much expectation, were less likely to attain economies of scale, had lower rates of tenant satisfaction and larger proportions of tenants not only in arrears, but also in large arrears, despite spending 50% more on housing management than their Council counterparts. However, Councils fared worse when it came to repairs and maintenance. In short, the report concluded that good management practice was not the exclusive preserve of either provider. As such, the government assumption that Housing Associations could offer a more efficient, effective and responsive service than Councils does not seem to be sustainable on current evidence.

Moreover, the legislation will impair the ability of Councils to meet their other statutory obligations:

"Tenants' Choice will obviously limit a local authority's ability to offer homes to people on the waiting list or to homeless households and to promote equal opportunities in housing. Local authorities have no formal right to nominate tenants to transferred estates. Existing tenants will be further trapped in the least desirable housing. As a local authority's stock is reduced the use of temporary accommodation, such as bed and breakfast hotels, to house the homeless is likely to increase."[6]

But, of course, the incentive for tenants to forsake municipal control could increase in the aftermath of the government's newly proposed Local Government and Housing legislation, designed to prevent local authorities subsidising Council rents from general rates or any surplus on the housing revenue account. The effect would be to hike up rents to a market level. Other provisions include restrictions on local authority borrowing, their discretion in how to allocate receipts generated by their asset sales, and their role in local economic development. Together with the Poll Tax and the 1988 Housing Act, the proposed legislation would be another large step in increasing central government control over local government finance.

The capacity of local authorities to sustain, never mind improve, their role in public sector housing is to be further restrained:

"Whether through capital constraints, hostile takeovers or ringfencing of housing revenue accounts, the council kitty for repairs and improvements will dwindle. Projections are that by 1990, council capital receipts will be only one-third of what they are now and rents will rise as much as £20 per week. New provisions in the Housing Act mean that desultory repair programmes could lead to litigation."[7]

The intention behind the recent legislative moves is a thinly veiled drive to greater privatisation of housing provision. Since 1980 around one million Council houses have been sold, while approximately 400,000 new ones have been built. Sales have netted some £3 billion. There are 1.2 million fewer rented homes than in 1979.[8] The DoE has predicted that house building by Housing Associations will overtake that by local councils, which would eventually play a primarily enabling role. In the words of Nicholas Ridley:

"Where they perceive a need for new housing, we want them to look at alternative ways of meeting those needs, working through Housing Associations and private developers before thinking about adding to their own stock."[9]

Government spending plans announced in 1990 indicate that by 1992-93 financial support for Housing Associations will be in excess of housing expenditure by local authorities for the first time. Labour has criticised government legislation for doing nothing to increase the stock of good low-cost homes at an affordable rent. Peter McGurk, Director of the Institute of Housing, has assessed the record in even more blunt terms, arguing that government "housing policy is not about housing, it's about tenure".[10] It has also been said that: "Housing policy emphasises the unacceptable core of Thatcherism — the pre-eminence of making money over making things and of the elevation of ownership above performance."[11]

The reliance on the private sector has come under other rebuke. A Shelter report[12] estimated that by the end of 1988 some 37,440 people were over six months in arrears with their mortgage repayments, nearly 4.5 times the 1979 figure of 8,420. In 1988, 16,150 properties were repossessed by the Building Societies and Banks, nearly 6.5 times the 1979 figure of 2,500. Meanwhile, the problem of homelessness has more than doubled compared to the 1979 figure of 56,750 households. An Audit Commission report on the homeless in February 1989 concluded that, though some Councils could manage stock better and bring back into use vacant property, those in the highest stress areas could not solve the problem without central government support for affordable rented properties. It charts the rise in the use of temporary accommodation from 5,000 households in 1982 to 30,000 by 1988, estimating the annual cost now to be £100 million.

Unusual for the government, it has been keen to infer that the problem is one of demand rather than supply, and that it has been aggravated by irresponsible social behaviour such as unmarried teenage pregnancies and young people prematurely leaving their parental home. This accords with a newspaper reference to:

> "....a confidential briefing pack for Tory MPs believed to have emanated from Conservative Central Office....It said 'Government's approach is designed to divide homelessness into a number of discrete issues, with a reasonable tale to tell on each, and to avoid treating it in general terms as a large amorphous issue which could only be approached by the injection of unrealistically large amounts of public money.'"[13]

## Some Political Implications

Tory housing policy has had an important political impact in Britain. Their 1979 victory was related to their pre-election promises about lower mortgage rates and privatisation of Council housing. The shift to the private sector was apparent by the time of Mrs Thatcher's third election victory in 1987, owner occupation having increased from 55% to 63% of all tenures. This transformation meant that Labour felt obliged to signal more clearly its approval of home ownership to ensure that its heartland support was not confined to a declining rented sector.

This shift to owner-occupation and the residualisation of Council housing under Mrs Thatcher has been accompanied by sharpening inequalities. Writing in the early 1980s, Le Grand had noted, in a review of the effects of government housing policy, the "substantial inequalities of public expenditure, with owner occupiers receiving more than private or public tenants and the better off receiving more than the less well off".[14] By the late 1980s, this pattern had been significantly accentuated. Mortgage interest tax relief— due to high interest rates and the privatisation programme — had risen to around £7 billion annually, disproportionately enjoyed by those on higher income. Taken together with the effects of the large capital gains consequent upon rapidly escalating house values, the abolition of capital gains tax and discounts on Council house sales, recent policy adds up to a sizeable subsidy to owner occupiers at a time when support for public sector tenants has considerably declined.

But as the government has pushed forward its strategy under the 1988 legislation, its assumption that the remaining tenants on the vast municipal estates would flock to register for liberation from uncaring local authorities has not so far proved accurate. As an article from the *Economist* noted:

"....Ministers' dreams may go pop. Few Council tenants love this government; fewer still know what a Housing Association is; most are frightened of private landlords.... [The idea of] alternative landlords.... seems insecure. Even if rigged rules allow a transfer to go ahead, will it? Housing Associations do not want hostile tenants."[15]

## Housing in Northern Ireland

The administrative system for public sector housing in Northern Ireland differs from that in Britain. Housing provision was one of the sensitive issues in the Civil Rights Campaign in the 1960s and a subsequent government Commission[16] acknowledged the use of housing allocation by some Unionist local authorities to gerrymander electoral wards in a manner that ensured a favourable political outcome for their party. Consequently, in 1971, a contentious reform was introduced whereby housing responsibility was taken away from local councils and vested in a single authority, known as the Northern Ireland Housing Executive (NIHE).

Over the last 15 years, Northern Ireland has been following quite closely housing policy developments in Britain. Under Labour, for example, the 1974 Housing Act came to Northern Ireland in the form of the 1976 Housing Order

(NI), similarly concerned with the establishment of Housing Action Areas and
statutory financial assistance for Housing Associations.

Under Mrs Thatcher's administration, the 1983 Housing Order (NI)
mirrored the 1980 legislation in Britain, though there had been some similar
provisions already in operation. For example, the switch in Britain after the
1980 Act to deficit financing was less relevant since the DoE in Northern
Ireland already exercised great control over the Housing Executive's budget.
Moreover, there had already been a 'right-to-buy' scheme in place since June
1979. In the period 1979 to 1987 the Housing Executive sold 35,546 dwellings,
but as in Britain, this privatisation process slowed down for most of the latter
half of the decade, declining from a peak of 6,622 in 1981 to around half that
figure by 1987. As in Britain, there has been a consequent shift towards owner
occupation. However, as Table 29 illustrates, public sector tenants still comprise just over one-third of all households compared to just over one-quarter
in Britain.

| Table 29 | Housing Tenure: Northern Ireland (NI) and Britain (GB), 1966-1986 (%) | | | | | |
|---|---|---|---|---|---|---|
| | Owner Occupation | | Rented from Local Authority | | Private Rented/Other | |
| | NI | GB | NI | GB | NI | GB |
| 1966 | 45 | 47 | 28 | 28 | 27 | 25 |
| 1971 | 47 | 52 | 34 | 31 | 19 | 18 |
| 1974 | 48 | 53 | 37 | 31 | 15 | 16 |
| 1979 | 52 | 55 | 39 | 32 | 9 | 13 |
| 1984 | 58 | 61 | 36 | 28 | 7 | 11 |
| 1986 | 60 | 63 | 34 | 27 | 5 | 10 |

Note: A change in calculation of the statistics results in the 1986 figures not being
directly comparable with those of other years.

*Source: Regional Trends, various years, Department of the
Environment, Northern Ireland.*

It is apparent that the public sector remains a significant component of
housing provision in Northern Ireland. In many ways, this is both the cause
and result of more generous public expenditure on housing in the region than
in Britain, even during the Thatcher period. The more significant role of owner
occupation in the 1980s can also be seen. In 1979 39% of Northern Ireland's
housing stock was Housing Executive rented. By 1986 this had fallen to 34%.
In the same period the rate of owner occupation had grown to nearly 60%.
Although the private rented sector continued to decline, Housing Associations,

while accounting for only a fraction of housing tenures, increased from 0.4% to 1.36%.

## Public Spending on Housing

In Britain, housing expenditure has been particularly vulnerable to cuts in public spending. This pattern did not start with Mrs Thatcher. During the last Labour government (1974-79), public expenditure on housing dropped 19%, and as a proportion of total government expenditure declined from 10% to 5.8%.[17] In the first term of the Thatcher administration, housing expenditure dropped by a further 53%, bearing about three-quarters of all spending cuts.[18] The 1980s also saw the continuation of the trend of the 1970s, whereby spending on rehabilitation rose while that on new build declined.

In Northern Ireland in the first period of the last Labour government, housing expenditure was given a significant boost. Responding to the evidence from the 1974 House Condition Survey,[19] which demonstrated that housing unfitness in the region stood at over twice the rate in England and Wales, Labour made a substantial increase in housing expenditure between 1974 and 1977. During this period, the real value of the spending more than doubled and it's share of total expenditure rose by two-thirds. However, after 1976-77, in the context of IMF intervention and consequent public spending restraint in Britain, government expenditure on housing in Northern Ireland was also cut. The year 1977-78 saw by far the sharpest drop in real terms (£23 million, a decrease of over 15% on the previous year). It should be noted, however, that its share of total public expenditure remained high. The reduction therefore was not specifically directed at housing but public expenditure in general which also fell in real terms. Under Mrs Thatcher, as we have seen, public expenditure on housing in Britain has fallen dramatically. Up to 1981-82 Northern Ireland paralleled this trend. The then chairman of the region's housing authority, Mr Brett, commented:

> "Over the past two years we have had a succession of cuts, moratoriums, and shifts in budget allocation, which have left the Board of the Executive reeling....do they [the government] or do they not accept the principle that different parts of the United Kingdom are entitled to aspire to parity of minimum housing standards?"[20]

A report in May 1981 by the Northern Ireland Economic Council[21] concluded that, in the context of the region's poorer housing relative to Britain, it required greater allocation of government resources. Mr Chris Patten, then Minister, did not demur, commenting that he had "no doubt at all that the housing statistics demonstrate the intensity of the problems in Northern Ireland."[22] In a subsequent report in 1985, the NIEC was able to record: "Over the past three years public expenditure on housing in Northern Ireland has increased by almost one-quarter in real terms."[23]

The Northern Ireland Economic Council had made a telling point in arguing that public expenditure on housing should not be characterised as wasteful consumption. It illustrated how, in terms the Tories could appreciate, public spending on housing was "good value for money". Being labour intensive and predominantly using local materials, the construction industry has a high public expenditure multiplier. Thus resources devoted to housing have a greater employment effect than other programmes.

The changes in expenditure were reflected in public housing starts. At its peak in 1977, 7,700 new dwellings were completed. This fell to 2,500 in 1980 and then began to rise again, reaching 4,500 starts in 1983-84. However, in subsequent years, the number of new starts once more declined. This was justified by a higher commitment to rehabilitation, a decline in the NIHE's waiting lists and the 1981 Census indication that there was a modest surplus of houses over households. But it was also a function of the shifting emphasis towards private sector new build. This is apparent in the pattern of dwelling completions over a recent ten-year period. It indicates the increasing role played in the Thatcher years by the private sector, which has raised its share of dwellings completed from 28.7% in 1977 to 71.1% a decade later. This has been mainly at the expense of the Housing Executive, whose share has declined from 71.3% to 28.9% over the same period, representing almost an exact reversal of roles.

Although new building in the late 1980s is comparable in scale to the mid 1970s, the role of the Northern Ireland Housing Executive has been dramatically reduced. The decline in the public sector's proportion of completions was substantial. In 1977 over 50% of all new starts were accounted for by Housing Executive contracts. In 1987 the equivalent figure was 16%. A comparison with other UK regions shows an even more significant reduction in the role of the public sector. In 1987 local authorities in the North, with a population twice that of Northern Ireland, managed only 765 completions and 473 starts. Wales with a 50% greater population has figures of 777 and 888 respectively. The comparable figures for Northern Ireland were 1,764 and 1,596. Allowing for population differences, new build activities of the public sector in Northern Ireland are three times greater than in Wales and four times that of the North. Public sector housing investment in Northern Ireland has retained a significantly higher priority than it has in Britain.

During the 1970s and early 80s public expenditure on housing in Northern Ireland grew about twice as fast as in Britain. In 1978-79 Northern Ireland's public sector housing expenditure was 4.1% of the UK total. By 1987-88 this figure had risen to 9.6%. In 1986-87 public expenditure on housing per head in Northern Ireland was nearly three times that of England and Wales and 20% higher than in Scotland.[24]

| Table 30 | Completed Permanent Dwellings in Northern Ireland, 1977-1987 | | | | | | |
|---|---|---|---|---|---|---|---|
| Year | Local Authority (NIHE) | Housing Association | Gov. Depts | Total Public Sector | Private Sector No. | % of Total | Total |
| 1977 | 7,676 | — | 1 | 7,677 | 3,085 | 28.7 | 10,762 |
| 1978 | 5,681 | 8 | 9 | 5,698 | 3,145 | 35.6 | 8,843 |
| 1979 | 3,436 | 231 | 71 | 3,738 | 3,574 | 48.9 | 7,312 |
| 1980 | 2,507 | 325 | 56 | 2,888 | 3,568 | 55.3 | 6,456 |
| 1981 | 2,859 | 129 | 223 | 3,211 | 3,557 | 52.6 | 6,768 |
| 1982 | 2,814 | 369 | 218 | 3,401 | 3,606 | 51.5 | 7,007 |
| 1983 | 4,044 | 528 | 49 | 4,621 | 4,971 | 51.8 | 9,592 |
| 1984 | 3,588 | 644 | 6 | 4,338 | 6,177 | 59.3 | 10,415 |
| 1985 | 3,233 | 626 | 2 | 3,861 | 6,940 | 64.3 | 10,801 |
| 1986 | 2,580 | 468 | 0 | 3,048 | 7,082 | 69.9 | 10,130 |
| 1987 | 1,683 | 423 | 0 | 2,106 | 5,193 | 71.1 | 7,299 |

Note: Figures for 1987 represent an annualised estimate based on

*Source: Housing and Construction Statistics, 1976-1986, Table 6.1; and Housing and Construction Statistics, Part 1, No. 24, September Quarter 1987, Northern Ireland Housing Executive.*

Nevertheless, during this period the share of total public expenditure in Northern Ireland (excluding Law & Order) allocated to housing fell slightly from 8.7% in 1983-84 to 7.8% in 1987-88. Public expenditure plans, published in 1989, revealed a projected fall in housing expenditure of 38% between 1987-88 and 1991-92 when its share of total expenditure would be reduced to 4.9%. This recent reduction represents a resource shortfall. The NIHE's Public Sector survey of 1985-86 suggested that the backlog on repair and improvement work totalled £875 million (at 1986 prices), Shelter (NI) has argued that this reflects a deeper problem:

"The government has been consistently underfunding the Executive since the beginning of the Eighties, but this has been hidden by the availability to the Executive of income from the sale of its dwellings to sitting tenants. Now that source is beginning to dry up and the underfunding is apparent to everyone."[25]

In the Executive's draft Housing Strategy Review 1990-93, it is claimed that there is a shortfall of £51 million between its planned expenditure and the likely government funding covering the period 1990-92. While the Northern Ireland public expenditure figures announced in the House of Commons in November 1989 indicated an increase in funds over the previous White Paper, the NIHE chief executive estimated that the new figure would still be £18 million less than was needed.[26] In January 1990 the Housing Executive announced that instead of the 1,300 houses it had intended to build in 1990-91, it could only build 1,000 due to government cuts in the budget. Faced with a decline in capital receipts from house sales, an increase in loan charges, and a real drop in government funding, the Executive has seen itself with four main options: persuading government to increase its financial support; persuading government to remove loan charges from budget calculations; raising private finance; or imposing substantial rent rises. It is apparent that, as in Britain, the government is keen to see rent levels rise. Whereas the Executive had recommended a rent rise for 1988 of 4%, in line with inflation, the government proposed a 9.2% increase.

Although the role of public sector housing and its share of public expenditure have been greater in Northern Ireland than in other regions, some aspects still reflect what has been happening elsewhere. For example, the average public sector rent has risen much faster than inflation. In 1974 the average Housing Executive weekly rent was £1.92. By November 1979 this figure had increased to £5.68, an increase of about 190%. However, by December 1987 the figure was £15.34. The percentage increase was slightly less than in the previous period, but in money terms it was a great deal more. Further, prices in general increased much faster in the former period than in the latter. Public sector housing thus became a greater burden on its inhabitants. Meanwhile, rent arrears also increased over the period. In 1974 they amounted to less than £4 million. By 1986 they were nearly £17 million.

Housing support for those on low incomes has taken the form of rent rebates/supplementary benefits or housing benefit. In 1979 about 18,000 tenants were in receipt of rent rebates with a much greater number having housing costs met by supplementary benefits. The introduction of housing benefit in Northern Ireland in 1984 (a year late) considerably changed that picture. Information on the operation of housing benefit for the four years 1984-87 is given in Table 31.

Despite strenuous efforts to cut back on expenditure, the cost has been increasing every year except 1987. Even in that year, the percentage receiving benefit and the number receiving full rebate increased. Housing benefit has been a particular target for expenditure cutbacks through the manipulation of conditions of eligibility and income tapers. Nevertheless, the government has not been able to save very much on this benefit in Northern Ireland.

| Table 31 | The Operation of Housing Benefit, 1984-87 | | | |
|---|---|---|---|---|
| | 1984 | 1985 | 1986 | 1987 |
| **Total No. of Tenants** | 216,000 | 207,000 | 202,000 | 199,000 |
| **No. Receiving Benefit** | 126,376 | 130,414 | 141,950 | 142,285 |
| **% Receiving Benefit** | 59.4% | 63.0% | 70.3% | 71.5% |
| **Total Benefit Paid (£000s)** | 92,815 | 103,059 | 119,810 | 117,927 |
| **Average Benefit** | 723 | 790 | 844 | 828 |
| **No. Receiving Full Rebate** | 76,897 | 79,535 | 80,831 | 82,969 |

*Source: Northern Ireland Housing Statistics, 1987.*

## Housing in Northern Ireland 1979-87: Sheltered from the Market?

While the backlog of housing neglect in Northern Ireland has still not been completely made up, substantial improvements have been achieved in two decades of the NIHE's existence. Evidence of the positive impact of a more active public policy on housing in Northern Ireland is given in successive House Condition Surveys, as the Table 32 illustrates.

| Table 32 | Changes in Housing Conditions in Northern Ireland, 1974-1987 | | | | | |
|---|---|---|---|---|---|---|
| | Lacking at least one basic amenity | | Requiring repairs in excess of £2,500 | | Unfit | |
| Year | % | No. | % | No. | % | No. |
| 1974 | 26.2 | 119,510 | N/A | N/A | 19.6 | 89,370 |
| 1979 | 17.9 | 84,132 | 25.4 | 119,000 | 14.1 | 66,208 |
| 1984 | 9.2 | 45,133 | 26.5 | 131,000 | 10.4 | 51,330 |
| 1987 | 5.5 | 28,330 | 22.5 | 115,000 | 8.4 | 42,900 |

*Source: Northern Ireland House Condition Surveys, 1974-1987.*

Of course, this general improvement disguises wide variation within the averages. For instance, the 1984 House Condition Survey showed that the unfitness figure for mainly rural Fermanagh was 27%, while in Castlereagh in Greater Belfast it was only 1.4%.

According to official figures, the NIHE waiting list in 1987 had dropped by nearly 25% from a 1980 peak of just under 32,500 applicants. This change is partly attributed to improvements in housing conditions. But it needs to be said that for one group in particular the problem is increasing. The number of single persons on the waiting list rose from 4,956 in 1981 to 8,627 in 1987, their share of the waiting list doubling from 17% to nearly 35%. Moreover, housing need as a result of sharing and overcrowding remains high. Of the 1988 waiting list total of 24,000, 50% were considered particularly urgent.

## Policy Changes in the Late 1980s

In recent years, the appropriateness of policy parity between Britain and Northern Ireland has been the subject of some contention. For example, it has been noted that:

> "....the controversial sections of the 1986 Housing and Planning Act
> — which enable other agencies to take possession of council
> tenancies and dispose of the management and ownership of estates
> (sections 9,10,11) — simply have no relevance to NI. The
> government and the NIHE are strongly opposed to such measures on
> the grounds that tenants might be exposed to control and exploitation
> by paramilitary groups."[27]

On the other hand, certain legislation in Britain, for example regarding homelessness, has been highly relevant but very slow in coming.[28] The Housing (NI) Order 1988, which began operation in April 1989, essentially brought Northern Ireland legislation on homelessness into line with that in Britain. Prior to that, responsibility rested with the Area Health Boards, since the 1977 Housing (Homeless Persons) Act and part of the 1985 Housing Act did not apply to Northern Ireland despite years of campaigning by the voluntary sector . Two distinguishing features of the Northern Ireland Order reflect the particular disruptive circumstances under which housing policy operates there. Article 28 relates to the Housing Executive taking over houses owned by people "who are unable or unwilling to occupy these as a result of acts or threats of violence or other intimidation"; and Article 29 refers to an emergency repair service to be applied to houses damaged as a result of "civil disturbance". But overall the new policy does not provide any guarantees against the discretionary powers of the housing authority in the assessment of genuine homelessness. As is evident from the experience in Britain, unless accompanied by appropriate extra resources, there will be an incentive for the Executive to interpret the provisions in a minimalist fashion.

Northern Ireland has yet to see the legislative equivalent to the 1988 Housing Act and the proposed legislation on local government and housing, which as we have seen, have as their goals extending owner occupation, resuscitating the private rented sector, demoting the role of the public sector, expanding the scope of Housing Associations and converting the function of local authorities to one of 'enabling' rather than direct provision. The Northern Ireland Housing Executive has acknowledged that it is likely to come under similar policy direction "to extend and diversify tenure choice and attract private funding for capital investment in new homes for sale and to rent, and to rehabilitate and upgrade run-down Public Housing Estates".[29]

Nevertheless, the Executive has produced a strategic paper which assesses the implications of changes in its future role — **Housing in the 1990s**[30] — and in it some reservations are expressed about its possible new functions. It acknowledges the keenness of government in Britain to revive the private rented sector. But it points out that in Northern Ireland, despite the lack of regulation on private rented properties built or converted since 1956, the sector's decline has continued. While it held a 27% share of the market in 1966, this had dropped to 9% by 1979 and declined further to 5% by 1986. This is an interesting trend since it suggests that, even with government moves in Britain to further de-control the private sector, the consequent results — at least in depressed regions — would likely disappoint expectation. Its significance for Northern Ireland is that even if owner occupation rises well above two-thirds of all tenures by the end of the century, a sizeable rented sector of around 150,000 dwellings is needed, most of which will have to be provided by means other than the private sector.

In Britain the role of Housing Associations is to be enhanced, and the Executive concurs that potential for them could also be tapped in Northern Ireland. Since the 1976 Order, 47 Associations have developed. But they are responsible for only 7,000 properties, equal to around 4% of the Housing Executive's stock. Unlike the situation in Britain, this third sector is not in a position to compete with, never mind replace, the public sector housing authority. But, as in Britain, there has been some concern expressed that, should the Associations be steered into a substantially increased role, their current social emphasis will likely give way to a more commercial one, reflected in more economic rents. The Executive suggests that as part of its comprehensive function to enable as well as to provide housing, it should be allowed to assume funding control over the Housing Associations. Presently, it only exercises a supervisory and facilitating role in relation to them. The campaign group, Shelter (NI), is sceptical about the Executive's proposal:

"....we are concerned that concentration of the debate on 'Housing in the '90s' on the Executive's proposal to monitor Housing Associations will deflect attention from the real issue, which is meeting housing need, the primary responsibility of government to provide the necessary funding, and secondly, the obligation on those who advocate the use of mixed public/private funding to set out the implications for rent levels and programmes for helping those in need".[31]

Indeed, the Executive does make a case for itself to assume "responsibility for the allocation of all government expenditure on housing, which should be maintained at an adequate level to satisfy the social housing needs of the province".[32] Moreover, it wants to be free to raise private capital to augment its housing budget and to facilitate in certain respects the private rented sector. Since it is already a single purpose housing body detached from local authority control, with responsibilities for run-down estates, it doesn't see any advantages in transporting the HAT experiment to Northern Ireland. The concept of tenants' choice to transfer to an alternative landlord is accepted, though each proposal it feels should be appraised "taking account of the particular circumstances in Northern Ireland".

The Executive's credentials to justify an enlarged rather than contracted role are also set out. These include its success in meeting targets set at its inception in 1971, establishment of a universal rent structure, facilitation of housing mobility and introduction of advanced estate management methods. Interestingly the greatest self-accolade is reserved for a wider achievement, that "given the particular circumstances in Northern Ireland, the Housing Executive has taken housing out of politics and ended allegations of sectarian discrimination in housing". But this impartiality is not immune from threat today since "indeed, in many respects the potential for paramilitary influence in housing matters is perhaps greater".

In summary, despite a decade of cajoling and coercion by government, with the carrot of sale discounts and the stick of rent increases, around one-quarter of all households in Britain still live in Council housing. Government's current concern centres around the best strategy to reduce this number further. But there has been some disagreement:

> "The Cabinet Minister responsible for housing, Mr Nicholas Ridley, does not disguise his contempt for local Councils. He believes that breaking their power as landlords will in itself be of great social benefit. His Housing Minister, the more centrist Mr William Waldegrave....envisages the Councils running a residual welfare-housing service which, together with a subsidised Housing Association sector, would attempt to cater for households in the greatest need".[33]

In other words, housing policy has been an important instrument in the Thatcher government's wider political strategy concerning the role of local authorities. This continues to be evident in the provisions of the 1988 Act, which seems to have been "framed more in a spirit of vindictiveness against the main providers of social housing, the local authorities, than as any real attempt to make life better for the homeless and inadequately housed."[34]

One of the problems is that government cannot even agree about the level of 'need'. Mr Ridley has said that "the quantity of housing available for renting overall is probably sufficient to cater for the number of households needing rented accommodation." But his then Ministerial partner, Mr Waldegrave has argued that "the quantity of housing available for renting is insufficient to cater for the number of households needing rented accommodation."[35]

At the same time, Northern Ireland continues to generate its own internal politics of housing. The transfer of authority to the NIHE in 1971 has not succeeded in depoliticising the issue. For example, community organisations in the Protestant Shankill area of Belfast have charged that their district's redevelopment has been deliberately designed to contract the Protestant population in the West of the city in order to facilitate military containment of sectarian conflict. Equally, a proposal to extend public sector housing on the edge of Catholic West Belfast to alleviate substantial overcrowding in that area, was fiercely resisted by an adjacent Unionist local authority. As a result the Department of the Environment scaled down the number of new houses in the plan. In another area of West Belfast, the inhabitants of a brutal redevelopment project, known as Divis Flats, campaigned for its demolition for years. The response from the NIHE never amounted to more than cosmetic renovation. However, quite recently, a commitment has been given to demolish the complex. There has been a debate about the reasons for this policy about-face between those who largely credit it to the unstinting campaign of local groups and those who see the hand of the Anglo-Irish Agreement influencing the British government to show good faith by making an initiative in West Belfast. Despite the agenda of Thatcherism, the specific politics of Northern Ireland continue to have their impact on housing.

# 8. Education: A Testing Time

The academic year 1989-90 began with concerns about a severe teacher shortage and prospects of cuts in real spending for the following year. The results of a comprehensive teacher union survey of 17,700 schools in England and Wales released on the 6th of November 1989 showed that permanent vacancies, at over 8,000, were double the level suggested by government. On the same day, government spending plans for the following year proposed a 3% expenditure increase, even though the inflation rate was 7.5%. By implication, thousands of children would be left deprived of proper tuition. The teacher shortage was itself symptomatic of both the various disputes afflicting the school system in recent years regarding pay and conditions, and the related staff demoralisation. Moreover, teachers' unions have charged that the government's imposition of constant new demands on teachers, such as the changed examination procedures implicit in GCSE, have often been accompanied by resource constraint rather than expansion. In February 1990 the senior Chief Inspector for Schools reported that inadequate accomodation, shortage of essential equipment and inappropriate teaching were combining to blight one third of all lessons. It is in this context that the government embarked upon what was billed as the most radical educational changes since the 1944 Butler reforms.

## Education Resources

The White Paper on government spending plans in January 1989 claimed that the rise in real terms in education spending over the previous decade was 10%. Total expenditure is set to increase from £5.7 billion in 1989-90 to £6.9 billion in 1992-93 — less than 20% in cash terms. Given current and projected inflation rates, this represents a spending cut over the three year period. Moreover, the effect of spending on the standard of the service is influenced by several considerations. Since it is labour intensive, its costs tend to rise faster than inflation. There are also transitional diseconomies related to the difficulty of trimming teacher numbers and building resources in neat correspondence with falling pupil numbers. Accordingly, government statistics which emphasise increased spending per pupil need to be treated cautiously.

In Northern Ireland total real expenditure by the Education and Library Boards has risen over the last decade. However, as Table 33 indicates, much of the increase has been in the latter years.

| Table 33 Total Real Expenditure By Northern Ireland Education and Library Boards, 1978-79 to 1988-89 | | |
|---|---|---|
| Year | GDP Deflater | £million |
| 1978-79 | 100 | 332.2 |
| 1979-80 | 117 | 324.9 |
| 1980-81 | 138 | 327.4 |
| 1981-82 | 152 | 323.2 |
| 1982-83 | 163 | 322.9 |
| 1983-84 | 170 | 327.4 |
| 1984-85 | 179 | 325.9 |
| 1985-86 | 188 | 321.4 |
| 1986-87 | 195 | 357.2 |
| 1987-88 | 205 | 366.6 |
| 1988-89 | 220 | 369.1 |

*Source: Calculated from data provided by the Department of Education (NI).*

Between 1978-79 and 1985-86 education expenditure, in real terms, varied only marginally. However, since then, each year has seen significant increase. At the same time the use of GDP deflators as a means of identifying 'real' growth in public expenditure is subject to dispute. Instead, it has been suggested that the use of a Relative Price Effect (RPE), which acknowledges that costs in the public sector — for instance resulting from greater labour intensity — may rise faster than general costs in the economy.

## Education Policy

In launching its 1988 legislation, the Thatcher government had three central objectives: one, to tap into the supposed widespread public unease about declining academic standards and erosion of discipline and respect for authority in schools; two, to ensure education becomes more in tune with the needs of business; and three, to subject the state system to the rigorous pressures of the market. There is, of course, nothing new about the first two concerns. Mr Callaghan, when Labour Prime Minister, promoted a loudly trumpeted 'grand debate' in 1976 about educational standards and simultaneously raised the issue of the relevance of the school curriculum to the skill needs of modern industry. As in some other policy areas, current government thinking on these issues is separated from its Labour predecessor by a matter of degree rather than kind.

It is again the emphasis on privatisation and the market which distinguishes educational change during the last decade. An early initiative was the 1980 scheme to fund assisted places in private schools. But this in itself could only provide a marginal boost to a sector, which still accounts for only 7% of pupils in England and Wales. The government remained confronted with the uncomfortable reality that the vast majority of pupils were dependent on the state sector. In its 1980 Education Act, it made several moves to restrict its public sector obligations. One related to pre-school facilities:

"....the Conservative government was embarrassed by the discovery that, under the 1944 Act, local education authorities could not close nursery schools as they had a statutory duty to provide schools for those under five. The Government acted quickly....(and) merely gave local authorities power to establish and maintain nursery schools. Thus the stage is set for a State retreat from pre-school education."[1]

Another retreat related to the school meals service. Charges were increased while the menu became no longer subject to prescribed nutritional standards. The effect was apparent within a few years. Between 1979-80 and 1984-85 real expenditure in this service dropped by 35%.[2]

But these measures were judged faltering and timid by the New Right ideologues who argued more ambitiously for a voucher scheme, whereby parents would receive a certain value in coupons to spend on their children's education as they chose. This idea represented a possible prelude to a fundamental transformation in the role of the public sector in education from direct provider to enabler. Though it received a sympathetic ear from prominent Thatcherites such as Sir Rhodes Boyson and Sir Keith Joseph, opposition both to its principle and practicality led to it being dropped from the serious educational agenda. However, as in the case of health policy, this rebuff for the radical solution did not see off its advocates. If that degree of privatisation could not be achieved at this stage, at least some kind of internal market could be introduced into the system.

The drive was, as usual, presented in terms of efficiency and value for money. For those Tories who believe that the educational 'product' has been deteriorating in quality, the fact that the budget consumes around 5% of GDP — twice its share in 1950 — is a matter of some indignation, never mind that the increase in costs is largely attributable to changes such as the raising of the school leaving age and the expansion of higher education. The 1988 Education

Act addressed this concern and can be examined under three main headings: content, the management structure and accountability.

## The Content of Education

The dramatic new requirements of a national curriculum mean that all children aged 5-16 in state primary and secondary schools (the omission of private schools being notable) are obliged to study three core subjects — English, Maths and Science — together with Foundation subjects — Geography, Music Art, Physical Education, History, Technology and Design — and in the case of secondary schools, also a Modern Language. In addition, Religious Education and a daily act of largely Christian worship became obligatory. Criticism has been made of the rigidity of the new curriculum structure, which over-packs the timetable; marginalises other creative and motivating learning opportunities; discourages the development of new courses; postpones specialisation; reduces teacher autonomy while massively increasing the burdens placed on them; and concedes to the central state unprecedented influence over subject content. Overall, it is seen by its critics as attempting to impose a standardisation just at a time when the multi-cultural nature of society requires greater diversity.

In its favour, it is argued that it removes the whimsical discretion exercised by schools, which can see subjects excluded or demoted for administrative rather than educational reasons. Transition from one educational stage to another is meant to be easier. The new curriculum also provides a universal structure throughout the country, which both facilitates the geographical mobility of teachers and pupils and provides a new consistency with which employers anywhere can better measure scholastic attainment. As such, it brings the UK into line with common European practice. Opportunity for cross-curricular project work remains, as does the capacity to respond to multi-cultural demands. Whatever view one takes of these opposing arguments, several points are apparent. First, the government explicitly aims to reverse what it sees as the anti-competition, anti-family and anti-authority values espoused in modern school curricula. Interestingly, the curriculum changes are not being forced on the private schools, from which traditionally the elite in Britain's central institutions, public and private, come. Nor do they address the argument, with which Thatcherites in particular are likely to concur, that the classical bias in the public schools, with its disdain for industrial culture, bears a significant responsibility for the nation's economic decline. Strangely, Thatcherism may not be averse to challenging the complacency of some Establishment institutions, but it has omitted to launch an assault on private education.

Second, the government has intimated its wish to see the school curriculum reflect and endorse a favourable — some might say glorified — version of Britain's position in the world. This is most obvious in the case of history. The working party established to devise new history syllabuses reported in August 1989 and broadly vindicated a traditional approach which weighted course content in favour of British history. The Education Secretary had specifically requested that more attention should be devoted to dates, events and people, a recommendation which could be interpreted as taking history away again from social movements and giving it back to the kings and generals.[3]

Third, there appears to be some tension between these kind of imperatives and the general support in Section One of the 1988 Act for "a broad and balanced curriculum which a) promotes the spiritual, moral, cultural, mental and physical development of pupils for the opportunities, responsibilities and experiences of adult life".

This new curriculum will be subject to national compulsory testing for all state school pupils aged 7, 11, 14, and 16. In what looks like an immensely complicated system, in each subject there will be 10 levels of attainment. At 7, the average child is expected to reach level 2, at 11 level 4, at 14 level 5 or 6, and at 16 level 10. Criticisms of this proposal include the educational validity of age-related tests, which ignore children's different rates of maturity; a tendency for such testing to promote coaching and cramming rather than learning; the pressures on teachers to skew classroom learning to what is readily examinable; the extensive monitoring required to comply with the new assessment format; and lastly, the emotional burden imposed on young people, who may, like their parents, attribute undue significance to the results.

The government counters these reservations by stressing that the purpose is to identify the child's progress to ensure that learning problems are detected early and acted upon. Moreover, the system provides a guarantee to parents that their child is receiving its entitled tuition by a more measurable teaching procedure. The standard assessment tests (SATs) are supposed to be non-competitive. "Each pupil will be compared, not with other pupils, but the attainment target laid down".[4] Attainment targets for each subject are used to construct what are called 'profile components', charting each pupil's performance. Results for individual pupils are intended for parents and teachers, and not for public consumption although the results of age groups will be published by schools as an indication of their overall achievement.

## The Management of Schools

The government's radical changes to the way schools are managed are supposed to improve their efficient use of resources and increase the parental consumer's choice as to the kind of school they want their children to attend.

Three of the important managerial measures in the new legislation reduce or potentially reduce the influence of the Local Education Authority:

a)   **Financial Management**

With the exception of primary schools of less than 200 pupils, school governors are now to be given a significant measure of control over their school's budget. The LEA is obliged to devolve the largest part of the school budget to individual schools on the basis of the number and ages of their pupils, retaining only what is necessary to cover costs such as central administration, capital building and debt charges. The school governors will be responsible for selecting and dismissing staff, buying equipment, and taking decisions about renovations and repairs. Recognising that this measure of financial delegation will be both demanding and time consuming, the government has made financial provision for appropriate training.

b)   **Admission Policy**

Prior to the 1988 Act, LEAs could disperse pupils around their comprehensive schools to achieve an appropriate balance in school numbers and efficient use of school buildings. Parents would receive notification of a designated school — usually in their immediate neighbourhood. If discontented with this allocation, they could nominate another school, and in 90% of cases the LEA was able to comply with this choice. The normal reason for turning down the choice of the disappointed 10% was that their selected school was full. Under the new legislation, this planned admission limit has given way to 'open enrolment', an obligation on all state secondary schools to accept the number of pupils for whom they have places. The government insists that this will improve parental choice. If their choice results in too low a demand for a school, closure may result. But it will be a decision effectively reached by parents not LEA administrators.

c)   **Opting Out**

Under the legislation, schools can 'opt out' of local education authority control and become 'grant maintained' directly by the Department of Education. This procedure can be initiated by a petition representative of at least 20% of the school parents or by the school's governing body. But the possibility of opting out is restricted to schools with over 300 pupils. The second stage is a secret postal ballot. If over half the parents voting agree to seek grant maintained status, that is sufficient. However, if less than half of all parents vote, a second ballot must be organised within a fortnight, for which a simple majority of those voting will be conclusive. If the proposal to 'opt out' wins favour, the school governors are obliged to draw up a plan to submit to the Secretary of State whose decision, after a period of consultation, is final.

To qualify for a vote, a person has to have a child at the school at the time of the vote. Eligible parents have one vote whatever the number of their children at the school. A particularly controversial issue concerns whether an 'opt out' school will retain its prior status, whether for example, a comprehensive school after becoming grant maintained will be permitted to adopt a

171

selective admissions policy. Guidelines suggest that no such change should occur for at least five years and would require further approval from the Secretary of State. The complications of the whole process have prompted government to allocate £0.25 million to a Trust established to advise schools on how to cope.

By mid 1989 some 60 ballots had taken place, about 75% of them resulting in a decision to 'opt out'. The Department had rejected only four, endorsed 21, with 22 still under consideration. Of those approved, over one-third were confronted with closure, one-third were keen to protect their Grammar school status, while the rest were apparently successful schools keen to reinforce their distinction.It was reported by the *Independent on Sunday* in February 1990 that under government cash allocations, each pupil in a grant maintained school in 1990 would get five times as much expenditure as his or her counterpart in a local authority school.

### 3) Accountability

As a stalwart of neo-conservative enthusiasm in education policy, Rhodes Boyson's comments on these ideas are interesting:

"A common curriculum being offered for 70% or more of the week to all pupils is an egalitarian concept. I am tempted to ask why the government should now want to 'nationalise' the school curriculum....Nor is it ever wise for any government to give powers to itself which it would not wish to be exercised by an alternative government." [5]

Sir Rhodes Boyson's concern about aspects of the legislation accord with the kind of criticism usually levelled at the political Left: that in the drive for uniformity, the virtues of pluralism and diversity have been abandoned while the central state has been further empowered.

Of course, the 1988 Education Act is presented in terms of increasing consumer choice and parental power by challenging the 'producer dominance' of administrators and teacher organisations. The very terms applied, such as 'opting out,' emphasise the choice factor. But choice for some parents, say to, desert one particular neighbourhood school for another, limits the choice of those parents whose children remain at the school, where because of a dwindling roll the comprehensive range of A level subjects is rendered unviable. Such processes could make schools in the poorest areas particularly vulnerable if they experience a pupil drain, consequent reductions in resources,and thereby become less attractive to parents. Put simply, the flourishing of one school may clearly blight the prospects of other schools, and their pupils, in the same locality. It is apparent that the nostrum of consumer sovereignty

An individual school's decision to 'opt out' involves other kinds of collective outcome. It has implications for the capacity of the LEA to forward plan for their area in a cost effective fashion. The new grant maintained schools will forfeit their claims on certain LEA resources and services, e.g. economies in bulk purchasing equipment and materials, and in-service teacher training.

It will be for the LEA to decide how far and at what price, these services continue to be offered to schools now outside their direct jurisdiction. Already, the Birmingham LEA has taken steps to reclaim library books from a Small Heath secondary school, which chose to leave the local fold.

A key criticism of the legislation has been that measures such as 'opting out' amount to a stalking horse for other non-egalitarian educational goals since the underlying motive is to achieve a move away from comprehensive education. It is certainly clear that, together with the abolition of planned admission limits, the scheme facilitates popular schools becoming more selective. The corollary is that other schools in less favourable environments may accumulate children with disproportionately high concentrations of social disadvantage. The government retorts that more competition amongst schools will raise academic standards and improve efficiency. Central to the operation of such 'free trade' amongst schools is the abolition of any protectionism which might fetter the market.

Markets are supposed to provide adequate information to signal to prospective consumers the implications of their choices. This is the purpose behind the responsibility now placed on schools to publish the general test results of pupils. But the point has been made that such results "measure output rather than value added".[6] In other words, a good pass rate for school A in a prosperous catchment area compared to a moderate pass rate for school B in a depressed area may,despite appearances, mean that school B's performance is more effective in its educational achievement.Unadjusted for social background and community advantage, such results contribute little to the goal of an informed consumer electorate and may actually be confusing. While the government would insist that it has now acknowledged this dimension, it remains unclear how results are to be socially contextualised in a meaningful way.

The decomposition of the state school system into a number of competing institutions is ultimately based on this government's theory of Social Darwinism — the survival of the fittest. The real agenda behind these reforms may be the construction of: "....a three tier system made up of independent schools (the existing public and private schools and the city technology colleges), public sector schools (both grant maintained and LEA), well enough reinforced by parental choice and voluntary funding, and a third tier, an underclass of schools located in areas of poverty, forced to exist on basic funding and less cushioned than previously by discretionary funding from the LEA."[7]

## Higher Education

In January 1989 the Secretary of State also announced plans for the long-term future of higher education. The central objective was for a substantial expansion in student intake but without a corresponding increase in government spending.Instead of the current one in seven teenagers attending college, the goal was to increase this to nearly one in three by year 2014. This proposal has to be seen in the context of the UK's current performance. Whereas 45% of school leavers go on to college in the USA, and European countries like France and West Germany average around 20%, the UK's 14% ranks as one of the lowest in the advanced economies. The government's ambitious projections are to be achieved by means other than substantial new state support. Its other policy commissions and omissions testify to that. For example, the idea of sixth form maintenance grants has not been pursued. After an earlier retreat on the issue in the face of middle-class opposition, the virtues of student loans have been rediscovered. In addition, despite difficulties in attracting and maintaining university staff in some disciplines, academic salaries have been allowed to slide by 20% relative to average earnings over the Thatcher decade.

University staff appointed after 20 November 1987, together with existing staff who get promotion or switch to another university, are no longer protected by academic tenure. Inefficiency, lack of demand for courses or lack of funds are the main criteria for dismissal. Considerations of academic freedom for lecturers espousing unpopular or controversial opinions are not conceded. The University Grants Committee is being replaced by a University Funding Council, of whose 15 members at least 6 must represent commerce and industry. Under the 1988 Act, around 60 polytechnics and colleges of higher education are to be financed through a new Polytechnics and Colleges Funding Council, whereas they were formerly under LEA control. The governing bodies will comprise between 13 and 25 members, half of whom must be from business. Clearly, the commercial orientation of higher education is set to be accentuated.

One of the most contentious government proposals is the student loan scheme, whereby from 1990 grants will be frozen and students will be obliged to borrow up to £420 annually to balance the deficit. Students, particularly from working-class backgrounds, who can rely less on parental support could be borrowing a substantial sum over the period of their course. Graduates whose initial earnings fall below 85% of average national earnings might be allowed reduced repayments at that early career stage. It has been estimated that it will cost government around £100 million annually to implement the scheme (assuming a 3% annual inflation rate) and that it will not break even until the year 2020. But if no public funds are to be 'saved', how can the scheme contribute to a diversion of resources to expand the service, as was originally claimed? Further problems beset the scheme when,in early 1990, it became clear that the banks were unwilling to participate. This was a bitter blow to the government's hopes for a smooth administration of their policy.

The Loan Scheme is a very interesting initiative from the Thatcher Tories. In its earlier incarnation,it was successfully opposed, mainly by a middle class lobby on Tory MPs. But after a strategic retreat, the government has returned to the offensive. Superficially, it appears to be another example of a staged privatisation of the costs of a public service. Certainly, student campaign literature raises the suspicion that the move is a thin end of a wedge — the preliminary to a complete withdrawal of grant and perhaps even fee support. But the proposal does not privatise the funding in the sense of introducing private sector money into the service. Students are to borrow in effect from the Treasury. It does, however, privatise the problem by the placing more of the onus on students and their families.

The scheme highlights a dilemma central to the redistributional claims of much of social policy. For instance, it could be argued that since the working class remains significantly under represented amongst UK university entrants, the existing grant system has been, on the one hand, a subsidy to the middle class, while, on the other, an insufficient incentive to the working class. As in the health service, the higher education system is mostly 'exploited' by the well off, since reducing or abolishing costs of a provision increases demand for it, and in the absence of a related increase in supply, sharpens competition. In education, it is the middle class candidate who is most favourably placed to be 'competitive'. This is the paradox to which Le Grand refers:

"Hence the subsidy to higher education, although lowering the cost to working-class students in one sense (through reducing the cost once they are at college), simultaneously raises the costs elsewhere (through increasing the amount of preparation that has to be done). The net effect may be actually to increase costs, and hence discourage working-class participation."[8]

## Education in Northern Ireland

The current administrative arrangements for education in Northern Ireland was constructed around the time of local government reorganisation and the institution of Direct Rule from Westminster. The Education and Libraries (Northern Ireland) Order 1972 established five Education and Library Boards with statutory responsibility for education, libraries and the youth service. Ministry nominations accounted for 60% of the seats on the Boards, the nominees being mainly representive of the Protestant and Catholic churches and teachers. The remaining seats were available for elected district councillors.

In other words, electoral accountability is extremely weak. The central influence of the Department of Education for Northern Ireland (DENI) is further reinforced by its control over the budget. Though, like England and Wales, education in Northern Ireland is funded on the basis of both rates and taxation, in Northern Ireland a regional rate is fixed to cover many services and is contributed directly to the Consolidated Fund. It is in this administrative context that the new education proposals must be considered.

## Education Reform: The Northern Ireland Version

The Education Reform (NI) Order 1990 parallels the 1988 legislation for England and Wales, but with some important distinctions. For example, the principle of a 'common' curriculum is upheld, though in a somewhat different form. It is intended that there will be six 'areas' — English, Maths, Science and Technology, the Environment and Society (mainly History, Geography and Politics), Creative and Expressive Studies and Language Studies. Everyone will be obliged to learn a language and, after some debate, Gaelic has been accorded equal status with other European languages. This is not so different from what is proposed for Wales, where in Welsh-speaking areas, Welsh is to be a 'core' subject and elsewhere a 'foundation' subject. Superimposed on these six 'areas' are six 'themes' — Cultural Heritage, Health Education, Information Technology, Economic Awareness, Careers Education and what is called Education for Mutual Understanding (EMU).

Unsurprisingly, it is the latter theme which has provoked most comment. Ian Paisley's DUP has characterised it as an insidious form of social engineering, designed to dilute the staunchness of Ulster Protestant witness. But overall, the curriculum proposals appear to accommodate greater potential experimentation and cross-subject project work than their counterpart in England and Wales. Inclusion of the EMU theme indicates a preparedness to engage with the controversial diversities and conflicts in Northern Irish society. The detailing of cross-curriculum themes pre dates such a move in Britain, and seems to have been shaped by pilot work in Northern Ireland schools in areas such as the 11-16 curriculum.

In November 1989 the Education Department announced that it was going to slow down the introduction of the curriculum changes. The new subjects will be phased in over a three-year period up to 1992, thereby granting schools and parents an extra year of adjustment compared to the original proposal. This concession to those critical of the rapid pace of reform has arguably been influenced as much by the Department's belated recognition of the substantial resources the changes demand as by the outcome of the consultation process itself.

The standard assessment test (SATs) are also to be applied, but starting with 8 rather than 7 year olds. And this is being introduced in a region where the compulsory school entrance age is to be reduced to 4, compared to 5 in Britain, to ensure 12 years compulsory education, and where the old 11+ examination has persisted, (though in recent years in a different form), as has a selective system for secondary education. This latter characteristic has influenced a distinctive departure from the 1988 Baker Act. The 'opting out' proposals in Britain, seen by some as a prelude to the restoration of selection, have less relevance in Northern Ireland where, for example, the Voluntary Grammar schools already deal directly with DENI. The major new provision being made for direct grant maintained schools in Northern Ireland is for the 'integrated' sector of mixed-religion schools. So, for any existing school to opt for direct grant maintained status will be not so much a change from Secondary Intermediate to Grammar as a conversion from religiously segregated to integrated.

Under the last Labour administration, the Cowan working party was established to propose how secondary education could be reorganised on a non-selective basis. The incoming Tory administration in 1979 removed responsibility from the Education Boards to pursue this path. Under the new proposals, the 11+ will be scrapped as will the opportunity for 'fee paying' into Grammar schools. But the selective nature of secondary education will remain intact, even though theoretically the obligation on all schools to follow a common curriculum minimises the old academic versus technical distinctions, and with it the disparity in esteem between the two types of school. The fact is that Grammar schools have, for over 40 years, had the chance to establish their reputation for 'excellence'. Any new competition between such institutions and secondary intermediate schools begins from a patently unequal base.

This inequality may well be reinforced by two other factors. First, provision for open enrolment will permit many Grammar schools to boost their pupil numbers, creaming off still more of the most able students. The government refutes the suggestion that this amounts to selection, arguing that if any school has a surplus of places it must grant one to any requesting pupil. Only if it faces over-subscription is it able to recruit selectively. But, of course, most likely it will be the Grammar schools that find themselves with a demand rather than supply problem, and so they will have the power to select. It is only the Grammar schools which will be able to include criteria of academic performance in their admissions policy.

Second, the existing resource disparities between the two types of school may continue. The chief officer of the North Eastern Education Board, Mr Hamilton, has noted this factor:

> "I am anticipating that when financial devolution comes it will include parity of treatment for Grammar schools and the maintained or controlled sectors. If not, we are going to have two tiers of schools. Voluntary Grammar schools are paid out in advance four times a year and can earn interest on the money...."[9]

Interestingly, this issue had loomed earlier, since throughout the 1980s there has been a significant drop in secondary enrolment, particularly affecting Belfast. In the context of this contraction, DENI proposed in 1983 that intake controls into Grammar and Secondary Intermediate schools should be abolished, a view not endorsed by a report from the then local elective Assembly,[10] which argued instead for a systematic rationalisation of school provision, within the existing 73:27 pupil ratio between the Secondary Intermediate and

Grammar sectors. The decision reached by DENI in 1985 was for some intake control to be maintained.

The corollary of Grammar school 'success' in the open enrolment procedure is the threat of closure for 'failing' Secondaries, a prospect which may in turn contradict the objectives of government inner city policy. A working party report in September 1989 for the Belfast Education Board, reviewing the education changes, referred to this aspect:

"If market forces are to prevail and thus determine the closure of schools where surplus places exist, it is quite possible that significant areas of Belfast could be left without school provision. Were such a scenario to develop, the government's attempts to encourage the revitalisation of Belfast could be affected significantly — people will be reluctant to move back to live in areas where no school provision exists."[11]

## More Parent Power?

As in England and Wales, budget control is to be devolved to local school principals working with the governors. Alongside this, new procedures for direct parental representation on school governing bodies were announced in September 1989. Compulsory public meetings of parents have to be organised by each school to elect parent governors, possibly complemented by a postal ballot if parental attendance should prove poor.

While, on the surface, this appears to democratise school management, many of the problems which have already emerged in England and Wales may also apply. Given that parents will be in a minority, will they be overwhelmed by the authority of professionals on the board? Or, will they seek to represent the interests of parents as a whole, or merely those of their own children? The new Education Order also offers parents new rights to information about how their children's schools are administered, partly from the Board of Governors Annual Report, and to raise matters of concern at an annual Parents' Meeting.

## The Role of Local Education Boards

In Britain the government's new legislation erodes the element of local accountability exercised by the LEAs. In Northern Ireland where, as earlier explained, local Education and Library Boards have limited electoral accountability in any case, the impact of the legislation appears to reduce the boards' powers even further than their counterparts across the water. For example, whereas LEAs in Britain retain a role in school inspection and monitoring of implementation of the National Curriculum, the Northern Ireland Order refers to Education Board officers inspecting schools only with the specific permission of the principals. The Local Education boards have also lamented the legislation's ambiguity in other aspects such as the extent of school governors' powers to dismiss and appoint staff and the legal responsibility for curriculum provision. Despite the fact that education policy in Britain and Northern Ireland have always had divergencies, the Boards are now pressing for the maintenance of parity. The Western Education and Library Board has said that the new Order would amount to:

"a serious break with the tradition that Northern Ireland remains in step with England and Wales....The apparent lack of authority which would enable boards to play a crucial role in determining the overall framework for the education service, in achieving a clear sense of direction and in planning ahead to meet future needs is evident throughout the Draft Order".[12]

The Southern Education and Library Board had earlier suggested that the proposals would create "a remote and authoritarian DENI Inspectorate which will increasingly be seen by schools as a hostile police force...."[13] In response to these criticisms, the Education Minister pledged that the 'partnership' between the Department, Area Boards and Schools would be sustained: "Successful implementation of the reforms depend on that partnership continuing and being strengthened, while ensuring that the key decisions about the curriculum and the school's budget are in the hands of those closest in the classroom — parents, teachers and school governors".[14] Yet, the Education Order contains a potential departmental power to compel any education authority to comply with ministerial directives.

The Belfast Education Board has argued that, given the already limited electoral accountability operating in Northern Ireland, further erosion of it in the Order is particularly regrettable:

"The Board considers it to be a matter of major concern that [Article 158] will permit the Department to impose, if it so chooses, its wishes or those of the Minister, on a community which is denied effective selective representation at provincial level".[15]

## Segregated Schooling

A key distinguishing feature of Northern Ireland education is that the vast majority of schools operate on the basis of religious segregation, a long-standing pattern, formalised by the 1930 Education Act (NI). This legislation gave rise to, in effect, two main types of schools — 100% funded state 'controlled' schools, which were almost exclusively Protestant, and 'voluntary' schools, which were predominantly Catholic and in receipt of similar subsidies to Catholic schools in Britain.[16] Since the 1960s the situation has become more complicated. Many former voluntary primary and secondary schools have acquired a 'maintained' status, whereby, apart from 15% of capital costs, they receive total financial support from government in return for accommodating a minority representation on their management committees from the local Education Board. Nevertheless, the essential character of the Northern Ireland school system remains one where the influence of the churches is dominant, and the ethos, ambience, pupil intake and management of each type of school reflects a distinct religious and cultural allegiance.

There has been much contentious debate — especially since the onset of the Troubles just over 20 years ago — concerning the potentially divisive effects of segregated education. While this is stoutly refuted by the Catholic Church,[17] research on this issue is more circumspect in its conclusions. For some, the interesting point is how far the two types of school provide a common education with regard to streaming, the curriculum, and the use of corporal punishment.[18] Others remark on the way separate schooling in both its official and hidden curriculum can reinforce the social distance and prejudice between the two communities.[19] The debate belongs to the familiar and inconclusive conundrum regarding how far schools shape or merely reflect their wider society. But this intellectual impasse has not dimmed the desire of some parents in Northern Ireland to press for a third sector of integrated schools, which could genuinely encompass the diversity of the two main cultural and religious traditions. But, by 1990 integrated education accounted for just over 1% of the school population.

The response of the last Labour government to this campaign was notably tentative. In 1978 it passed an 'enabling order' to permit existing schools to change their status to 'controlled integrated schools'. But since this left the initiative still largely in the hands of a church-influenced school management system, no practical progress emerged. In the early 1980s, the integrationist lobby adopted a new tack, and established two voluntary schools of their own in Belfast, only achieving 'maintained status' when they clearly demonstrated to the Education Department the viability of their pupil numbers. Since then, a small number of similar ventures throughout Northern Ireland have operated on the same basis of self initiative and risk, receiving no significant Departmental support until they had demonstrated their viability. But recently, the government has indicated its intention to move from a passive to an active role in this regard. Integrated status will be easier to establish. Rather than being tied to a fixed percentage of pupils from each of the two religions, the school now has to demonstrate, in the words of the Education Reform Order, that it will be "likely to attract reasonable numbers of Protestant and Roman Catholic pupils". Once endorsed by the Department as an integrated school, it will receive 100% funding, whereas under current 'maintained' status it has to raise 15% of the capital costs. Moreover, integrated schools are to receive priority treatment when decisions are taken about funding new building. There is also to be provision to compensate existing trustees of segregated schools where parents vote into the integrated sector.

Those sympathetic to integrated education have welcomed these steps, albeit with some reservations. The Order does not appear to apply to nursery and special schools. The reference to a 'reasonable' mix does not encourage a serious and genuine effort to embrace the principles of integration; rather it may simply offer some schools faced with closure an expedient way to boost pupil numbers and restore their viability. And although governors of a proposed integrated school are obliged to create a school ethos capable of attracting cross-community parental support, there is no stipulation that the make-up of the governing body itself should be appropriately representative of both traditions. To achieve this might ironically infringe other government anti-discrimination legislation:

"The government is statutorily prohibited from funding bodies which discriminate. Unless integrated schools are permitted an exemption, they will have to pretend to ignore religion and culture——the converse of what integrated education is all about".[20]

The Catholic Bishops, on the other hand, have charged that the new provisions for integrated education contravene the guarantees in the Northern Ireland Constitution Act (1973) against religious discrimination. Further, they take exception to the possibility of a parental vote to transfer a school out of the Catholic system into the integrated sector:

"As the Draft Order's text now stands, a transient group of present parents can thus override the rights of other parents and the whole Catholic community. This, in our view, amounts to a serious departure from the long established tradition of governmental recognition of the rights of Catholic parents to a Catholic education for their children."[21]

In response to this concern, the Education Minister has agreed to consult the Catholic Council For Maintained Schools should a Catholic school vote to switch to integrated status. A different kind of criticism has come from Enoch Powell who has accused the government of "blatant sectarianism and discrimination" in according preferential treatment to integrated schools. In his view, it typifies how people in Northern Ireland are being induced:

"....to give up exercising a right in education which is accorded to people in Great Britain....That is what belonging to the UK ought to mean — the same law for all in Northern Ireland and the same law in Northern Ireland as in Great Britain....[instead of] holding Ulster at arms length in the hope of getting rid of it altogether".[22]

Those in Northern Ireland, like Mr Powell, who see the solution to the conflict in terms of complete political integration between the province and Britain, argue that such policy differences give succour to the IRA because they are symptomatic of an ambiguity in Britain about its relationship to Northern Ireland. But the Education Minister has given a more mundane explanation for this preference, arguing that because those parents keen on integrated education have been long deprived of the choice, justice demands a compensatory allowance, not in perpetuity, but for a few years.

Interestingly, this whole argument may have repercussions soon for schools in Britain, where presently voluntary aided or controlled church schools make up nearly one-third of the total number of schools, though educating only about 10% of all pupils. The Labour Party's education policy review suggests that equity demands that Muslim schools should also be entitled to voluntary aided status, whereby 85% of their capital costs and 100% of their running costs would be met from the public purse. For some, keen to achieve a more secular and multi-cultural character for British education, this portends of deepening separatism. Nor can Muslim feminists view with equanimity the prospect of fundamentalist schools relegating female pupils to a narrow and subservient role. But if Muslims or any other significant religious group do not feel comfortable within the existing system, withdrawal is always possible. In Northern Ireland, Ian Paisley's Free Presbyterians have taken that step and set up a number of independent schools. Only if they did depend on state support would they be obliged to teach in a less sectionalist manner under the provisions of the National Curriculum. So if Muslim schools did receive subsidy, the new legislation might help limit any tendency to instil a theocratic and sexist view of the world.

## The Business of Education?

Educational reform in Britain explicitly aims at a change in the relationship of education to the world of work. In the 1980s this concern has also been very evident in Northern Ireland. A major study relating to the experience of YTP[23] and a jointly funded DENI/EEC project, known as the Transition to Adult and Working Life (TRAWL) 1983-87, addressed aspects of this link. At a wider policy level, the Department of Economic Development (DED), in its reference to the need for a move from an 'employment' to an 'enterprise' culture, is implicitly addressing the question of what the local education system produces. Indeed the DED has co-operated with DENI in producing a version of the Compact initiative, which has been operating for some time in parts of Britain. Basically, the idea involves particular schools being connected to particular employers, who outline their skill needs so that the schools can 'bend' their courses — including day release schemes — to meet the requirement. But in one important respect its operation in Northern Ireland is to be different to that in Britain. As an editorial in the *Belfast Telegraph* commented:

> "Not only is there a scarcity of manufacturing employment, into which students can be fitted, but because of the divided school system it is impossible to offer guaranteed places — unlike the Compact system operated in Britain."[24]

One of the telling features of Northern Ireland education is the particularly skewed examination results of its pupils. While its students do better than their counterparts in England and Wales in A and O levels and CSE, it also has a higher share of students with 'no graded results' compared to England and Wales.[25] This apparent failure to provide for a substantial number of school children has implications for a weak regional economy: "....the large proportion of children in Northern Ireland who are under achieving is a potentially disadvantageous factor in securing the longer-term development of the local economy".[26]

Nominally, a primary concern of the 1988 Education Act is to address the needs of the bottom 40% of school pupils. Clearly this is a highly relevant aim in the case of Northern Ireland. But, if a major consequence of education reform in Britain is to restore selection, then it may well reproduce the negative effects of selection so evident in Northern Ireland.

## Higher Education in Northern Ireland

Higher Education in Northern Ireland has been subject to great change over the last quarter of a century. The Lockwood Report[27] followed the optimism of the Robbins Report in Britain and endorsed the need for two universities and an advanced further education college (in effect a polytechnic). Sufficient student demand to fill this capacity did not materialise for various reasons, including the impact of the Troubles, which deterred outside students while inducing greater numbers of Northern Ireland students to apply to institutions in Britain, where there was also increasing surplus capacity, post-Robbins. The recommendations of the Chilver Review,[28] charged with recommending a rationalisation of this unsatisfactory outcome, went largely unheeded by government, whose own solution has since included the amalgamation in 1984 of the region's one Polytechnic with the New University of Ulster at Coleraine and Magee College in Derry to form the University of Ulster.

This first 'polyversity' in the UK has ostensibly contributed to:

"....a widening of access to higher education along with a unique diversification of institutional provision under the umbrella of a 'university'....We are still a long way away from mass higher education but, unlike secondary level provision, higher education in Northern Ireland displays certain innovatory features worthy of future monitoring".[29]

Besides these local developments, Northern Ireland's higher education system has been subject to similar imperatives as in Britain. As in other parts of the system a more instrumental view is being taken. The intrinsic value of learning continues to receive official lip-service. But the relevance to entrepreneurial endeavour is now high on the agenda. The new business of higher education is 'business', so to speak.

Particular changes such as the removal of academic tenure; the proposed 'tracking' between those staff who will concentrate on teaching and those who will mostly research; and the overall restructuring of courses and research output, which maximises 'excellence', efficiency, private sector funding, and 'relevance' all apply to Northern Ireland as in Britain.

Also applicable is the student loan scheme. The local Minister has asserted: "Under the new proposals, the resources available to students will be increased — not reduced. This should benefit Northern Ireland students".[30] But a review[31] of the local implications suggests the possibility of a different result, including a diminished participation rate particularly among vulnerable groups such as women and lower-income families, a category in Northern Ireland which includes a disproportionately large share of Catholics. The interesting point is that women and Catholics have been increasing their representation at higher education level, a trend which may be reversed should students face new financial burdens. Moreover, Northern Ireland is already meeting another goal set by Mr Baker — increasing working-class access. Whereas, in the mid 1980s, one-fifth of all university entrants in the UK came from manual backgrounds, in Northern Ireland the corresponding figure was over one-third. Such patterns suggest that the idea of 'the middle-class sub-sidy', which worries Mr Baker on the Right and Mr Le Grand on the Left for different reasons, is less applicable in Northern Ireland. The review concludes with the observation: "There can be no doubt that in Northern Ireland there will be substantial numbers of graduates who will take a long time to earn sufficient salaries to rise above the 85% threshold , if, in fact, they ever do."

## The Current Agenda

Educational debate in the 1960s and for much of the 1970s concerned the issue of equality in terms particularly of access to, and an equitable share of, educational resources. It was apparent from a substantial body of research,[32] that social class remained a key determinant of educational attainment despite the goals of equal opportunity and meritocratic assessment in the 1944 Butler Act. The basic judgement on the post-war system was conclusive: "In none of its interpretations has equality of educational opportunity been reached".[33] Nevertheless, in these decades the emphasis in educational policy was to innovate and extend provision in an effort to improve equality of opportunity. The Plowden Report into primary education in 1967 led to an experiment in positive discrimination in favour of designated 'Priority Areas'.[34]. At the other end of the spectrum, the Robbins Report[35] declared as a key principle that: "Courses of higher education should be available for all who are qualified by ability and attainment to pursue them and who wish to do so". It might be argued that the intent behind many of these, and other policies, was always more nominal than real. Certainly, their results proved disappointing: "....despite the celebration of the four 'C's of comprehensive, compensatory, community and continual education, the gap between the least and the most favoured shows little sign of narrowing".[36]

With some resignation, educationalists discovered the simple but problematic axiom that school cannot compensate for the inequities of the wider society. But the policy drive to, at least, ameliorate the educational impact of social disadvantage retained a legitimacy, and the debate turned to the relative efficacy of improving the educational relevance, affinity and opportunity for working-class children within the system in comprehensive or community schools as compared to a more radical solution of deschooling or 'free' schooling outside the system. By the late 1970s, such concerns were overtaken by other pressing realities such as expenditure restraint. During much of this period the Far Right had been on the fringes of the debate, producing a series of so called Black Papers edited by people like Cox and Boyson, which basically mourned the passing of discipline and competition in the vain pursuit of egalitarianism.

The Thatcher decade has seen a further demotion of equality issues and a promotion instead of some of the Black Paper agenda. The notion of 'relevance' now stresses the role of education as a function of the economy. Despite falling pupil rolls, complaints from educationalists about inadequate resourcing have increased. The government's response hinges on the marketisation of the service, while at the same time devolving authority to local schools and increasing the centralisation of political control. In a range of measures Northern Ireland has followed closely in step with Britain though in some aspects, such as the contracting out of ancillary services, the pressure to follow suit has been delayed.

In the case of the Education Reform Act 1988, it is likely that DENI basically assessed the legislation for England and Wales clause by clause and replicated those parts considered applicable to the circumstances of the Northern Ireland system. But in some instances, even where Northern Ireland's divergent circumstances do pertain, there has been a policy parity, as in higher education with such measures as the student loans scheme and the abolition of academic tenure. However, the positive push towards integrated education in the Northern Ireland legislation is a significant step, leading the Director of the Northern Ireland Council for Integrated Education to predict in 1990 that this sector would account for one third of the school population within ten years.[37]

Interestingly, educational reform has been much more incremental in Scotland. While it has only had 'opting out' procedures since the Self Governing Schools Etc. (Scotland) Act 1989, it has had open enrolment since the Education (Scotland) Act 1981. The long experience of the latter has allowed some evaluation of its effects. It has been suggested that it has created a two-tier system in which those schools suffering a pupil exodus have endured subsequent resource restraint. This had in turn debilitated their efforts to deliver a quality service and thereby reinforced their decline.[38] Not all the recent educational changes in Scotland, which have paralleled those in England and Wales have been instigated by the Tory administration. For instance, in February 1990 Labour-controlled Strathclyde started a pilot project for financial devolution in 33 schools — quite similar to the proposals for local school budget control in the 1988 Education Reform Act.

# 9. Health Care: Operating Under Thatcherism

## The Northern Ireland NHS

In 1948 the Northern Ireland Parliament passed legislation to create a National Health Service in the region. There were a number of differences in organisation with the British NHS. Doctors were to be paid on a per capita basis rather than a salary plus fees for the number of patients on their register. Also, if a doctor was disqualified, he or she could appeal to the High Court rather than the Minister. Hospital property was transferred to the Hospital's Authority rather than the state, while hospitals retained their individual endowments rather than having them pooled for general distribution.

The purpose of these changes achieved the same end as in Britain but was "more in keeping with Unionist principles than those adopted in the system across the water."[1] The major dispute concerned the refusal of the main Catholic hospital, the Mater, to be fully integrated within the NHS. Nevertheless, as in Britain, the NHS became the most popular and consistently supported arm of the welfare state although it was criticised for the under-representation of Catholics in the many new jobs created.

In the 1970s, as part of the reorganisation of local services in Northern Ireland, four Health and Social Services Area Boards were established. Their function was to offer comprehensive health care, including personal social services which in England and Wales remained the responsibility of local government. Their size was expected to create economies of scale and offer greater opportunity for rational management. Moreover, the Area Boards, with a minority of elected representatives, were expected to eliminate the political bias of which previous hospital management committees had been accused.

187

# Health Care: Britain and Northern Ireland Compared

Health care expenditure per head in Northern Ireland has been greater than in England, in recent years by around 25%,[2] though if greater average morbidity is allowed for the figure would be closer to 15%. Nevertheless, there have been considerable changes in certain areas of health care.

| Table 34 | Infant Mortality Ratios as a % of the UK Average by Region | | |
|---|---|---|---|
| | 1971 | 1981 | 1987 |
| North | 104 | 96 | 96 |
| South East | 89 | 93 | 99 |
| South West | 89 | 93 | 93 |
| Wales | 103 | 113 | 104 |
| N.Ireland | 127 | 118 | 95 |
| *Source: Regional Trends, 1989.* | | | |

Table 34 indicates that the improvement in Northern Ireland's infant mortality has been dramatic. The ratios have been reduced by more than a quarter over 16 years. As for mortality rates, these show that heart disease, pneumonia and accidents are more prevalent causes of death in Northern Ireland than other areas. Cancer is a less frequent cause of death. On average, Northern Ireland citizens obtain more prescriptions (8.7 per head at a cost of £38.21 in 1987) than in the other regions, with the exception of Wales. In response, hospital provision is more extensive.

| Table 35 | Hospital Beds per 1,000 Population by Region, 1986 | |
|---|---|---|
| | Available Beds | Occupied Beds |
| Northern | 7.5 | 6.0 |
| North Thames | 6.9 | 5.8 |
| South West Thames | 7.1 | 6.0 |
| Wales | 7.7 | 6.0 |
| N.Ireland | 10.2 | 8.0 |
| *Source: Regional Trends, 1989.* | | |

Northern Ireland not only has more beds, but has the lowest occupancy rate. This fact has been used to argue for better cost improvement programmes within the Northern Ireland health authorities. Additional beds are reflected in greater expenditure per head. In 1986-87 average health expenditure per head was £386.61 in Northern Ireland compared to, for example, only £233.15 in the Northern Board. Moreover, the Northern Ireland Boards have the equivalent of 247.5 full-time staff per 10,000 population, which is 40 more than the next highest area, Wales. Thus, while Northern Ireland does have specific problems of health, its NHS has enjoyed much greater relative resources than elsewhere.

## The Economics of Health Care

Despite the unwavering popularity of the NHS in Britain, there has been a long standing debate about the economics of health care. There are two reasons:

☆ First, the growth of health care expenditure exceeded all early predictions. At the introduction of the service, it was believed that the consequent general improvement of the nation's health would, in real terms, reduce the resources that would have to be devoted to it. Yet inflation within the NHS has been faster than the rise of the retail price index, while standards of what is considered acceptable health care have risen. Further, the growing population of old people consumes greater resources and so adds to the overall cost of the system. As such, health care seems to be a bottomless pit for public expenditure. This poses particular problems for a government which has consistently claimed to be careful with the tax payers' money;

☆ Second, because health care for the majority of the population, with the exception of prescription, dental and optical charges, has been provided free of charge, it has been difficult to assess whether the NHS has been efficient in its use of resources allocated. Indeed, whatever the system of health care, this is a very thorny question. Even where the consumer pays directly for their health care, lack of knowledge can lead either to over-consumption (through hypochondria) or underconsumption (through ignorance of the meaning of symptoms). In addition, those on lower incomes would be more likely to be denied proper health care, so generating a major problem of equity.[3] Personal payment in the form of private insurance cannot resolve the situation since those who diagnose the problem, doctors, also supply the service. This results in over-supply to the few (those adequately insured) and high returns to the suppliers (in the United States, doctors' earnings are over five times higher than average earnings compared to about two and a half times in Britain). Further, it is not clear that the health of the general population benefits from this system. Thus, it is not easy to design a health care system which can simultaneously demonstrate an efficient use of resources and provide comprehensive care for the population as a whole.

The NHS has attempted to deal with the problem by using an allocation formula (RAWP), which allows for the morbidity and mortality characteristics of the recipient populations. What this cannot do is provide detailed evaluation of micro decisions. As Willetts comments:

> "Why is it that one-third of all people waiting for over a year are concentrated in one-sixth of districts? Why is it that one coronary unit operates on 200 patients a year whereas another nearby manages 600 patients for roughly the same budget? Why is it that death rates vary so much between doctors?"[4]

Clearly, for a government so preoccupied with reforming the supply side in industry and with the priority of market discipline, these are crucial questions. There is also the issue of how a universal service with free access 'subsidises' many of its users who would otherwise be able to pay through private insurance. The use of a fiscal claw-back from the higher income groups to compensate for this anomaly has not been considered acceptable in an era of reductions in personal taxation which are designed disproportionately to favour precisely such groups. From the perspective of New Right economics, the NHS is, a priori, inefficient.

## Thatcherism and the NHS

It is perhaps surprising that the task of restructuring the health service was left to the third term of Mrs Thatcher's government and that this was more in response to the unpalatable fact of babies dying for the lack of operating capacity, while nurses were up in arms about low pay, than a careful long-term strategy. Prior to that, the government only embarked on piecemeal changes. Early ministerial predictions that as much as a quarter of all health care would be provided through private insurance by the mid 1980s, proved wildly over-optimistic. The figure stabilised at around 10%.[5] Efforts to ensure more cost effective prescribing by family practitioners, through publishing a list of generic drugs, made sense in the light of the profit levels of the drugs industry. The government in fact increased prescription charges between 1979 and 1990 by over 1,500%, and raised charges for dental care. Certain changes in management, with the establishment of general managers, were implemented in line with the Griffiths proposals to increase NHS efficiency. A new emphasis on community as opposed to residential care emerged in the mid 1980s. This was designed to provide a low cost alternative to the residential needs of the elderly and has been condemned as putting a new burden on female relatives in the community. And the privatisation of certain ancillary services was enforced on health authorities. But the central structure of the NHS remained untouched.

Nevertheless, the system of health care continued to encounter many problems. In 1985 the death of an Oxfordshire mother, who had been left ignorant of a positive test for cervical cancer, sharply highlighted the weaknesses of the screening system. The government had ignored the recommendations of one of its own committees to restructure the programme.[6] In the following year, it was revealed that a majority of hospital kitchens failed to meet food hygiene standards. In the late 1980s Listeria and Salmonella scares abounded and ended the career of one government Minister.

Following the general election of 1987 amid an intense debate about the quality of health care in Britain, the Prime Minister defended her government as having a record to be proud of in spending on the NHS — a real increase of 30% since 1979. In cash terms public spending on health had increased from £8 billion in 1978-79 to £23 billion in 1988-89. In fact, an annual increase of at least 2% is necessary to allow for changes in demography and patterns of care. Moreover, a large part of the increase in NHS pay levels followed from the recommendations of the Clegg Commission, established by the previous Labour government. This cannot be attributed to the generosity of the Conservatives.

Taking such factors into account, the House of Commons Social Services Select Committee calculated that health and community services were underfunded by £1.325 billion between 1980 and 1986.[7] In this respect, Webster comments: "Taking Mrs Thatcher's term of office as a whole, the average real rise in NHS expenditure on current goods and services is smaller than that of any previous administration."[8]

Moreover, in the international context, Britain spends a relatively low proportion of GDP on health. In 1987 public health expenditure in Britain was 5.3% of GDP compared to 6.5% in France. In the United States' largely private system, the proportion of GDP spent on health care is nearly twice that of Britain.[9] Yet, on indicators like life expectancy and infant mortality, Britain out-performs the United States. The explanation lies with the greater number and higher cost of medical inputs in the United States — more caesarians per 1,000 births, more hysterectomies etc. — while the impact of health care has to be measured by outputs, i.e., less illness in the population. Even with greater expenditure, higher cost supply and more limited access to the system can reduce the overall standards of health care. Nevertheless, by European standards, spending in Britain has been insufficient. If Britain increased its health spending in 1989-90 to match the OECD average, the figure would have been £36.6 billion rather than the £25 billion allocated.

Greater pressure has also been put on the NHS as a result of other social and economic changes, principally the growth of unemployment, poverty and homelessness. The publication of the Black Report on inequalities in health was delayed because its conclusions found little favour with government. But another report in the late 1980s, from the British Medical Association, argued·

"Allowing deprivation to persist on the present scale is neither strategically advisable nor morally defensible".[10]

This growth of need consumed health care resources without allowing for significant improvement in service. Notwithstanding the failure of the Conservatives' record to match their rhetoric (the NHS is "safe in our hands"), an undoubted sensitivity to health care issues has remained. It has been suggested[11] that this has much to do with the special character of the NHS in which the middle-classes are both the primary suppliers and consumers of the service. The NHS provides substantial employment for the professional and managerial classes, who also make much greater use of its services than those in manual occupations.[12] While this group are in favour of public expenditure restraint in general, because of its implications for their personal tax burden, it is unwilling to see the NHS, as opposed to say public sector housing, bear the brunt of expenditure cuts.

The prediction that the middle-class would turn overwhelmingly to private health care proved unfounded and so the defence of the existing NHS remained explicitly in its interest. Since this group is also crucial to the electoral fortunes of Conservativism, the government has had to be more cautious about adopting measures that would alienate it. It was only in January 1988, after nearly 9 years in office, that the government announced a wide ranging review of the NHS. The battle that ensued between the government and the British Medical Association exploded any easy assumptions about a cosy relationship between the Conservatives and health care professionals.

## The NHS Review

There are two interpretations about why a fundamental review of the NHS was initiated in 1988. Robin Cook, Labour's spokesman on health, argued that the long-term aim of the Tories has been to replace a public health service with one based on market criteria. The difficulty in effecting this transformation was that research and opinion poll evidence strongly indicated that the electorate remained attached to the NHS. Since the political cost of their hostility was too high, the government has tried to claim that it was restructuring rather than dismantling the NHS. Kenneth Clarke was appointed in order to disarm critics and he was given a £1 million budget for the presentation of the White Paper, an expensive piece of packaging.

According to this view, the Tories aim to move to a model based on private insurance, possibly with vouchers for those on low incomes; to bring private money into state medical care; and to encourage cost-cutting by means of competition within the system. An additional goal was to depoliticise health care by devolving more responsibility to practitioners/managers so that waiting lists and child deaths would no longer be blamed on the government but on those who directly ran the system. The proposals emerging from the review have been a most significant step in that direction. The NHS is yet another victim of the Thatcher 'permanent revolution', the drive to press on with changes rather than consolidate those already implemented and move remorselessly towards an uncontaminated social market economy.

An alternative interpretation is that the government initiated the NHS Review in response to severe political problems resulting from claims that the health service was in a terminal state. By the end of 1987, medical practitioners, the Royal Colleges and a wide range of political figures were claiming an acute crisis in health care. The most potent symbol of the crisis was the Birmingham baby, David Barber, whose vital heart operation was only carried out after five postponements and a court case. It was claimed that this dreadful case was merely the tip of an iceberg of falling standards, ward closures and growing waiting lists. The proportion of GDP spent on health care was actually falling in contrast to what was happening in almost every other developed country. The level of protest, and the potential political difficulties associated with it, created a dilemma for government policy. It could not give a blank cheque to the NHS since that would contradict more general political and fiscal objectives. Nor could it appear to be inactive because of the damage being done to its standing in the opinion polls. Its solution was to announce a review in order to create the space needed to consider the options carefully. Moreover, the Prime Minister was convinced that much of the difficulty lay in inefficient practices rather than a lack of resources, and this conviction heavily influenced the subsequent White Paper's proposals. Whether the review was an element in a long-term strategy or an ad hoc response to political pressure, its proposals published in January 1989 sought fundamentally to reorganise the basis of NHS operation. The claim by the Health Minister, Kenneth Clarke, that it was "a change of pace rather than a fundamental change of direction" is hard to sustain. There were three key proposals:[13]

☆ "Major hospitals will be able to apply for a new self-governing status as NHS hospital trusts". Although technically within the NHS, these trusts would be able to market their services freely, negotiate their own rates of pay and even borrow funds for capital development. They would be in a competitive environment and therefore have an incentive to attract patients.

☆ "Each health authority's duty will be to use the funds available to it to secure a comprehensive service, including emergency services, for its population...." Thus the function of authorities would be to buy care from NHS hospitals, NHS trusts or the private sector within the limits of their budgets. A market for major health care is to be created in which hospitals may sell their services freely and authorities will be equally free to buy.

☆ The attempt to create a surrogate internal market for health care was to be completed by reorganising GP practices. "Large GP practices will be able to apply to have their own budgets for buying a range of services direct from hospitals." Similarly, GPs were to be encouraged to compete for patients, while patients would be equally free to choose their GPs.

The proposals were clearly based, once again, on a belief in the efficacy of competition, even in a field as complicated as health care. Earlier, we pointed to arguments which suggest that free competition does not necessarily lead to either the optimal use of resources or the best standards of care for the maximum number of patients. Peter Kellner of *The Independent*[14] has summarised the arguments against the proposals. While the government's rhetoric emphasised consumer sovereignty, the consumers would in fact be GPs and health authorities rather than patients. The possibility then exists that the interests, and hence decisions, of the real consumers will diverge from those of patients. For example, bulk order contracts signed between a health authority and a hospital for a certain type of operation may mean that patients are forced to go to that hospital even if inconvenient. The quality of health care may also deteriorate: "It is impossible to introduce incentives to greater efficiency by saving costs — as the reforms do — without also putting downward pressure on quality."[15]

One of the most serious concerns is that patients with chronic illnesses, who are therefore expensive to treat, might, if for example they moved house, find it difficult to get onto a GP's register. The latter's concern with managing a budget might inhibit him or her from accepting "hard to treat" patients. Robin Cook described the reforms as: "A prescription for a health service run by accountants for civil servants and written by people who will always put a healthy balance sheet before healthy patients."[16]

Following the White Paper's publication, eight detailed working papers were produced and 29 project groups were set up to introduce the changes. In an internal Health Department document,[17] it was mentioned that: "The Secretary of State is anxious to minimise the latter [consultation with interested parties] which could seriously slow up the process of implementation". In public the Minister welcomed "contributions, constructive criticism and alternative suggestions, so long as they are aimed at putting the White Paper proposals into practice by 1991". The contradictions in that statement seem to have escaped the Minister.

The NHS reforms, rather than solving problems for the government, generated many more. The medical establishment in the shape of the Royal Colleges and the BMA were sceptical about the benefits and incensed by the virtual absence of consultation. During 1989 the BMA engaged in a Saatchi & Saatchi-style publicity campaign against the proposals, making use of the same kind of clever advertising so often employed by the government itself. In August the Commons Social Services Committee reported that there were significant gaps in the proposed changes and that the programme could jeopardise standards of health care. The aim of creating an internal market within the NHS by 1991 was branded as impossibly optimistic and it was suggested that the government was trying to move too fast. Into the 1990s, typified by the long running ambulance drivers' dispute, the NHS continued to be a thorn in the side of the Conservative government.

## Rationalising Health Expenditure in Northern Ireland

Even before the NHS Review, the Department of Health and Social Services in Northern Ireland was attempting to rationalise the costs of health care. The Regional Strategic Plan for the Health and Personal Social Services 1983-88 assumed that resources would not increase in real terms by more than 1% per year, half of which was to be found from greater efficiency. The then Health Minister, Chris Patten, summarised the position: "....until the national economy recovers and the industrial base is strengthened, it would be unrealistic to expect further substantial growth in spending."[18]

The plan attempted to prioritise a number of key areas which would be the major recipients of resources: selected acute hospital services; services for the elderly; services for the mentally handicapped; maternal and child care services; social services for children and young persons. At the same time, the general emphasis was on raising efficiency, improving cost effectiveness and mobilising voluntary effort.

In 1987 the new Health Minister, Richard Needham, introduced a further five-year plan. In line with developments in the British NHS, the focus was on the development of community care, health education and prevention. The theme of achieving greater efficiency in the hospital services was reiterated.[19] Targets for cash savings and improvements in productivity were in line with those for health authorities in Britain.

When Richard Needham announced the following year's spending allocations in November 1987, it became clear that cost reduction in the health service was a priority. Spending was to rise by just over 5% compared to 6.4% in England. The Minister acknowledged that:

"In maintaining the momentum of change and development, Boards will face difficulties....Boards will have to sustain their efforts to maximise cost improvement programmes. There is also a margin available for development but the pace of that development will obviously depend to some extent on the efforts made by Boards to improve efficiency and thereby release resources for use within the service."[20]

The higher spending per head on health in Northern Ireland was to be reduced through the more efficient use of resources. It was argued, for example, that the proportion of empty beds in the region's hospitals was greater than in equivalent regions, while the duration of time spent in hospitals was also greater. Though as Odling-Smee pointed out: "To people who only look at throughputs and percentage bed occupancy, allowing an old man to stay in hospital an extra day whilst social workers get his house warmed up is not a mark of quality."[21]

The four Area Health Boards were to receive additional resources of £31 million, an increase of 5.2% on the previous year's total. Since inflation was forecast at 4.5%, the real addition was only about £4.5 million or less than 1%. In any case, the prediction for inflation was an underestimate, so health care received no real increase for the year. For the level of service to correspond to the resources allocated, there was to be a 20% reduction in the number of acute hospital beds and in the number of people in long stay psychiatric and mental handicap hospitals.[22] A public row over this between the chairman of the Eastern Health Board, by far the largest, covering nearly half of Northern Ireland's population, and the Minister coincided with the former not being reappointed for another term. However, in March 1988, £5 million was transferred from housing expenditure while Belfast saw some of its biggest demonstrations against cuts in health care. In the end the Area Boards received over £630 million for 1988-89.

For 1989-90, total resources were increased to £692.9 million.[23] However, the impact of the Review Body pay awards, including a 17.4% increase in the wages bill for nurses, accounted for much of the increase. Boards were expected to maintain cost improvement programmes of at least 1%—double what had been set as the goal in the 1983 regional strategy. The Eastern Health Board announced plans to save £3.5 million over the financial year. This was to be achieved by "closing beds, reviewing staffing levels, getting tougher on overtime and hoping for savings through competitive tendering." A working party was recommended to look at the overlap of services between the three Belfast central hospitals and to examine the opportunities for rationalisation. In turn, this has led to proposals to curtail emergency services. At the same time, the Eastern Board embarked on a process of centralising certain services at the cost of rural provision. A report prepared by doctors, councillors and district committee members, 'A Patient's View',[24] argued that many potential patients did not possess cars and would have extreme difficulties in travelling to Belfast. By 1989-90 the level of expenditure per head in Northern Ireland was 23% greater than in England, demonstrating greater convergence than before. Thus, although health spending has tended to remain higher than in Britain for most of the 1980s, the Northern Ireland Health Service has experienced similar pressures on resources as the NHS. In Chapter Two we argued that the "lavishly endowed" health service in the region had to be seen in the context of the levels of deprivation and violence as well as greater morbidity rates. In the absence of precise analysis of the relationship between health and other social characteristics, it is difficult to say what should be the exact level of health expenditure in Northern Ireland. What the government is undoubtedly doing, however, is trying to harmonise health care expenditure with that in Britain.

## Privatising Ancillary Services

A further aspect of the health reforms in Britain has been the enforced privatisation of hospital ancillary services. In Northern Ireland, the attempts by the DHSS to effect similar changes have encountered considerable opposition. In August 1989 the health union, NUPE, claimed to have access to documents of the Eastern Board which proposed to cut 500 jobs through privatisation. The union called a day-long strike in protest. However, at the beginning of September the Eastern Board rejected a proposal from its general purposes committee that three private firms should be given cleaning contracts. The reasons given for the decision referred to the loss of jobs, the problem of ensuring quality and the maintenance of good staff relationships. Although the health unions were delighted, there were fears that the Minister, now Lord Skemersdale, would either force the Board to carry out the government's directive, or deduct the anticipated savings of £250,000 from future fund allocations. In any case, the resistance of the Board was short-lived. At its next meeting, under pressure from the Department, it agreed to implement the competitive tendering exercise after all. Thus, while the pace of privatisation has been slower in Northern Ireland, the level of opposition from Area Boards has not been a match for the power of the Department. Even though the Board members, largely appointed by the Minister, were anxious to demonstrate their autonomy from Departmental diktat and a certain amount of solidarity with their workforce, the reality of centralised control and centralised funding was decisive in the end.

## The NHS Review and Northern Ireland

The central provisions of the NHS Review are to be fully applied in Northern Ireland. The major hospitals will be able to opt for trust status and the larger GP practices will be able to control their own budgets.[25] Given differences in structure and legislation, the timetable for the introduction of the reforms is to be slightly different. In addition, a number of measures specific to Northern Ireland will also be introduced:

☆ The Health and Social Services Boards are to be reconstituted so as to eliminate representatives of professional bodies and District Councils. The Minister described their role as "mission impossible" attempting to combine a representative with a managerial role. The Boards are to be exclusively managerial bodies.

☆ The previous monitoring bodies, the District Committees, are to be abolished and replaced with four Area Committees. This will significantly reduce the number of monitoring bodies.

☆ Major acute hospitals are to have unit general managers to provide a "local management focus".

☆ Boards are to be allocated funds in proportion to the populations they serve.

☆ And a unified management structure is to be introduced for the Belfast teaching hospitals, the Royal Victoria and the City Hospital.

Seven working papers have been produced to provide greater detail of the changes.

Within the region, the Review proposals attracted similar criticism to that made in Britain. The deputy Northern Ireland officer of the Irish Congress of Trades Unions claimed: "These pressures will result in a two-tier health service, the loss of comprehensive local services and the closure of 'less competitive' hospitals".[26] The local secretary of the Institute of Health Services Management was more cautious in expressing a similar concern: "The Institute believes that safeguards would need to be developed to ensure that comprehensive services can be provided to communities." The Association of District Committees (to be abolished as a result of the reforms) argued that: "The government is trying to introduce too many new ideas without being sure that they will work...."[27] and warned that they would lead to a reduction of consumer representation within the region. There is no evidence that any of these reservations will modify or delay the implementation of the proposals.

The Health Service in Northern Ireland has borne almost the full brunt of the Thatcher revolution. Although its funding base was higher than in England and Wales and the levels of provision remain superior, there have been consistent attempts to enforce rationalisation, bed closures and productivity increases in order to bring funding more into line with Britain. Competitive tendering has also been introduced as means of saving resources, but has encountered greater obstacles. The Area Boards were unable to hold out for long, given the wide degree of coercive powers possessed by the Department. The proposals of the NHS Review are to be fully implemented with the additional removal of levels of participation and consumer accountability.

# 10. Conclusion

## Thatcherism and Northern Ireland: An Agenda of Change or a Change of Agenda?

Throughout this book, two questions have predominated. To what extent can Thatcherism be regarded as a distinctive and coherent political entity? And what has been its impact on Northern Ireland?

In our view, Thatcherism can be regarded as a distinctive development in British politics. In the first instance, Thatcher and a relatively small group of confidantes were able to mount a successful struggle for control of the Conservative Party. Even though at the time it was not obvious who was the most powerful figure within the group, they all shared the belief that both Britain and the Tory Party had been steadily undermined by the compromises and indecision of 30 years of social democracy. The transition was all the more remarkable because almost the first formal electoral process within the Conservatives to choose a party leader, produced not only a female leader but one who espoused a brand of politics that had earlier marginalised Enoch Powell. The effect has been described by Denis Healey as taking the Conservative Party from the landlords and giving it to the estate agents.

The process of change was fed by a ferment of ideas generated by the Radical Right. Such ideas were given a new legitimacy and seriousness through having access to a sympathetic leader of a major party, while the ideas, in turn, helped provide her with an agenda. The combination has resulted in a new and clear Conservative project. Its basic rationale has been to restore market supremacy in the belief that Britain's long-term economic decline was attributable to the erosion of enterprise through the growth of welfarism and corporatism. In addition, there had been a failure of resolute leadership in domestic and foreign policy generally. The nature of the project was to reverse both in order to create a reinvigorated Britain. Thatcherism emerged as a response to a 'crisis of governability'. It was a dynamic politics determined to unsettle the complacency of many British institutions, operate a Cabinet unimpeded by internal debate or doubt, and resist being 'bossed around' by foreigners.

This does not imply that a pre-existing blueprint of strategic changes was available at the beginning. Rather, there was a general assumption about the efficacy of market forces which were to be applied to a variety of economic and social policies. As a recent *Guardian* editorial commented: "She believed, in 1979, that she had inherited the leadership of a land enmeshed in liberal pessimism to which bracing poultices could be applied."[1]

But, in practice, this conviction was moderated in a number of ways. Certain areas, like the NHS, had proved historically popular and their reform had to be approached with caution. In addition, there were political restraints on imposing changes in regions where both the Thatcher ideology has had less legitimacy and where a greater tradition of political autonomy existed — Scotland, Wales and in particular, Northern Ireland. And finally, there have been fields of policy which have not been subject to a consistent application of principle — the abandonment of certain monetary targets in the mid 1980s being a classic example, or the jittery raising of interest rates in 1989 in response to the overheating of the economy particularly in the South East, itself a product of the dilution of regional policy.

A further dimension to this political transformation was a changing relationship between government and the civil service, between a political party and the state. The traditional view of the neutrality of the state, long dismissed as a figment by Marxists like Miliband,[2] has now been called into question by even liberals and social democrats. Examples abound of ways in which the security of the state has been treated as indistinguishable from the needs of the government. The Thatcher administration's conduct of a secret war in the South Atlantic was protected to the extent of prosecuting a senior civil servant, Clive Ponting, for exposing unwanted detail. There has been constant interference with those sections of the civil service responsible for the gathering and publishing of statistics. This has been most obvious in sensitive areas like unemployment and poverty, but has also extended to the trade figures and the calculation of inflation. There have also been claims that government information has become party propaganda, for instance, with issues like the poll tax and water privatisation, while government's advertising budget has increased from £20 million to £120 million since 1979. Speculation persists that the Information Service in Downing Street, under Bernard Ingham, has not merely significantly increased its powers of control over the flow of departmental information, but has, on occasion, been more than 'economical with the truth'. The real stories behind sagas such as Westland and Stalker may never emerge. Finally, it has been argued that the process of public appointments, particularly in the fields of broadcasting and the arts, has been more than usually susceptible to political influence.

Thus, the party which entered office with the slogan of 'rolling back the state' has overseen an aggrandisement of state power, an attempt to amalgamate government with the state and a much increased centralisation of state control. This needs perhaps to be qualified by a recognition that, after 10 years in office, the policies of a government tend to become the new norm. A high proportion of the civil service will not have served under any other government. Moreover, its partisan activities do not mark a complete departure from, as much as a development of, previous practices. As Bernard Crick comments: "She has only carried to a destructive extreme the already dangerously swollen powers of her predecessors."[3] Indeed, the latest publication of the diaries of Tony Benn demonstrates a similar desire to subordinate civil servants, only from a Left perspective. However, in that case, the Minister was restrained by the Prime Minister whereas, over the past decade, this impulse has come from the Prime Minister herself.

Thatcherism is characterised, therefore, by both a shift of power within the Conservative Party, as well as a distinctive political and economic project. Its implementation has seen a centralisation of authority, erosion of the 'autonomy' of the civil service and enhancement of the power of the state.

A further dimension, much discussed by the Left, concerns the issue of hegemony. Martin Jacques,[4] for example, has argued that Thatcherism has to be understood in terms of a crisis of hegemony generated by Britain's international decline, by changes in the nature of class and production and by the emerging contradictions in welfarism and Keynesianism. These produced a sense of insecurity and loss of traditional national identity. The arrival of a dominant figure, apparently with clear ideas about what was required, with very little capacity for self-doubt and with a strong tendency towards an anti-intellectualist populism, fitted well with the nation's desire to be rescued. Thatcherism thus represented a shift in hegemony, a radical change in popular consciousness, as significant as the Post-War Settlement. By implication, it would therefore be deeply rooted and durable.

It is important, of course, to analyse the phenomenon of Thatcherism in terms of fundamental changes taking place outside the arena of formal politics. The evidence of the past decade, however, suggests that the ideological impact of Thatcherism has been less than universal or even consistent. This has been manifest in the results of Social Attitudes surveys which, in key areas, demonstrate a stubborn resistance to her world view. Indeed, in the very recent period, the Prime Minister herself has shown signs of growing introspection and even defeatism. Her September 1989 speech at the Guildhall reflected a belated recognition that human nature was less mutable than she had supposed ten years earlier and that certain fundamental problems remained untouched by her revolution. And even those who argued most forcefully that Thatcherism was a formidable, long-term phenomenon, are beginning to predict its demise. It would appear that its forward march has been halted.[5] An NOP survey for the *Independent* (30 October 1989) registered one of the lowest popularity ratings for a Prime Minister (only 24% support) since polling began.

It may be that Mrs Thatcher has finally exhausted the appeal of an autocratic leader, having mistaken obduracy for consistency and confused prejudice with principle. In the aftermath of the Lawson affair, she did appear to accept her mortality by referring in an interview for the Sunday Correspondent to her probable departure after the next election. However, she quickly retreated from this position and in later interviews declared that by 'popular acclaim' she was persuaded to stay on and on. Nevertheless, this new flush of confidence did not pre-empt a leadership election. Although her campaign was run with the seriousness of a general election effort and she obtained 85% of the votes cast by Tory MPs, the election fed fresh doubts about her staying power.

However, even if Thatcherism is approaching its autumn, the broader economic and social forces which helped create the phenomenon are still in place. Pervasive transformations in the global economy have exercised a decisive influence both on the scope and content of her agenda. Current British politics does have to be set in the context of the international reorganisation of industry that is occurring, both in terms of its global relocation and the introduction of systems of production. The new international division of labour, in part a function of the greater mobility enjoyed by transnational capital, has disturbed the traditional dichotomy in the world economy between a dependent and primarily agricultural periphery and a dominant industrial core.[6]

Modern capitalism is no longer characterised by medium-sized companies with particular urban and regional loyalties, and operating primarily within national boundaries. Rather, it is a system dominated by international financial and industrial corporations, with monopolistic tendencies and an expansive global reach. In their quest for optimum conditions for capital investment and accumulation, they have been internationalising their operations more intensively in recent times.[7]

The related emergence of newly industrialising countries (NICs), together with the current pre-eminence of Japan, has tilted the world's economic axis heavily in favour of the Pacific Basin. A recent publication from the European Commission comments: "New factories employing 10, 15 or 20,000 people are a feature of China and the Pacific Basin, not of Europe today".[8]

Britain, as a relatively weak economy within the European Community, which is itself less significant within the global economy, has felt the effects of such trends in a particularly acute form. Since the late 1970s, the trend in manufacturing trade between the UK and the rest of the EC has been one of increasing deficit, reaching nearly £5 billion by the mid 1980s. Indeed between 1979 and 1984, when UK manufactured exports to the EC had an increase of 66% by volume, imports from the EC increased by 300%. In 1986 the UK's imports of EC goods and services were equal to 12% of its GDP, while its exports were equal to only 9.3%.[9]

Europe may be central to the fate of Thatcherism. Her inability to adapt to the next steps in building more powerful EC institutions and the reordering of Eastern Europe has isolated her within the Council of Ministers and generated enemies within her own party. In the past it was the Labour Party that appeared to flounder over its attitude to the EC. Now a similar set of ambiguities has afflicted the ruling party. The resistance to the Exchange Rate Mechanism, the Social Charter and faster European integration have given the Prime Minister, if not the entire party, an isolationist label. In July 1989 a report by two members of the West German Chancellor's office developed a sophisticated schema for a Europe of 'concentric circles'. The original Community of six, together with other countries committed to the concept, would form a United States of Europe. By implication, Britain would be excluded from the process. The second circle would comprise the remaining EC members, together perhaps with new entrants like Austria and Norway in a looser federation, something like the existing Community. The third circle would involve a structure similar to EFTA covering not only Switzerland, Sweden and Finland but also some of the East European economies like Hungary and Poland. The final component would be a European-wide trading system that would also embrace the Soviet Union. If this scenario was to be realised, then the existing structure of the EC would be disrupted as some members embarked on full integration while others, like Britain, held back. Previous allies, like the United States, would appear to have abandoned Britain in this respect and sought a closer relationship with West Germany. In such circumstances, Britain's influence would be even further diminished.

One approach made by the Thatcher government in response to Britain's decline, relative to its European partners, has been to liberalise not only labour but also capital markets. The government has argued that with industrial and financial capital increasingly operating at an international level, the British economy must be progressively opened up to the global market. In this respect, it is interesting to note that the Westland crisis, which was perceived primarily in political terms, also indicated the degree to which predatory transnational companies regard ailing British industries as ripe for takeover. One result could be that dynamic sectors of the UK economy might predominantly consist of the branch plants of Japanese and US corporations seeking access to EC markets. Another alternative would be for the UK, despite its relatively weak position in the EC, to place its hope in greater industrial collaboration at the European level. Both choices imply a resignation to the demise of much of the UK's independent manufacturing base.

There is thus a sharp disjuncture in Thatcherism between its populist rhetoric about the pursuit of national sovereignty and the virtues of a small business mentality as an approach to economic regeneration, and the government's constant accommodation with transnational corporations, facilitating their ability to operate in Britain. Admittedly, many of these are companies based in Britain, but their strategic perspective and sphere of activity are essentially global. The Thatcher agenda, therefore, is not only a set of ideas espoused by the Prime Minister, but is heavily influenced by these wider processes.

This analysis suggests that many Conservative policies must be understood in the context of such broader changes. Traditional, and now declining, industries as large employers of labour have been as much the victim of the changing nature of world industrialism as of an uncaring Prime Minister. From a trade union perspective, Mrs Thatcher is frequently perceived as an avenging force, for example, crushing the miners for the victory they achieved in 1974. But, in fact the government regarded the traditional British trade union form of labour organisation as an obstacle to industrial restructuring and consequently the legal and other rights of trade unions have been undermined. Similarly, the Left has viewed the government's original deliberate policies to increase unemployment as a vindictive attempt to discipline the working class; but it must be appreciated that changes in the technology of production were decimating the numbers employed in any case.

However, the political dimension remains of considerable importance. In other European countries with stronger economies, the opportunity has existed to buy off organised labour so as to achieve the necessary changes — hence the Social Charter for 1992. The British government's strategy has been to secure compliance more through coercion than consent. But though the role of Thatcherism has been to facilitate rather than originate industrial restructuring, to regard her government as simply the instrument of transnational capital would be mistaken.

This issue is part of a wider discussion about the role of the state in modern capitalism. As a very truncated account of the debate, one view claims that the state operates primarily at the behest of capital. While the degree of the state's autonomy and the general independence of politics from economics is debatable, this view portrays the state as acting in a facilitative rather than directive relationship to capital, if only because political success is held to be mostly contingent on the performance of the economy. In this way the imperative of the private sector to maximise profit becomes scarcely distinguishable from the public good of growth and affluence.[10]

Our contention is that while the state does operate in general in the interests of capital, and therefore must take account of shifts in the location of investment and transformations of the production process, its autonomy may be reduced in times of crisis but is never eliminated. Thus, although the Thatcher agenda has been heavily influenced by structural changes in the economy, it has not been completely determined by these.

So far, we have indicated our understanding of Thatcherism and its relationship to broader changes that are taking place. This leaves the question of its relevance to Northern Ireland. Some local commentators are certain that

Thatcherism has had a clear cut impact on the region. Responding to the prospect of the Tory Party starting its own organisation in Northern Ireland, an editorial in the main local evening newspaper commented:

"Local Tory candidates will have to support the Conservative election manifesto, and economic policy will prove hard to sell to a Northern Ireland electorate which has felt the full force of the chill wind of Thatcherism."[11]

Yet, the review of several areas of policy undertaken in previous chapters indicates that the application of Thatcherism in Northern Ireland has been notably uneven. The significance of this should not be overstated, since some divergence from the agenda is also apparent in Scotland and Wales. For at least two recent Secretaries of State (James Prior in Northern Ireland and Peter Walker in Wales), their regions have been places of exile, the consequence of irredeemable 'wetness'. One compensation to soften the blow of exile has been the central government's acceptance of their greater freedom to develop interventionist strategies, even where these run contrary to the general tenor of Thatcherite policy. However, in the future Northern Ireland will be less favoure. Public expenditure projections up to 1993 suggest that growth in Northern Ireland has come to a halt and may even fall behind growth rates in Britain.

In addition, Northern Ireland has been largely immune to the hegemony of Thatcherism. The government's social agenda has been resisted not only by social democrats like the SDLP, Alliance and the Workers' Party, but even by right-wing Unionists in Ian Paisley's DUP. There has been an attempt to import Toryism into Northern Ireland, but, despite the recognition of local Conservative Associations and limited electoral success in local government, their showing in the European election was only about 50% of what had been anticipated. Nevertheless, at various times, different groups have silently applauded Mrs Thatcher's resolution. For instance, the Loyalists were gratified to see her stand firm against the demands behind the Republican hunger strike. Similarly, Nationalists approved her stout resistance to the opposition mounted by Loyalists against the Anglo-Irish Agreement. Indeed, the Anglo-Irish Agreement itself is an interesting example of her capacity occasionally to transcend her own prejudices and instincts. Just as the Lancaster House settlement reached an accommodation with radical Zimbabwean leaders such as Robert Mugabe, so this Agreement involved a diminution of British sovereignty which runs counter to her strong posturing on sovereignty in other areas.

This inconsistency corresponds with the notion that, in any case, Thatcherism is not a uniform political experience embracing the whole of the UK. Some have emphasised the relative insulation of the Celtic Fringe. But in large areas of the North, where Labour continues to have strong electoral representation, there also persists a political culture inimicable to many of the appeals of Thatcherism.

In the case of Northern Ireland, one important factor accounting for the divergence has been a history of an independent administration. A legislative and administrative framework pre-existed Direct Rule and had to be accommodated in the development of policy. The necessity to produce special legislation for Northern Ireland in the form of Orders in Council alone helps to account for the time lag in introducing particular measures. Also, legislation had to be drafted to fit in with the forms of existing provision. For example, prior to 1979, local authorities in Northern Ireland had already lost much of their substantive powers. One key feature of Conservative strategy in Britain has been to bring local government under greater control. This has been unnecessary in Northern Ireland. Indeed, it is all the more remarkable that similarities do appear where legislation has been largely informed by this imperative. Moreover, the delay involved in Orders in Council allows time to provide for some of the unforeseen problems which, by that stage, may have emerged in its implementation in Britain. For instance, it may well be the case that Housing Action Trusts (HATS) will not feature in the new Northern Ireland Housing Order. This is not merely because the Northern Ireland Housing Executive already possesses potential powers in this regard, but also because of the disappointing experience of the HATs implementation so far in Britain. Further, the higher level of social need in Northern Ireland has been generally recognised, and this has afforded an opportunity to obtain a greater share of public spending. This again has two dimensions: the necessity to make up for a backlog of Unionist neglect; and second, because of an ailing economy, the greater concentration of social need. This has to be qualified it must be said, by the recognition that in more recent years, there has been a greater degree of policy convergence, as exemplified by recent statements from the Department of Economic Development about the necessity for an 'enterprise culture'.

Another feature of the situation has been the fact that a substantial minority in Northern Ireland not merely reject the Thatcher government, but oppose British rule itself. A certain section of this minority carry their opposition to the point of guerrilla war. The last Labour Secretary of State, Roy Mason, responded by relatively generous social policies on the one hand, and a strong military posture on the other. Undoubtedly, aspects of this policy persisted under the Conservatives. Nearly all the Conservative Secretaries of State have referred to the need for a comprehensive policy, involving the social and the economic as well as the military dimension, in resolving the crisis. This backdrop of violence remains an important factor affecting the whole range of Conservative policy options. In some respects, it has influenced the agenda. This has been particularly so in the aftermath of the Anglo-Irish Agreement by which the government of the Irish Republic has had a greater, though still very limited, capacity to influence social policy.

Additionally, speculation has persisted that the United States has taken a greater interest in Northern Ireland affairs in recent years. Both the US and Irish governments seem to believe that a more visibly fair allocation of social resources can help to undermine violence. Also, British governments have been anxious to claim that they have no interest in reproducing the patterns of sectarian disadvantage that persisted under Unionism. Even marginally to alleviate these problems in a period of unsteady economic growth, requires acceptance that more public resources will be required. Of course, many critics of the British government are cynical about its determination in this respect, and, would in any case argue that patterns of sectarian disadvantage are too deeply entrenched to be ameliorated by such modest levels of intervention.

The argument so far has addressed the degree to which policies developed in Britain in the 1980s have been applied to Northern Ireland. There is, however, also a sense in which some of these British policies have been informed by prior developments within the region. The debate about the degree to which policies of repression have been exported to Britain has been well rehearsed. As *Labour Research* comments:

"Northern Ireland remains the testing ground for many government policies. The use of rubber and plastic bullets, together with CS gas, as a method of crowd control was first seen in operations in Northern Ireland in the 1970s. Since the Conservatives took office, these methods have been transported to the rest of the UK. In 1986 the UK police were given the right to use plastic bullets and CS gas regardless of the views of the relevant police authority."[12]

The Colin Wallace affair is illustrative of the way undercover security and intelligence operations conducted in Northern Ireland, have had a spill-over effect in Britain. But, there are other examples in the sphere of social policy. In Northern Ireland the centralisation of local services and the emasculation of local government occurred in the 1970s before Mrs Thatcher came to power. By the 1980s these objectives were prominent in the agenda of the Conservative party. Or, to take another example, Northern Ireland has always maintained selection for secondary education. This has now become, in effect, a desired objective among many Tories in Britain.

Finally, it is ironic that the British government is prepared in some ways to be more progressive in the region than in Britain. As we have already noted, despite many flaws in the new Fair Employment legislation, it does incorporate the notion of contract compliance, which, to date, has been firmly resisted in Britain.

Just as earlier, we emphasised the need to locate an understanding of Thatcherism within the context of wider economic and social changes, so also is it necessary to contextualise the changes in Northern Ireland in the last decade by reference to the same processes. In the early 1980s, the contraction and closure of certain sectors of the regional economy, like artificial fibres, was linked to decisions by transnational corporations to relocate investment.

This led to speculation that the prospects for new inward investment in the future were bleak. Yet the Industrial Development Board has claimed that its recent activities have generated an impressive list of job promotions. Notwithstanding the scepticism about how many jobs 'promoted' will actually materialise and endure,[13] it would appear that the possibilities for new inward investment have improved. While these successes may reflect inflows of capital from countries outside the EC anxious to penetrate EC markets in the run up to 1992, it may also illustrate the dynamic nature of capital movement in the process of uneven development whereby depressed regions may recreate new conditions for profitability.

A decade of Thatcherism has affected wage rates in Northern Ireland to the point where such conditions apply. Thus, many of the companies new to Northern Ireland have sought single union agreements with compliant trade unions and have offered wage rates which, in real terms, compare most unfavourably with what was obtained in the 1970s. For these reasons the shift of capital to the newly industrialising economies in the 1970s may not have been permanent. Once the decline in the core economies produced political responses like Thatcherism, which was determined to recreate market conditions for greater profitability and eagerly encourage industrial restructuring, the incentive for some of that investment to flow back to the core was greater.

The problems of applying macro theories to small environments have led some 'locality' researchers to be more circumspect about their value. It is worth remembering that in the 1950s theorists were proclaiming 'the end of ideology', 'the embourgeoisment of the working class' and the onset of 'post-capitalism'. However, by the 1960s, poverty was being 'rediscovered', ideological conflicts were spilling onto the streets and in the late 1970s, the post war-consensus collapsed. Today, the 'end of history' is being proclaimed once again with the universal establishment of liberal capitalism, only 200 years after Hegel had first proclaimed the end of history through the establishment of the Prussian state. While such constructs can be insightful and interesting, they need to be treated cautiously. Perhaps the easy use of the concept of Thatcherism is also an example of a kind of theoretical sloganising. It permits definite insights but cannot provide detailed and comprehensive explanations at the local level. And so, while the history of Northern Ireland in the 1980s cannot be understood without reference to Thatcherism, it cannot be understood exclusively in such terms.

# References

## Chapter 1

1. Quoted in the *Liverpool Daily Post*, June 1974.
2. 'Margaret Thatcher's Ten Years', *The Economist*, 29 April 1989.
3. For example, F.A. Hayek, *The Political Order of a Free People*, RKP, 1960 and M. and R. Friedman, *Free to Choose*, Pelican, 1980.
4. Quoted in *The Guardian*, 6 March 1989.
5. For example, see K. Minogue and M. Biddiss (eds.), *Thatcherism: Personality and Politics*, Macmillan, 1987.
6. B. Jessop, K. Bonnett, S. Bromley and T. Ling, *Thatcherism: A Tale of Two Nations*, Polity Press, 1988, p.61.
7. E. Hobsbawm in M. Jacques and F. Mulhern (eds.), *The Forward March of Labour Halted?*, Verso, 1981.
8. C. Leadbetter, 'Thatcherism and Progress', in S. Hall and M. Jacques (eds.), *New Times: The Changing Face of Politics in the 1990s*, Lawrence & Wishart, 1989, p.396.
9. R. Mishra, *The Welfare State in Crisis*, Wheatsheaf Books, 1984.
10. C. Offe, *Contradictions of the Welfare State*, Hutchinson, 1984.
11. S. Hall, 'The Great Moving Right Show', *Marxism Today*, January 1979.
12. S. Hall and M. Jacques (eds.), *The Politics of Thatcherism*, Lawrence & Wishart, London, 1983, p.13.
13. H. Young, *One of Us*, Macmillan, 1989.
14. B. Jessop et al., op.cit.
15. D. Marquand, 'Now's the Hour', *New Statesman & Society*, 28 April 1989.
16. R. Williams, 'Problems of the Coming Period', *New Left Review*, 140, July-August 1983, pp. 7-18.
17. J. Krieger, *Reagan, Thatcher and the Politics of Decline*, Polity Press, 1986.
18. B. Jessop et al., op.cit.

19. Ibid.
20. A. Gamble, *The Free Economy and the Strong State: The Politics of Thatcherism*, Macmillan, 1988, p.227.
21. Ibid. p.230.
22. Ibid.
23. Ibid. p.237.
24. L. Abse, *Margaret, Daughter of Beatrice*, Jonathan Cape, 1989.
25. Quoted in *The Economist*, 29 April 1989.
26. P. Riddell, *The Thatcher Government*, Martin Robertson, 1983.
27. H. Young, op.cit.
28. I. Gilmore, *Britain Can Work*, Martin Robertson, 1983.
29. F. Pym, *The Politics of Consent*, Hamish Hamilton, 1984.
30. J. Prior, *A Balance of Power*, Hamish Hamilton, 1986.
31. R. Miliband et al. (eds.), *'Conservatism in Britain and America: Rhetoric and Reality'*, *Socialist Register, 1987*, Merlin Press, 1987.
32. P. Armstrong, A. Glyn, J. Harrison, *Capitalism Since World War II: The Making and Breakup of the Great Boom*, Fontana, 1984, p.401.
33. A. Lipietz, *Mirages and Miracles: The Crises of Global Fordism*, Verso, 1987.
34. D. Massey, *Spatial Divisions of Labour: Social Structures and the Geography of Production*, MacMillan, 1984, p.116.
35. For example, see D. Greaves, *The Irish Crisis*, Lawrence & Wishart, 1971.
36. G. Adams, *The Politics of Irish Freedom*, Brandon, 1986, p.88.
37. S. McBride, 'The Debate Continues', in M. Collins (ed.), *Ireland After Britain*, Pluto, 1985, p.26.
38. R. Crotty, *Ireland in Crisis*, Brandon, 1986
39. H. Patterson, *Sectarianism and Class Conflict*, Blackstaff, 1982.
40. D. Byrne, 'Northern Ireland and the Crisis', unpublished paper, 1981.
41. B. Rowthorn and N. Wayne, *The Political Economy of Northern Ireland*, Polity Press, 1988.
42. J. Hume, 'The Irish Question in a Changed World', *The Irish Times*, 14 August 1989.
43. R. Johnston, *New Ireland Forum Report, Public Session*, No.6., 1984, p.4.
44. MO. Loinsigh, ibid., p.52.
45. P. Bew, P. Gibbon and H. Patterson, *The State in Northern Ireland, 1921-1972*, Manchester University Press, 1979.
46. R. Hall, *Capital and Space in Northern Ireland*, unpublished Ph.D. Thesis, University of Ulster, 1987.
47. J. Freeman, F. Gaffikin and M. Morrissey, *Making the Economy Work*, ATGWU, 1988.
48. B. Probert, *Beyond Orange and Green: The Political Economy of the Northern Ireland Crisis*, Zed Press, 1978.

49. For example, see N. Poulantzas, *State, Power,Socialism*, New Left Books, 1978.
50. C. O'Halloran, *Partition and the Limits of Irish Nationalism: An Ideology Under Stress*, Gill and Macmillan, 1987, p.177.
51. J. Hume, op. cit.
52. From an interview with members of the IRA's General Headquarters Staff and its Northern Command, *Republican News*, 17 September 1989.
53. J. Wickham, 'The Politics of Dependent Capitalism', in A. Morgan and B. Purdie, (eds.) *Divided Nation, Divided Class*, Ink Links, 1980, p.72.
54. H. Young, op. cit.,1989.
55. I. Aitken, *The Guardian*, 26 July 1989.
56. Mrs Thatcher, quoted in *Belfast Telegraph*, 18 March 1989
57. Queen's University Ulster Unionist Association, *Ulster: The Internal Colony*, November 1989.
58. Peter Robinson, quoted in *Belfast Telegraph*, 10 November 1989.
59. The Cameron Report (*Disturbances in Northern Ireland: Report of the Commission appointed by the Governor of Northern Ireland*), HMSO, Belfast, September 1969.

## Chapter 2

1. Northern Ireland Economic Council, *Economic Strategy: Overall Review*, Report 73: March 1989.
2. *The Government's Expenditure Plans 1980-81*, HMSO, 1979.
3. R. Klein, M. O'Higgins (eds.), *The Future of Welfare*, Basil Blackwell, 1985.
4. C. Thain, M. Wright, 'Coping With Difficulty: The Treasury and Public Expenditure, 1976-89', *Policy and Politics*, Vol.18, No.1, 1990.
5. 'Britain: Dividends of Death', *The Economist*, 26 March 1988, p.26.
6. 'Regional Accounts 1987', *Economic Trends*, November 1988.
7. *Economic Assessment: April 1989*, Northern Ireland Economic Council, 1989.
8. J. Simpson, 'Government Spending Probe', *Belfast Business Telegraph*, 20 February 1990.
9. Northern Ireland Information Service, 30 November 1988.
10. G. Gudgin et al., *Job Generation in Manufacturing Industry*, Northern Ireland Economic Research Centre, 1989.
11. *A Plan to Combat Long-Term Unemployment and to Assist the Occupational Integration of Young People in Northern Ireland*, Northern Ireland Office, 1989.
12. H. Morrissey, *Women in Ireland: The Impact of 1992* , ATGWU, 1989.

13. *Northern Ireland House Condition Survey 1989*, Northern Ireland Housing Executive, 1989.
14. *The Economist* op. cit. p.26.
15. Northern Ireland Information Service, 8 September 1987.
16. D. Piachaud, 'The Growth of Poverty', in A. Walker and C.Walker (eds.), *The Growing Divide*, Child Poverty Action Group, 1987.
17. *Regional Trends 1989*, Central Statistical Office, 1989.
18. Northern Ireland Information Service, 26 September 1988.
19. W. Keegan, 'Taxing Times on the Way to the Polls', The *Observer*, 4 March 1990.

# Chapter 3

1. 'Unemployment Index', *Unemployment Unit Bulletin*, January 1989.
2. *Social Trends*, HMSO, London, 1989.
3. Sir J. Ball, 'The United Kingdom Economy: Miracle or Mirage?' *National Westminster Bank Quarterly Review*, February 1989.
4. G. Maynard, *The Economy Under Mrs Thatcher*, Basil Blackwell, 1988 and HM Treasury, April 1989.
5. D. Smythe and A. Sentance, UK Productivity — Closing the Gap?, *PA/CBI Productivity Survey*, 1988.
6. S. Brittan, 'The Thatcher Government's Economic Policy', in D. Kavanagh and A. Seldon (eds.), *The Thatcher Effect*, Oxford University Press, 1989, p.13.
7. G.Wright (ed.), *The ABC of Thatcherism*, Fabian Society, 1989.
8. W. Godley, 'The Mirage of Lawson's Supply-Side Miracle', The *Observer*, 2 April 1989.
9. *CBI Industrial Trends Survey*, CBI, August 1989.
10. *The UK Economy*, OECD, August 1989.
11. W. Godley, 'Economic Disaster in Slow Motion', The *Observer*, 27 September 1989.
12. *The Guardian* editorial, 9 December 1987.
13. HM Treasury, *Medium Term Financial Statement*, HMSO, London, 1981.
14. V. Keegan, 'The Government's Credibility Comes Under the Hammer', *The Guardian*, 6 November 1989.
15. *OECD Labour Force Statistics* and *ILO Bulletin of Labour Statistics*, 1988.
16. A. Dunnett, 'The Role of the Exchange Rate in the Decline of UK Manufacturing', *The Royal Bank of Scotland Review*, No.161, March 1989.
17. Ibid., pp.20-21.

18. C. Leys, 'Thatcherism and British Manufacturing: A Question of Hegemony', *New Left Review*, No.151, May-June 1985.
19. G. Maynard, op.cit.
20. OECD *Economic Survey: UK*, HMSO, 1988, p.84.
21. Sir J. Ball, op.cit. p.56.
22. 'The British Economy Since 1979', *National Institute Economic Review*, No.122, 1987, p.46.
23. The 7 leading OECD countries are USA, Japan, West Germany, France, Italy, UK and Canada. They are sometimes referred to as G7.
24. R. Rustin, 'London Markets Get an Overdose of Gloomy News', *Wall Street Journal*, 27 October 1989.
25. Coopers & Lybrand Deloitte, *The Northern Ireland Economy: Review and Prospects*, January 1990.
26. G. Gudgin et al., op. cit.
27. Coopers & Lybrand, *The Northern Ireland Economy: Mid Year Review*, August 1989.
28. Coopers & Lybrand, *The Northern Ireland Economy*, January 1989.
29. Northern Ireland Economic Council, *Economic Strategy: Overall Review*, Report No. 73, 1989.
30. Coopers & Lybrand Deloitte, op.cit.
31. Northern Ireland Economic Council, op.cit. 1988.
32. Ibid.
33. Coopers & Lybrand Deloitte, op.cit. 1990.
34. Northern Ireland Economic Council, op.cit., 1989.
35. Coopers & Lybrand Deloitte, op.cit., 1990.
36. I. Isles and N. Cuthbert, *An Economic Survey of Northern Ireland*, HMSO, Belfast, 1957, p.316.
37. Hall Report, *Report of the Joint Working Party on the Economy of Northern Ireland*, Cmnd. 446, 1962, p.4.
38. D. Canning, B. Moore and J. Rhodes, 'Economic Growth in Northern Ireland: Problems and Prospects', in P. Teague (ed.), *Beyond the Rhetoric: Politics, the Economy and Social Policy in Northern Ireland*, Lawrence & Wishart, 1987, p.221.
39. J. Freeman, F. Gaffikin and M. Morrissey, op.cit. 1988.
40. *The Quigley Report*, Department of Finance & Personnel, Northern Ireland, 1976.
41. D. Canning, B. Moore and J. Rhodes, op.cit., 1987, p.223.
42. *Regional Industrial Development*, DTI, HMSO, London, December 1983.
43. Department of Economic Development, *The Pathfinder Process*, HMSO, Belfast, 1987.
44. D. Fell in the *Trustee Savings Bank Review*, 1986
45. Northern Ireland Economic Research Centre, op.cit., 1989.
46. Ibid.

47. N. Gibson and J. Spenser, 'Unemployment and Wages in Northern Ireland', *Political Quarterly*, Vol.52, No.1, January-March 1981. For evidence on changes in the patterns of earnings see *New Earnings Survey*, Northern Ireland, 1974, 1979, 1984, 1986.

48. For example see P.N. O'Farrell and DMWN. Hitchens, 'The Comparative Performance of Small Manufacturing Companies in South Wales and Northern Ireland: An Analysis of Matched Pairs', *Omega*, Vol.16, No. 5, pp. 429-438, 1988, and DMWN. Hitchens and JE. Birnie *Manufacturing Productivity in Northern Ireland: A Comparison with Great Britain, Northern Ireland* Economic Research Centre, 1989.

49. 'Pro-Consul of the New Wales', The *Observer*, 12 February 1989.

50. *News From The Labour Relations Agency*, Information Note No. 12, July 1989

51. JBH. Black, 'Collaboration or Conflict' in *Industrial Relations Journal*, Vol. 18, No. 1, pp. 14-25, 1987.

52. Northern Ireland Information Service, 5 July 1989.

53. Irish Congress of Trade Unions, *Into the 1990s*, ICTU, 1986.

54. Quoted in R. Wilson, 'If It Moves, Sell It', *Fortnight*, September 1989.

55. Northern Ireland Information Service, 9 November 1988.

56. Standing Advisory Committee on Human Rights, *Religious and Political Discrimination and Equality of Opportunity in Northern Ireland*, Cmd.37, HMSO., London, 1987.

57. P. Compton, (ed.), *The Contemporary Population of Northern Ireland and Population Related Issues*, Queen's University, Belfast, 1981.

58. D. Eversley, *Religion and Employment in Northern Ireland*, Sage Publications, 1989.

59. *Fair Employment in Northern Ireland*, Department of Economic Development, Northern Ireland, 1989, p.5.

60. Northern Ireland Economic Council and the National Economic and Social Council, *The Economic Implications for Northern Ireland and the Republic of Ireland of Recent Developments in the European Community*, 1988.

61. See for example, P. Ekins (ed.), *The Living Economy: A New Economics in the Making*, RKP, 1986.

62. B. Laurance, The Brutal Truth: Britain Has Joined the Forth World, *The Guardian*, 1 March 1990.

## Chapter 4

1. See E. Evason *Poverty: The Facts in Northern Ireland*, 1976, or *On The Edge*, 1985, Child Poverty Action Group.

2. D. Piachaud, *The Growing Divide*, op. cit., 1987.

3. G. Wright, op.cit.,1988.

4.  'Poverty Reaches Record Levels', *Labour Research*, July 1988.
5.  D. Byrne, *The Growing Divide*, op. cit.
6.  R. Holman, *Poverty*, Martin Robertson, 1978.
7.  S. Stitt, *Rowntree, Poverty and Supplementary Benefits*, Undergraduate Dissertation 1986.
8.  B. Abel-Smith and P. Townsend, *The Poor and The Poorest*, Bell & Sons, 1965.
9.  Ibid., p. 17.
10. A. Dilnott, JA. Kay and CN. Morris, *The Reform of Social Security*, The Clarendon Press, 1984.
11. P. Townsend, *Poverty in the United Kingdom*, Penguin, 1979.
12. J.Mack and PS. Lansley, *Poor Britain*, Allen & Unwin, 1984.
13. D. Piachaud, 'Peter Townsend and the Holy Grail', *New Society*, 10 October 1981.
14. AK. Sen, *Poverty and Famine: An Essay on Entitlement and Deprivation*, Oxford, 1981, p. 17.
15. L. Sawhill, 'Poverty in the United States: Why is it so Persistent?' *Journal of Economic Literature*, September 1988.
16. P. Townsend 'A Theory of Poverty and the Role of Social Policy', in M. Loney, D. Boswell and J.Clarke (eds.), *Social Policy and Social Welfare*, Open University Press ,1983.
17. J. Le Grand, *The Strategy of Equality*, Allen & Unwin, 1982.
18. M. O'Higgins, 'Welfare Redistribution and Inequality: Disillusion, Illusion and Reality', in P.Bean et al. (eds.), *In Defence of Welfare* , Tavistock, 1985.
19. E. Powell, *Still To Decide*, Batsford, 1972, p.11.
20. R. Boyson, *Down With The Poor*, Churchill Press, 1971.
21. R. Nozick, *Anarchy, State and Utopia*, Basil Blackwell, 1974.
22. A. Sinfield and B. Showler, *The Workless State*, Martin Robertson, 1981.
23. R. Bacon and W.Eltis, *Britain's Economic Problems: Too Few Producers*, MacMillan, 1976.
24. M. Nevin, *The Age of Illusions*, Victor Gollanz, 1981.
25. Quoted in O'Higgins, op. cit.
26. W. Beckerman, 'The Impact of Income Maintenance Payments on Poverty in Britain', *Economic Journal*, Vol. 86, June 1979.
27. P. Golding and S. Middleton, *Images of Welfare: the Press and Public Attitudes to Welfare*, Basil Blackwell and Martin Robertson, 1982.
28. P. Minford et al., *Unemployment: Cause and Cure*, Basil Blackwell, 1985.
29. Quoted in T. Novack, *Poverty and the State*, Open University Press, 1988, p.183.
30. Quoted in *Economic Progress Report*, The Treasury, No.203, August 1988, p.4.

31.    Quoted in M. Loney, 'A War on Poverty or on the Poor' in *The Growing Divide*, op. cit., p.10.
32.    N.Timmins, 'Moore Says Poverty Levels Exaggerated', The *Independent*, 12 May 1989.
33.    R. Oakley, 'Poor Britons Have Never Had It So Good', The *Times* 12 May 1989.
34.    'The Poverty of Moore's Thought', Leader in The *Independent*, 12 May 1989
35.    The *Times*, op. cit.
36.    *Low Income Statistics: Report of a Technical Review*, Department of Health and Social Services, March 1988.
37.    *Social Security Statistics* 1983 & 1987, DHSS, 1983, 1987.
38.    *The Independent*, op. cit.
39.    Townsend, op. cit.
40.    Evason, 1985, op. cit.
41.    Ibid, p. 14.
42.    GC. Feighen, S.Lansley and AD.Smith, *Poverty and Progress in Britain 1953-1973*, Cambridge University Press, 1977.
43.    'The Family Expenditure Survey', *PPRU Monitor*, The Department of Finance and Personnel (NI), 1988, p.12.
44.    See Press Release, 'Social Security Changes Cause Upheaval', NIACAB, 14 April 1988.
45.    Northern Ireland Information Service, 14 April 1988.
46.    Letter From Michael Meacher to ATGWU, 2 April 1986.
47.    Northern Ireland Association of Citizens' Advice Bureaux, *Social Security Changes: An Initial Appraisal of the Impact upon Claimants*, September-November 1988.
48.    *Hansard*, 16 December 1987.
49.    Information provided by the Belfast Law Centre.
50.    Ibid.
51.    B. Rolston and M. Tomlinson, *Winding Up West Belfast*, Obair, 1988.
52.    L. Noakes, 'Hearing the Cry of the Poor', *Unity*, 9 December 1989.
53.    Statistics from *Making Belfast Work*, Northern Ireland Information Service, 1988.
54.    Noakes op. cit.

## Chapter 5

1.    M.P. Smith and J.R. Feagin (eds.), *The Capitalist City*, Basil Blackwell, 1989, p.17.
2.    'It is Worse to Travel Hopefully', The *Economist*, 24 June 1989.
3.    National Audit Office, (DoE), *Urban Development Corporations*, HMSO, London, 1988.

4.      'Development for Yuppies', *Labour Research*, January 1989.
5.      J. Edwards, 'Positive Discrimination as a Strategy Against Exclusion: The Case of the Inner Cities', *Policy and Politics*, Vol.17, No.1, 1989, pp.11-24.
6.      B. Appleyard, 'Miracle at Salford', *The Sunday Times Magazine*, 29 November 1987.
7.      'Needham's 'Maritime Glory' — Can Earl Attain His Dream?', *Boardroom*, April 1987.
8.      'Up-Market Tide Turns On the Working Class', *Sunday News*, 23 July 1989.
9.      *The Employment Effects of Urban Development Corporations*, Employment Committee Third Report, Session 1987-88, HMSO, London, August 1988.
10.     *LDC Review* 1988, London Docklands Development Corporation, 1988.
11.     R. Weiner, *The Rape and Plunder of the Shankill: Community Action-the Belfast Experience*, Farset, 1978.
12.     D. Birrell et al., *Housing in Northern Ireland*, Centre for Environmental Studies, October 1971.
13.     J. Ditch, *Social Policy in Northern Ireland Between 1939-1950*, Gower, 1988.
14.     *Location of Industry in Northern Ireland: Interim Report of the Planning Advisory Board*, Cmd. 225, HMSO, 1944.
15.     I. Isles and U. Cuthbert, *An Economic Survey of Northern Ireland*, HMSO, Belfast, 1957 and *Report of the Joint Working Party on the Economy of Northern Ireland* (Hall Report), Cmd. 446, 1962.
16.     Matthew Report (*Belfast: Regional Survey and Plan*), HMSO, Belfast, 1964.
17.     McCrory Commission, (*Review Body on Local Government in Northern Ireland*), Cmd.596, HMSO, Belfast, 1970.
18.     Cameron Report (*Disturbances in Northern Ireland: Report of the Commission appointed by the Governor of Northern Ireland*), Cmd.532, HMSO, Belfast, 1969.
19.     C. Cockburn, *The Local State: Management of Cities and People*, Pluto, 1977.
20.     *Northern Ireland Discussion Paper: Finance and the Economy*, HMSO, Belfast, 1974.
21.     Coopers & Lybrand, Building Design Partnership in association with Drivers, Jonas and Milhench Crothers, *Retail Study, The Belfast Urban Area Plan 1986 — 2001*, DoE, NI, December 1986.
22.     Northern Ireland Housing Executive, T*he Northern Ireland Household Survey 1985*, NIHE, 1986
23.     S. Brown, 'Shopping Centre Development in Belfast', *Land Development Studies*, 1987, No.4, pp.193-207.

24.  *Major Retail Developments, Planning Policy's Guidance Note*, DoE/Welsh Office, HMSO, January 1988.

25.  P. Wilkinson, 'City Centre Planning and Promotion', *The Planner*, July 1988.

26.  P. Healy, *Local Plans in British Land Use Planning*, Pergamon Press, 1986.

27.  Quoted in R. Wilson, 'Putting the Gloss on Belfast', *New Society*, 13 May 1988.

28.  N. Milner and D. John, 'Hey, Big Spenders — It Looks Like the Party's Over', *The Guardian*, 27 September 1988.

29.  C. Hasluck, *Urban Unemployment*, Longman, 1987.

30.  P. Cheshire, 'Urban Revival In Sight: The End is Where We Start From?', *Local Economy*, Vol.3, No. 2, August 1988.

31.  *Labour Research* 1986, Distributive Trades EDC, 1985.

32.  D. Byrne, *Beyond the Inner City*, Open University Press, 1989, p.139.

33.  *Technical Supplement, Belfast Urban Area Plan 2001, Industry & Commerce*, Town & Country Planning Service, DoE (NI), 1987, p.5.

34.  D. Massey, *Spatial Division of Labour: Social Structures and the Geography of Production*, Macmillan, 1984.

35.  For example, S. Fothergill and G. Gudgin, *Unequal Growth: Urban and Regional Employment Change in the UK*, Heinemann, 1982.

36.  C. Hasluck, op.cit., 1987.

37.  *Economic Trends*, HMSO, London, November 1987.

38.  Coopers & Lybrand, *The Northern Ireland Economy*, 1988.

39.  *Treasury Autumn Statement*, 1989.

40.  C. Ree and P. Pashardes, *Who Pays Indirect Taxes*, Institute for Fiscal Studies, Report Series No. 32, 1988.

41.  D. Byrne, op.cit., p.145.

42.  P. Ambrose, *Whatever Happened to Planning*, Methuen, 1986, p.251.

43.  T. Brindley, Y. Rydin and G. Stoker, *Remaking Planning: The Politics of Urban Change in the Thatcher Years*, Unwin Hyman, 1989.

44.  Adam Smith Institute, *Omega Report: Local Government Policy*, 1983.

45.  A.D. Sorensen, 'Toward a Market Theory of Planning', *The Planner*, May-June 1983, pp. 78-80.

46.  A.D. Sorensen, 'Planning Comes of Age: A Liberal Perspective', *The Planner*, November-December, 1982, pp.184-88.

47.  G. Kirk, *Urban Planning in a Capitalist Society*, Croom Helm, 1980, p.32.

48.  A. Blowers, *The Limits of Power: The Politics of Local Planning Policy*, Pergamon, 1980.

49.  T. Brindley, Y. Rydin, and G. Stoker, op.cit., p.182.

50.  C. Moore and S. Booth, 'Urban Policy Contradictions: The Market Versus Redistributive Approaches', *Policy and Politics*, Vol. 14, No.3, 1986, pp.361-387.

51.  Quoted in *The Guardian*, 21 October 1989.

## Chapter 6

1.  For example, M. Young and P. Willmott, *Family and Kinship in East London*, RKP, 1957, or K. Coates and R. Silburn, *Poverty: The Forgotten Englishman*, Penguin, 1973.
2.  P. Lawless, *Britain's Inner Cities*, Harper & Row, 1981.
3.  *Belfast Areas of Special Need*, Department of Finance and Personnel, Northern Ireland, 1977.
4.  *Belfast: Areas of Relative Social Need-1981 Update*, PPRU, 1988.
5.  *Municipal Journal*, 1980, p.466.
6.  D. Finn, 'Within the City Walls', *Unemployment Bulletin*, No. 25, December 1987, p.22.
7.  Audit Commission (DoE), *Urban Regeneration and Economic Development: The Local Government Dimension*, HMSO, London, 1989.
8.  See M. Linton, 'Message of a Better Life From Battersea,' *The Guardian*, 14 September 1987.
9.  Kenneth Clark quoted in *British Business*, 23 October 1987.
10.  Audit Commission, op.cit., 1989.
11.  Quoted in *The Guardian*, 8 October 1987.
12.  Quoted in *The Guardian*, 26 November 1987.
13.  Quoted in *Belfast Telegraph*, 13 September 1989.
14.  Editorial, *Belfast Telegraph*, 13 September 1989.
15.  DoE written Parliamentary Answer, 30 June 1987.
16.  C. Hasluck, *Urban Unemployment*, Longman, 1987.
17.  P. Balchin, *Housing Policy: An Introduction*, Croom Helm, 1987.
18.  *Enterprise Zones*, Committee of Public Accounts Report, No. 293, HMSO, June 1986.
19.  A. Edwards, J. Leslie, G. O'Donovan, L. Carter, 'Simplified Planning Zones — A Reaction to the Proposals', *Planning Outlook*, Vol.29, No.1, 1986.
20.  S. Hall, *New Socialist*, September-October 1981.
21.  *Hansard*, Col.974, 14 July 1981.
22.  S. Mooney and F.Gaffikin, *Reshaping Space and Society*, Belfast Centre for the Unemployed, 1988.
23.  Northern Ireland Information Service, 19 July 1988.
24.  Northern Ireland Housing Executive, *Belfast Household Survey 1985*, 1986.
25.  Ibid.
26.  C. Daly, *West Belfast-Time for a New Deal*, Shanway Press, 1988.

27.  N.Acheson, 'Ace Vetting For Community Groups', *Scope*, November-December 1985.
28.  P. Townsend and N. Davidson, (eds.), *Inequalities in Health*, Penguin, 1982.
29.  We are grateful for data provided by Les Allemby of the Belfast Law Centre.
30.  NIHE, op.cit., 1986.
31.  Figures calculated from the statistical appendix of *Making Belfast Work* op. cit.
32.  V. Keegan, 'Lawson's Miracle: Is It All Done With Mirrors?', *The Guardian*, 7 November 1988.
33.  *Making Belfast Work*, op.cit.
34.  Northern Ireland Information Service, July 1988.
35.  P. McGinn and M. Morrissey, *Survey of Belfast's Long Term Unemployed*, Belfast Centre for the Unemployed, 1987.
36.  P. Lawless, 'British Inner Urban Policy Post-1979: A Critique', *Policy and Politics*, Vol.16, No.4, 1988, p.262.
37.  Ibid.
38.  D.Massey, *Spatial Divison of Labour: Social Structures and the Geography of Production*, MacMillan, 1984.

## Chapter 7

1.  S. Platt, 'The Lost Decade', *New Society*, 25 July 1986.
2.  G. Parket-Jervis, 'The Great Council House Sell Off', The *Observer*, 26 March 1989.
3.  Housing Minister, Lord Caithness, interviewed by *On The Record*, BBC Television, 6 November 1988.
4.  'Cooking Votes To Taste', *The Guardian*, 5 November 1988.
5.  Glasgow University Centre for Housing Research, *The Nature and Effectiveness of Housing Management in England*, HMSO, London, 1989.
6.  *Caught in the Act, A Critical Guide to the 1988 Housing Act*, SHAC, December 1988, p.13.
7.  M. Brimacombe, 'Could Ridley's Revolution Put Councils in the Dock?', *Surveyor*, 8 December 1988, p.11.
8.  A. Booth, *Raising the Roof on Housing Myths*, Shelter, 1989.
9.  A. Travis, 'Ridley Sounds the Death Knell for Council House Building', *The Guardian*, 24 November 1988.
10.  Quoted in J. Connolly, 'DOE Sits Tight on Damning Homes Report', The *Observer*, 9 October 1988.
11.  V. Keegan, 'It's Too Easy To Be Homeless in the Conservative Property Owning Democracy', *The Guardian*, 7 July 1986.

12. A. Booth, op.cit.
13. A. Travis, 'Time for Cathy to Come Home Again?', The *Guardian*, 23 November 1988.
14. J. le Grand, *The Strategy of Equality*, Allen and Unwin, 1982, p.100.
15. 'Yes, But Will the Horse Drink?', The *Economist*, 19 November 1988.
16. Cameron Report *(Disturbances in Northern Ireland: Report of the Commission appointed by the Governor of Northern Ireland)*, HM SO, Belfast, September 1969.
17. PN. Balchin and GH. Bull, *Regional and Urban Economics*, Harper & Row, 1987.
18. HM Treasury, *The Government's Expenditure Plans, 1986/87 to 1988/89*, Cmd. 9720, HMSO, London, 1986.
19. Northern Ireland Housing Executive, *House Condition Survey, 1975*.
20. C. Brett, quoted in the *Belfast Telegraph*, 9 July 1981.
21. Northern Ireland Economic Council, *Public Expenditure Priorities: Housing*, Report No. 22, May 1981.
22. Interview in *Scope*, September, 1983, p.5.
23. Northern Ireland Economic Council, *Review of Recent Developments in Housing Policy*, Report No. 48, February 1985, p.1.
24. Northern Ireland Economic Council, op. cit. 1988.
25. Shelter (NI), *Response to NIHE's Draft Report, Housing in the 1990s*, (Draft), November 1988.
26. M. Kelly, 'Fund Still £18 million Short Warns Executive', *Belfast Telegraph*, 30 November 1989.
27. Northern Ireland Housing Executive Board Press Statement, 25 November 1987.
28. D. Graham, 'Northern Ireland Let Off Lightly', *Roof*, September-October 1987.
29. Northern Ireland Housing Executive, *Housing Strategy Review (Draft) 1990-1993*, June 1989.
30. Northern Ireland Housing Executive, *Housing Into the 1990s, (Draft)*, July 1988.
31. Shelter (NI), op.cit.,1988.
32. Northern Ireland Housing Executive, op.cit., 1988.
33. Quoted in *The Economist*, 'Rachman On One Side, Council Blocks On the Other', 2 July 1988.
34. C. Gossop, 'Wrong Solutions', *Town and Country Planning*, February 1988, p.37.
35. Both quoted in 'Thatcher's Rent Boys', *Roof*, September-October 1987.

## Chapter 8

1. M. Wicks, *A Future For All: Do We Need a Welfare State?*, Penguin, 1987, p.81.
2. *Government Expenditure Plans 1985/86*, Vol.11, p.149.
3. See C. Weston, 'History Syllabus Group Endorses British Bias', *The Guardian*, 11 September 1989.
4. C. Martin, *Schools Now: A Parents' Guide*, Lion, 1989, p.159.
5. Sir R. Boyson, 'The Government Must Try Harder', *The Sunday Times*, 29 November 1987.
6. C. Huhne, 'Education: A Lesson in Economics', *The Guardian*, 9 December 1987.
7. JRG. Tomlinson, 'The Schools' in D. Kavanagh and A. Seldon, *The Thatcher Effect: A Decade of Change*, Oxford University Press, 1989, p.193.
8. J. le Grand, *The Strategy of Equality*, Allen & Unwin, 1982, p.76.
9. 'End Cash Disparity In Schools, Says Official', *Belfast Telegraph*, 25 July 1989.
10. *Northern Ireland Assembly Report*, HMSO 1984.
11. Belfast Education and Library Board, Working Party Report on NI Education Order, September 1989.
12. 'Belfast Education and Library Board in Parity Protest', *Belfast Telegraph*, 1 August 1989.
13. 'Warning on "Hostile Police" Over Schools', *Belfast Telegraph*, 13 February 1989.
14. 'School Shake-up Gets More Time for Talking', *Belfast Telegraph*, 10 August 1989.
15. Belfast Education and Library Board, op.cit.,1989.
16. D.H. Akenson, *Education and Enmity: The Control of Schooling in Northern Ireland 1920-50*, David and Charles, 1973.
17. W. Conway, *Catholic Schools*, Veritas, Dublin, 1974.
18. J. Darby et al., *Education and Community in Northern Ireland: Schools Apart?*, New University of Ulster, 1977, and AE. Sutherland, A. O'Shea and R. McCartney, *Curriculum Projects in Post Primary Schools*, Northern Ireland Council for Educational Research, 1983.
19. For example, D. Murray, *Worlds Apart: Segregated Schools in Northern Ireland*, Appletree Press, 1985.
20. C. Moffat, 'Schools Need New Terms', *Fortnight*, September, 1989.
21. Quoted in *Belfast Telegraph*, 9 November 1989
22. 'Powell Slams School "Bias"', *Belfast Telegraph*, 5 September 1989.
23. *YTP Cohort Study Stage 1 (1984), Stage 2 (1985) and Stage 3 (1986)*, Policy Planning and Research Unit, Department of Finance and Personnel, Northern Ireland.

24.   'Pilot Hopes', *Belfast Telegraph*, 6 October 1989.
25.   *Regional Trends 23*, HMSO, London, 1989.
26.   Northern Ireland Economic Council, *Economic Strategy: Overall Review*, Report No. 73, March 1989, p.27.
27.   *Report of the Committee on Higher Education in Northern Ireland Under the Chairmanship of Sir John Lockwoo*d, Cmd. 475, HMSO, Belfast, 1965.
28.   *The Future of Higher Education in Northern Irelan*d, HMSO, Belfast, 1982.
29.   RJ. Cormack, RL. Miller and RD. Osborne, 'Education and Policy in Northern Ireland', in RD. Osborne, RJ. Cormack and RL. Miller (eds.), *Education and Policy in Northern Ireland*, Policy Research Institute, 1987, p.7.
30.   Quoted in N. McAdam, 'Getting Into Debt By Degrees', *Belfast Telegraph*, 8 February 1989.
31.   RJ. Cormack, RD. Osborne and RL. Miller, Student Loans: A Northern Ireland Perspective, *Higher Education Quarterly*, Vol.43, No.3, Summer 1989, pp.229-245.
32.   E. Midwinter, *Priority Education*, Penquin, 1972; D. Byrne, B. Williamson and B. Fletcher, *The Poverty of Education*, Martin Robinson, 1975; R. Davie, N. Butler, and H. Goldstein, *From Birth to Seven*, Longman in association with the National Children's Bureau, 1972.
33.   J. le Grand, op.cit., p.77.
34.   A.H. Halsey (ed.), *Educational Priority, Vol.1: EPA Problems and Policies,* HMSO, London, 1972.
35.   *Higher Education* (The Robbins Report), 1963, p.8.
36.   P. Robinson, *Education and Poverty*, Methuen, 1976, p.27.
37.   N. McAdam, 'More Schools Seek Integrated Status in Ulster: Claim', *Belfast Telegraph*, 5 February 1990.
38.   M. Adler, A. Petch, and J. Tweedie, *Parental Choice and Educational Policy*, Edinburgh University Press, 1989.

# Chapter 9

1.   Quoted in J. Ditch, *Social Policy in Northern Ireland Between 1939-1950*, Gower, 1988, p. 99.
2.   Northern Ireland Information Service, 6 August 1987.
3.   See N. Barr, *The Economics of the Welfare State*, Weidenfeld and Nicholson, 1987.
4.   D. Willetts, 'The NHS Remedy — To Be Taken Internally', *The Guardian*, 1 February 1989.

5.      C. Huhne, 'The NHS: A Suitable Case For Much Better Treatment', *The Guardian*, 20 January 1988.
6.      C. Webster, 'The Health Service', in D. Kavanagh and A. Seldon (eds.), *The Thatcher Effect*, Oxford University Press, 1989.
7.      M. Philips, 'Why Mrs Thatcher's NHS has a Hole in its Heart', *The Guardian*, 27 November 1987.
8.      Webster, op. cit., p. 171.
9.      'An Investigation of the NHS in Crisis', *The Sunday Times*, 24 January 1988.
10.     'Mrs Thatcher Makes You Sick', *The Guardian*, 23 December 1987.
11.     J. Le Grand and D. Winter, 'The Middle Classes and the Defence of the British Welfare State', in R.Goodin and J.LeGrand (eds.), *Not Only The Poor*, Allen & Unwin, 1987.
12.     P. Townsend and N. Davidson, *The Black Report*, Penguin, 1982.
13.     A. Ferrinau, 'Cash Will Go Where Work Is Done Best', The *Observer*, 29 January 1989.
14.     P. Kellner, 'Market Pegs That Won't Fit The Holes', The *Independent*, 6 February 1989.
15.     C. Huhne, 'Useful Reforms, But the Health Service is Still Anaemic', *The Guardian*, 15 February 1989.
16.     Quoted in *The Guardian*, 1 February 1989.
17.     N. Timmins, 'Clarke To Force Through Changes', The *Independent*, 21 February 1989.
18.     *Regional Strategic Plan For The Health & Personal Social Services in Northern Ireland: A Summary*, DHSS, 1983.
19.     Northern Ireland Information Service, 6 August 1987,
20.     Northern Ireland Information Service, 12 November 1987.
21.     W. Odling-Smee, 'Sorry, Sir, We Need Your Bed', *Fortnight*, 15 March 1988.
22.     Northern Ireland Information Service, 22 January 1988.
23.     Northern Ireland Information Service, 6 December 1988.
24.     D. Curley, 'Report Warns on Cost of Health Care', *Belfast Telegraph*, 7 February 1989.
25.     Northern Ireland Information Service, 1 February 1989.
26.     D. Curley, 'Needham Opens White Paper Debate', *Belfast Telegraph*, 27 February 1989.
27.     J. Kane, 'Health Board Set to Give Reasons for its Decision', *Belfast Telegraph*, 10 August 1989.

## Chapter 10

1.      Editorial, *The Guardian*, 27 September 1989.

2.   R. Miliband, *Capitalist Democracy in Britain*, Oxford University Press, 1984.
3.   B. Crick, The *Observer*, 5 March 1989.
4.   M. Jacques and S. Hall (eds.), *The Politics of Thatcherism*, Lawrence & Wishart, 1983.
5.   E. Hobsbawm, 'The End of Thatcherism', *Marxism Today*, October 1989.
6.   F. Froebel, J. Heinrichs & O. Kreye, *The New International Division of Labour*, Cambridge University Press, 1980.
7.   P. Dicken, *Global Shift: Industrial Change in a Turbulent World*, Harper and Row, 1986.
8.   European Commission Annual Report 1988-89, *The European Economy: Preparing For 1992* , 1989.
9.   European Commission, *Employment in Europe*, 1989.
10.  N. Poulantzas, *State, Power, Socialism*, New Left Books, 1978.
11.  Editorial, *Belfast Telegraph*, 10 November 1989.
12.  'A Decade of Inequality', *Labour Research*, May 1989.
13.  See *Belfast Telegraph*, 26 January 1990.

# Bibliography

## Books and Booklets

B. Abel-Smith and P. Townsend, *The Poor and The Poorest*, Bell & Sons, 1965.

L. Abse, *Margaret, Daughter of Beatrice*, Jonathan Cape, 1989.

Adam Smith Institute, *Omega Report*: Local Government Policy, 1983.

G. Adams, *The Politics of Irish Freedom*, Brandon, 1986.

M.Adler, A.Petch, and J.Tweedie, *Parental Choice and Educational Policy*, Edinburgh University Press, 1989.

D.H. Akenson, *Education and Enmity: The Control of Schooling in Northern Ireland 1920-50*, David and Charles, 1973.

P. Ambrose, *Whatever Happened to Planning*, Methuen, 1986.

P. Armstrong, A. Glyn, J. Harrison, *Capitalism Since World War II: The Making and Breakup of the Great Boom*, Fontana, 1984.

R.Bacon and W.Eltis, *Britain's Economic Problems: Too Few Producers*, MacMillan, 1976.

PN. Balchin, *Housing Policy: An Introduction*, Croom Helm, 1987.

PN. Balchin and GH. Bull, *Regional and Urban Economics*, Harper & Row, 1987.

M.Ball, F.Gray and L.McDowell, *The Transformation of Britain*, Fontana, 1989.

N. Barr, *The Economics of the Welfare State*, Weidenfeld and Nicholson, 1987.

P.Bean et al. (eds.), *In Defence of Welfare*, Tavistock, 1985.

P. Bew, P. Gibbon and H. Patterson, *The State in Northern Ireland, 1921-1972*, Manchester University Press, 1979.

D. Birrell et al., *Housing in Northern Ireland*, Centre for Environmental Studies, October 1971.

A. Blowers, *The Limits of Power: The Politics of Local Planning Policy*, Pergamon, 1980.

A. Booth, *Raising the Roof on Housing Myths*, Shelter, 1989.

R. Boyson, *Down With The Poor*, Churchill Press, 1971.

EA. Brett, *The World Economy Since The War: The Politics of Uneven Development*, MacMillan, 1985.

T. Brindley, Y. Rydin and G. Stoker, *Remaking Planning: The Politics of Urban Change in the Thatcher Years*, Unwin Hyman, 1989.

D. Byrne, B. Williamson and B. Fletcher, *The Poverty of Education*, Martin Robinson, 1975.

D. Byrne, *Beyond the Inner City*, Open University Press, 1989.

K. Coates and R. Silburn, *Poverty: The Forgotten Englishman*, Penguin, 1973.

CBI, *CBI Industrial Trends Survey*, August 1989.

D.Coates, G. Johnston and R. Bush, *A Socialist Anatomy of Britain*, Polity, 1985.

C. Cockburn, *The Local State: Management of Cities and People*, Pluto, 1977.

M. Collins (ed.), *Ireland After Britain*, Pluto, 1985.

P. Compton, (ed.), *The Contemporary Population of Northern Ireland and Population Related Issues*, Queen's University, Belfast, 1981.

W. Conway, *Catholic Schools*, Veritas, Dublin, 1974.

Coopers & Lybrand, *The Northern Ireland Economy*, January 1989.

Coopers & Lybrand, *The Northern Ireland Economy: Mid Year Review*, August 1989.

Coopers & Lybrand Deloitte, *The Northern Ireland Economy: Review and Prospects*, January 1990.

R. Crotty, *Ireland in Crisis*, Brandon, 1986.

J.Curran (ed.) *The Future of the Left*, Polity Press/New Socialist, 1984.

C. Daly, *West Belfast-Time for a New Deal*, Shanway Press, 1988.

R. Davie, N. Butler, and H. Goldstein, *From Birth to Seven*, Longman in association with the National Children's Bureau, 1972.

A. Dilnott, JA.Kay and CN.Morris, *The Reform of Social Security*, The Clarendon Press, 1984.

J. Darby et al., *Education and Community in Northern Ireland: Schools Apart?*, New University of Ulster, 1977.

J. Ditch, *Social Policy in Northern Ireland Between 1939-1950*, Gower, 1988.

P. Ekins (ed.) *The Living Economy: A New Economics in the Making*, RKP, 1986.

E. Evason, *Poverty: The Facts in Northern Ireland*, Child Poverty Action Group, 1976.

E. Evason, *On The Edge*, Child Poverty Action Group, 1985.

D. Eversley, *Religion and Employment in Northern Ireland*, Sage Publications, 1989.

GC. Feighen, S. Lansley and AD. Smith, *Poverty and Progress in Britain 1953-1973*, Cambridge University Press, 1977.

S. Fothergill and G. Gudgin, *Unequal Growth:Urban and Regional Employment Change in the UK*, Heinemann, 1982.

J. Freeman, F. Gaffikin and M. Morrissey, *Making the Economy Work*, ATGWU, 1988.

M. and R. Friedman, *Free to Choose*, Pelican, 1980.

F.Froebel, J.Heinrichs & O.Kreye, *The New International Division of Labour*, Cambridge University Press, 1980.

A.Gamble, *Britain in Decline*, MacMillan, 1981.

A. Gamble, *The Free Economy and the Strong State: The Politics of Thatcherism*, Macmillan, 1988.

I. Gilmore, *Britain Can Work*, Martin Robertson, 1983.

P. Golding and S. Middleton, *Images of Welfare: the Press and Public Attitudes to Welfare*, Basil Blackwell and Martin Robertson, 1982.

R.Goodin and J. Le Grand (eds.), *Not Only The Poor*, Allen & Unwin, 1987.

D. Greaves, *The Irish Crisis*, Lawrence & Wishart, 1971.

G. Gudgin et al., *Job Generation in Manufacturing Industry*, Northern Ireland Economic Research Centre, 1989.

R. Hall, '*Capital and Space in Northern Ireland*', unpublished Ph.D. Thesis, University of Ulster, 1987.

S. Hall and M. Jacques (eds.), *The Politics of Thatcherism*, Lawrence & Wishart, London, 1983.

S. Hall and M. Jacques (eds.), *New Times: The Changing Face of Politics in the 1990s*, Lawrence & Wishart, 1989.

A.H. Halsey (ed.), *Educational Priority, Vol.1: EPA Problems and Policies*, HMSO, London, 1972.

C. Hasluck, *Urban Unemployment*, Longman, 1987.

F.A. Hayek, *The Political Order of a Free People*, RKP, 1960.

P. Healy, *Local Plans in British Land Use Planning*, Pergamon Press, 1986.

DMWN. Hitchens and JE. Birnie, *Manufacturing Productivity in Northern Ireland: A Comparison with Great Britain*, Northern Ireland Economic Research Centre, 1989.

R. Holman, *Poverty*, Martin Robertson, 1978.

ILO, *Bulletin of Labour Statistics*, 1988.

Irish Congress of Trade Unions, *Into the 1990s*, ICTU, 1986.

M. Jacques and F. Mulhern (eds.) *The Forward March of Labour Halted?*, Verso, 1981.

B. Jessop, K. Bonnett, S. Bromley and T. Ling, *Thatcherism: A Tale of Two Nations*, Polity Press, 1988.

D. Kavanagh and A. Seldon, *The Thatcher Effect: A Decade of Change*, Oxford University Press, 1989.

W.Keegan, *Mrs Thatcher's Economic Experiment*, Penguin, 1984.

W. Kennet (ed.), *The Rebirth of Britain*, WEidenfeld and Nicolson, 1982.

N. Kinnock, *Making Our Way*, Basil Blackwell, 1986

G. Kirk, *Urban Planning in a Capitalist Society*, Croom Helm, 1980.

R. Klein and M.O'Higgins (eds.), *The Future of Welfare*, Basil Blackwell, 1985.

J. Krieger, *Reagan, Thatcher and the Politics of Decline*, Polity Press, 1986.

S. Lash and J. Urry, *The End of Organised Capitalism*, Polity, 1987

P. Lawless, *Britain's Inner Cities*, Harper & Row, 1981.

J. Le Grand, *The Strategy of Equality*, Allen & Unwin, 1982.

A. Lipietz, *Mirages and Miracles: The Crises of Global Fordism*, Verso, 1987.

M. Loney, D.Boswell and J.Clarke (eds.), *Social Policy and Social Welfare*, Open University Press, 1983.

London Docklands Development Corporation, *LDC Review 1988*, 1988.

M.McCarthy (ed.), *The New Politics of Welfare*, MacMillan, 1989.

G.McLennan et al, *State and Society in Contemporary Britain*, Polity, 1984.

G.McLennan, D.Held and S.Hall, *The Idea of the Modern State*, Open University Press, 1987.

J.Mack and PS. Lansley, *Poor Britain*, Allen & Unwin, 1984.

C. Martin, *Schools Now: A Parents' Guide*, Lion, 1989.

D. Massey, *Spatial Division of Labour: Social Structures and the Geography of Production*, Macmillan, 1984.

G. Maynard, *The Economy Under Mrs Thatcher*, Basil Blackwell, 1988

E. Midwinter, *Priority Education*, Penquin, 1972.

R. Miliband, *Capitalist Democracy in Britain*, Oxford University Press, 1984.

R. Miliband et al. (eds.), 'Conservatism in Britain and America: Rhetoric and Reality', *Socialist Register*, 1987, Merlin Press, 1987.

P. Minford et al., *Unemployment: Cause and Cure*, Basil Blackwell, 1985.

K. Minogue and M. Biddiss (eds.),*Thatcherism: Personality and Politics*, Macmillan, 1987.

R. Mishra, *The Welfare State in Crisis*, Wheatsheaf Books, 1984.

S. Mooney and F.Gaffikin,*Reshaping Space and Society*, Belfast Centre for the Unemployed, 1988.

A.Morgan and B.Purdie, (eds.) *Divided Nation, Divided Class*, Ink Links, 1980.

H.Morrissey, *Women in Ireland: The Impact of 1992* , ATGWU, 1989.

D. Murray, *Worlds Apart: Segregated Schools in Northern Ireland*, Appletree Press, 1985.

M.Nevin, *The Age of Illusions,* Victor Gollanz, 1981.

Northern Ireland Association of Citizens' Advice Bureaux, *Social Security Changes: An Initial Appraisal of the Impact upon Claimants*, September-November 1988.

Northern Ireland Economic Council, *Public Expenditure Priorities: Housing*, Report No. 22, May 1981.

Northern Ireland Economic Council, *Review of Recent Developments in Housing Policy*, Report No. 48, February 1985.

Northern Ireland Economic Council and the National Economic and Social Council, *The Economic Implications for Northern Ireland and the Republic of Ireland of Recent Developments in the European Community*, 1988.

Northern Ireland Economic Council, *Economic Assessment: April 1989*, 1989.

Northern Ireland Economic Council, *Economic Strategy: Overall Review*, Report No. 73, 1989.

T.Novack, *Poverty and the State*, Open University Press, 1988.

R. Nozick, *Anarchy, State and Utopia*, Basil Blackwell, 1974.

C. O'Halloran, *Partition and the Limits of Irish Nationalism: An Ideology Under Stress*, Gill and Macmillan, 1987.

OECD, *Labour Force Statistics* ,1988

OECD, *Economic Survey: UK*, HMSO, 1988

OECD, *The UK Economy*, August 1989.

C. Offe, *Contradictions of the Welfare State*, Hutchinson, 1984.

RD. Osborne, RJ. Cormack and RL. Miller (eds.), *Education and Policy in Northern Ireland*, Policy Research Institute, 1987.

H. Patterson, *Sectarianism and Class Conflict*, Blackstaff, 1982.

N.Poulantzas, *State, Power,Socialism*, New Left Books, 1978.

E. Powell, *Still To Decide*, Batsford, 1972.

J. Prior, *A Balance of Power*, Hamish Hamilton, 1986.

B. Probert, *Beyond Orange and Green: The Political Economy of the Northern Ireland Crisis*, Zed Press, 1978.

F. Pym, *The Politics of Consent*, Hamish Hamilton, 1984.

Queen's University Ulster Unionist Association, *Ulster: The Internal Colony*, November 1989.

C. Ree and P. Pashardes, *Who Pays Indirect Taxes*, Institute for Fiscal Studies, Report Series No. 32, 1988.

P. Riddell, *The Thatcher Government*, Martin Robertson, 1983.

B. Rolston and M. Tomlinson, *Winding Up West Belfast*, Obair, 1988.

P. Robinson, *Education and Poverty*, Methuen, 1976.

B. Rowthorn and N. Wayne, *The Political Economy of Northern Ireland*, Polity Press, 1988.

AK. Sen, *Poverty and Famine: An Essay on Entitlement and Deprivation*, Oxford, 1981.

SHAC, *Caught in the Act, A Critical Guide to the 1988 Housing Act*, December 1988.
A. Sinfield and B. Showler, *The Workless State*, Martin Robertson, 1981.
D.Smith, *The Rise and Fall of Monetarism*, Pelican, 1987.
D.Smith, *North and South*, Pelican, 1989.
MP. Smith and JR. Feagin (eds.), *The Capitalist City*, Basil Blackwell, 1989.
D. Smythe and A. Sentance, *UK Productivity — Closing the Gap?*, PA/CBI Productivity Survey, 1988.
AE. Sutherland, A. O'Shea and R. McCartney, *Curriculum Projects in Post Primary Schools*, Northern Ireland Council for Educational Research, 1983.
P. Teague (ed.), *Beyond the Rhetoric: Politics, the Economy and Social Policy in Northern Ireland*, Lawrence & Wishart, 1987.
P. Townsend, *Poverty in the United Kingdom*, Penguin, 1979.
P. Townsend and N. Davidson, (eds.), *Inequalities in Health*, Penguin, 1982.
A. Walker and C.Walker (eds.), *The Growing Divide*, Child Poverty Action Group, 1987.
R. Weiner, *The Rape and Plunder of the Shankill: Community Action-the Belfast Experience*, Farset, 1978.
M. Wicks, *A Future For All: Do We Need a Welfare State?*, Penguin, 1987.
G.Wright (ed.), *The ABC of Thatcherism*, Fabian Society, 1989.
H. Young, *One of Us*, Macmillan, 1989.
M. Young and P. Willmott, *Family and Kinship in East London*, RKP, 1957.

## Articles

Sir J. Ball, 'The United Kingdom Economy: Miracle or Mirage?' *National Westminster Bank Quarterly Review*, February 1989.
W.Beckerman, 'The Impact of Income Maintenance Payments on Poverty in Britain', *Economic Journal*, Vol. 86, June 1979.
JBH. Black, 'Collaboration or Conflict', *Industrial Relations Journal*, Vol. 18, No. 1, 1987.
M. Brimacombe, 'Could Ridley's Revolution Put Councils in the Dock?', *Surveyor*, 8 December 1988.
S. Brown, 'Shopping Centre Development in Belfast', *Land Development Studies*, No.4, 1987.
P. Cheshire, 'Urban Revival In Sight: The End is Where We Start From?', *Local Economy*, Vol.3, No. 2, August 1988.

A. Dunnett, 'The Role of the Exchange Rate in the Decline of UK Manufacturing', *The Royal Bank of Scotland Review*, No.161, March 1989.

*The Economist*, 'Britain: Dividends of Death', 26 March 1988.

*The Economist*, 'Yes, But Will the Horse Drink?', 19 November 1988.

*The Economist*, 'Margaret Thatcher's Ten Years', 29 April 1989.

*The Economist*, 'It is Worse to Travel Hopefully', 24 June 1989.

A. Edwards, J. Leslie, G. O'Donovan, L. Carter, 'Simplified Planning Zones — A Reaction to the Proposals', *Planning Outlook*, Vol.29, No.1, 1986.

J. Edwards, 'Positive Discrimination as a Strategy Against Exclusion: The Case of the Inner Cities', *Policy and Politics*, Vol.17, No.1. 1989.

N. Gibson and J. Spenser, 'Unemployment and Wages in Northern Ireland', *Political Quarterly*, Vol.52, No.1, January-March 1981.

C. Gossop, 'Wrong Solutions', *Town and Country Planning*, February 1988.

D. Graham, 'Northern Ireland Let Off Lightly', *Roof*, September-October 1987.

S. Hall, 'The Great Moving Right Show', *Marxism Today*, January 1979.

E. Hobsbawm, 'The End of Thatcherism', *Marxism Today*, October 1989.

*Labour Research*, 'Northern Ireland: A Double Dose of Thatcherism', February 1990.

P. Lawless, 'British Inner Urban Policy Post-1979: A Critique', *Policy and Politics*, Vol.16, No.4, 1988.

C. Leys, 'Thatcherism and British Manufacturing: A Question of Hegemony', *New Left Review*, No.151, May-June 1985.

D. Marquand, 'Now's the Hour', *New Statesman & Society*, 28 April 1989.

C. Moffat, 'Schools Need New Terms', *Fortnight*, September, 1989.

C. Moore and S. Booth, 'Urban Policy Contradictions: The Market Versus Redistributive Approaches', *Policy and Politics*, Vol. 14, No.3, 1986.

*National Institute Economic Review*, 'The British Economy Since 1979', No.122, 1987.

P.N. O'Farrell and DMWN. Hitchens, 'The Comparative Performance of Small Manufacturing Companies in South Wales and Northern Ireland: An Analysis of Matched Pairs', *Omega*, Vol.16, No. 5, pp. 429-438, 1988.

W. Odling-Smee, 'Sorry, Sir, We Need Your Bed', *Fortnight*, 15 March 1988.

RD. Osborne, RJ. Cormack and RL. Miller, 'Student Loans: A Northern Ireland Perspective', *Higher Education Quarterly*, Vol.43, No.3, Summer 1989.

D. Piachaud, 'Peter Townsend and the Holy Grail', *New Society*, 10 October 1981.

S. Platt, 'The Lost Decade', *New Society*, 25 July 1986.

L.Sawhill, 'Poverty in the United States: Why is it so Persistent?' *Journal of Economic Literature*, September 1988.

A.D. Sorensen, 'Planning Comes of Age: A Liberal Perspective', *The Planner*, November-December, 1982.

A.D. Sorensen, 'Toward a Market Theory of Planning', *The Planner*, May-June 1983.

P. Wilkinson, 'City Centre Planning and Promotion', *The Planner*, July 1988.

R. Williams, 'Problems of the Coming Period', *New Left Review*, 140, July-August 1983.

R. Wilson, 'Putting the Gloss on Belfast', *New Society*, 13 May 1988.

**Government and Other Official Publications**

Audit Commission (DOE), *Urban Regeneration and Economic Development: The Local Government Dimension*, HMSO, London, 1989.

Belfast Education and Library Board, Working Party Report on NI Education Order, September 1989.

The Cameron Report (*Disturbances in Northern Ireland: Report of the Commission appointed by the Governor of Northern Ireland*), HMSO, Belfast, September 1969.

Committee of Public Accounts, *Enterprise Zones,* Report No. 293, HMSO, June 1986.

Coopers & Lybrand, Building Design Partnership in association with Drivers, Jonas and Milhench Crothers, *Retail Study, The Belfast Urban Area Plan 1986 — 2001*, DoE, NI, December 1986.

Department of Economic Development, Northern Ireland, *The Pathfinder Process*, HMSO, Belfast, 1987.

Department of Economic Development, Northern Ireland, *Fair Employment in Northern Ireland* 1989.

DoE/Welsh Office, *Major Retail Developments, Planning Policy's Guidance Note*, HMSO, January 1988.

Department of Finance and Personnel, Northern Ireland, *Belfast Areas of Special Need*, 1977.

Department of Health and Social Security, *Social Security Statistics, 1983*, 1983.

Department of Health and Social Security, *Social Security Statistics, 1987*, 1987.

Department of Health and Social Security, *Low Income Statistics: Report of a Technical Review*, March 1988.

*The Employment Effects of Urban Development Corporations*, Employment Committee Third Report, Session 1987-88, HMSO, London, August 1988.

*Economic Trends*, HMSO, London, November 1987.

*Economic Trends*, HMSO, London, November 1988.

European Commission Annual Report 1988-89, *The European Economy: Preparing For 1992* , 1989.

European Commission, *Employment in Europe*, 1989.

*The Future of Higher Education in Northern Ireland*, HMSO, Belfast, 1982.

*The Government's Expenditure Plans 1980-81*, HMSO, 1979.

*The Government Expenditure Plans 1985/86*, Vol.11. HMSO, 1984.

Glasgow University Centre for Housing Research, *The Nature and Effectiveness of Housing Management in England*, HMSO, London, 1989.

The Hall Report, *Report of the Joint Working Party on the Economy of Northern Ireland*, Cmnd. 446, 1962.

*Higher Education* (The Robbins Report), HMSO, 1963.

HM Treasury, *Medium Term Financial Statement*, HMSO, London, 1981.

HM Treasury, *The Government's Expenditure Plans, 1986/87 to 1988/89*, Cmd. 9720, HMSO, London, 1986.

I. Isles and N. Cuthbert, *An Economic Survey of Northern Ireland*, HMSO, Belfast, 1957.

*Location of Industry in Northern Ireland: Interim Report of the Planning Advisory Board*, Cmd. 225, HMSO, 1944.

The McCrory Commission, (*Review Body on Local Government in Northern Ireland*), Cmd.596, HMSO, Belfast, 1970.

The Matthew Report *(Belfast: Regional Survey and Plan)*, HMSO, Belfast, 1964.

National Audit Office, (DoE), *Urban Development Corporations*, HMSO, London, 1988.

National Audit Office, *Regenerating the Inner Cities*, HMSO February 1990.

Northern Ireland Housing Executive, *House Condition Survey 1974*, 1975.

Northern Ireland Housing Executive, *The Northern Ireland Household Survey 1985*, 1986.

Northern Ireland Housing Executive, *Northern Ireland House Condition Survey 1989*, 1989.

*Northern Ireland Annual Abstract of Statistics*, HMSO, 1989.
*Northern Ireland Annual Abstract of Statistics*, HMSO, 1988
*Northern Ireland Annual Abstract of Statistics*, HMSO, 1981
*Northern Ireland Assembly Report*, HMSO, 1984.
*Northern Ireland Discussion Paper: Finance and the Economy*, HMSO, Belfast, 1974.
Northern Ireland Information Service, *Making Belfast Work*, 1988.
*The Quigley Report*, Department of Finance & Personnel, Northern Ireland, 1976.
Policy Planning and Research Unit, Department of Finance and Personnel, Northern Ireland. *YTP Cohort Study* Stage 1 (1984), Stage 2 (1985) and Stage 3 (1986),
Policy, Planning and Research Unit, Department of Finance, Northern Ireland, *Belfast: Areas of Relative Social Need-1981 Update*, 1988.
*Regional Industrial Development*, DTI, HMSO, London, December 1983.
*Regional Strategic Plan For The Health & Personal Social Services in Northern Ireland: A Summary*, DHSS, 1983.
*Regional Trends 1989*, Central Statistical Office, 1989.
*Regional Trends 1985*, Central Statistical Office, 1985
*Regional Trends 1984*, Central Statistical Office, 1984.
*Regional Trends 1974*, Central Statistical Office, 1974.
*Report of the Committee on Higher Education in Northern Ireland Under the Chairmanship of Sir John Lockwood*, Cmd. 475, HMSO, Belfast, 1965.
*Social Trends*, Central Statistical Office, 1989.
*Social Trends*, Central Statistical Office, 1990.
*Standing Advisory Committee on Human Rights, Religious and Political Discrimination and Equality of Opportunity in Northern Ireland*, Cmd.37, HMSO., London, 1987.
Town & Country Planning Service, DoE (NI), *Technical Supplement, Belfast Urban Area Plan 2001, Industry & Commerce*, 1987.

235

# Index

## A

Adam Smith Institute · 128
Americanisation · 12
Anglo-Irish Agreement · 1, 34, 37, 43, 139, 142, 146, 165, 205 - 206
arithmetical particularism · 19
Audit Commission · 129, 133, 154
authoritarian populism · 18

## B

Belfast Areas of Need · 131
Belfast politics · 126
Belfast Urban Plan · 116 - 117, 120, 122, 124 - 125, 144, 146
Benn, Tony · 25, 31, 102, 201
Boyson, Rhodes · 87, 101, 168, 172, 185
Brooke, Peter · 33
business
    failure · 82
    small · 11, 26, 84, 128, 203

## C

Canning, Moore & Rhodes · 82, 89, 123
CDP · 130 - 131
child benefit · 102, 105, 145
Clarke, Kenneth · 134, 192 - 193
Community Development Project · 130
contract compliance · 92, 207
Cook, Robin · 192, 194
corporatism · 9, 13, 19, 25 - 26, 88, 199
Crosland, Tony · 102

## D

debt · 68 - 70, 171
deindustrialisation · 50, 121
dependence · 9, 30, 107
dependency · 9 - 10, 21, 30, 61, 79, 84, 101, 107 - 108, 111, 124, 141, 143, 145
deprivation · 3, 51, 62, 99, 106, 111, 128 - 129, 131 - 132, 139 - 141, 146, 148, 192, 196
deregulation · 26, 64, 119, 125, 136, 146

discrimination · 132, 185
    positive · 130
    religious · 3, 83, 91, 93, 146, 164, 181

# E

enterprise culture · 11, 13, 84, 110, 143, 206
Enterprise Zones · 133, 136 - 139, 146
entrepreneurship · 9, 20, 55, 84 - 85, 110, 128, 131, 184

# F

Fair Employment · 92, 142, 207
Fordism · 26

# G

Gamble · 20 - 21, 26
Government overload · 10

# H

Hall, Stuart · 16 - 20, 139
Harland & Wolff · 77, 88, 123
Heath, Ted · 8, 14, 22, 37, 101
Hegemony · 17, 21, 133, 201, 205

# I

Income Distribution · 52 - 53, 96, 98, 100, 104, 107
Industrial Development Board · 84 - 85
Industrial Restructuring · 4 - 5, 8, 11, 15, 20, 73, 83, 112, 131, 149, 184, 190, 192, 204, 208
International Capital · 19 - 20, 27 - 28, 30 - 31, 67, 82 - 83, 115, 117, 202 - 204, 208
Irish Republic · 5, 28, 30 - 31, 34, 37, 41, 43, 62, 93, 142, 206

# J

Japan · 25, 65 - 66, 70 - 71, 93, 202 - 203
Jessop, Bob · 17, 19
Job Creation · 65, 83, 85, 90, 111, 122, 129, 142

# K

Keynes · 8 - 9, 35, 63, 73, 87, 201
King, Tom · 49, 62, 91

# L

Lawson, Nigel · 14, 64, 66, 68, 202

# M

| | |
|---|---|
| Massey, D. | 27, 123 |
| Meacher, Michael | 109 |
| Monetarism | 10, 13, 15, 35, 73, 102, 119 |

# P

| | |
|---|---|
| privatisation | 11, 14, 18, 62, 64, 70, 88 - 91, 93, 125 - 126, 135, 151, 153 - 156, 168, 175, 190, 197, 200 |

# R

| | |
|---|---|
| Radical Right | 4, 8, 16, 199 |
| Republicanism | 1 - 3, 27 - 32, 34, 36, 41 - 42, 62, 126, 128, 140, 142, 205 |

# S

| | |
|---|---|
| Sinn Fein | 2, 28, 33 - 34, 42, 139 - 140, 142 |
| sovereignty, | 28 - 29, 31, 37, 172, 203, 205 |
|        consumer | 12, 172, 194 |
| Student Loans | 174, 185 |
| supply side economics | 9 - 10, 13, 102 - 103 |

# T

| | |
|---|---|
| Townsend, P. | 98 - 99, 107 |
| Transnational Companies | 203 |

# U

| | |
|---|---|
| Unemployment | 3, 5, 8, 15, 25, 28, 43, 54, 64, 74 - 75, 85, 103, 141, 146, 191, 200 |
| Unionism | 3, 28 - 29, 31 - 32, 36 - 39, 43, 62, 90 - 91, 115 - 116, 135, 155, 165, 187, 206 |
| Urban Regeneration | 106, 115, 118, 120, 124, 136, 146 |

# W

| | |
|---|---|
| Welfare State | 5, 10, 16, 27, 40, 43, 97, 100, 110, 130, 187 |
| West Belfast | 1, 90, 110, 117, 126, 134, 139, 143, 149 |
| Westland Affair | 13 - 14, 200, 203 |